Inequality and Social Mobility in Brazil

Inequality and Social Mobility In Brazil

José Pastore

Translated by
Robert M. Oxley

THE UNIVERSITY OF WISCONSIN PRESS

Published 1982

The University of Wisconsin Press
114 North Murray Street
Madison, Wisconsin 53715

The University of Wisconsin Press, Ltd.
1 Gower Street
London WC1E 6HA, England

First printing   73067

Printed in the United States of America

Originally published by T. A. Queiroz, Editor, Brazil, as *Desigualdade e mobilidade Social no Brasil*.
© T. A. Queiroz, Editor, 1979.

For LC CIP information see the colophon

ISBN 0-299-08830-8

Contents

Tables

Foreword

So far as is known, every society large enough to be worthy of the name has been stratified in terms of power, economic status, and social status. Over the centuries considerable objective scholarship has been devoted to attempts to explain why this is so and to describe the exact forms stratification systems take.

In relative terms, however, only a small part of the concern generated by stratification has been dispassionately analytical. Much of it has been devoted to peoples' impassioned attempts to change the stratification systems of societies or to change the position of one group or another within them. Those who initiate such actions may be convinced that they know what they are doing, and to some extent they might. But stratification systems and the changes they undergo are too abstract, too complex for most people to understand very well.

To assert that they are complex and that to date the actors within them may have only a vague understanding of them does not imply that they are chaotic. Presumably their structures and the variations they may undergo are orderly. Given adequate data and careful theoretic work it might well be possible to identify concepts elucidating their implicit order.

Beginning at least as far back as the Athenian philosophers to whom we in the West attribute the origins of our scientific theorizing, many serious students of social behavioral phenomena have attempted to explicate the structure and variations of such systems. Yet down to the present day, such efforts have been only partially successful. Upon reflection, it is easy to understand why this has been so. To be valid, theories always require a comprehensive and detailed knowledge of the phenomena to which they are addressed. The kinds of observations this requires simply could not be obtained until recently. Empirically valid theory of stratification is almost wholly a product of this century. Its most general aims are: 1. to measure the structural variations of stratification systems under all the circumstances in which they are found—that is, across time and place—and to measure the positions people occupy within these systems; 2. to determine what happens to other aspects of society as a result of variations in stratification systems and to individual people as a result of variations in their positions in such systems; and 3. to determine the factors that lead to variations in stratification systems and in the positions people hold within them.

If secure answers could be provided to questions posed by such aims they might help people to determine whether, when, and how to try to modify stratification systems. Surprising as it may seem, people tamper with the stratification systems of their societies all the time—and sometimes with those of other societies. On rare occasions this is done deliberately, sometimes in struggles that assume titantic proportions, as in the Russian Revolution early in the century and in the revolution in China from 1948 to Mao's death. More frequently, the changes that occur are less dramatic and more or less accidental. Still, stratification phenomena matter a great deal to those implicated in them. It seems self-evident that with a realistic understanding of these phenomena, people will be more successful in avoiding their more sanguinary consequences.

By the end of the 1960s the concepts and methods of stratification research had become sufficiently well developed to permit stratification systems to be described in ways which are at once panoramic, precise, and concise. This, a viable descriptive theory of stratification, was the work of countless thinkers from several thought domains. Techniques by which to elicit observations had to be developed to obtain data on samples of persons such that valid estimates could be made of the parameters of the populations from which the data were drawn. This in turn required an infrastructure consisting of survey research establishments and the trained personnel they employ. These began to appear less than 50 years ago. A logic by which specific classes of valid observations on persons could be conceived as comprising variables measuring similarities and differences among them had to be devised. This is the logic of measuring human behavior. It began to appear about the turn of the century, but only within the past generation has it come to be rather fully elaborated. Various aspects of mathematical statistics had to be developed and their application to human phenomena had to be worked out. Mainly, this involves two kinds of thinking, the theory of statistical sampling and the theory of statistical estimates of effects. This work began over a century ago and is still going on. But only since World War II have we learned how to identify and contact samples of human beings in ways that permit probabilistic estimates of parameters. Statistical methods by which to estimate the effects of sets of variables began to appear around 1920. But these did not come into wide use until high speed computers became generally available, largely in the 1960s. Finally, specialists in stratification had to learn to think about their phenomena in terms of measurable variables describing the "content dimensions" of economic status, power, and social status, and in terms of over-arching variables—"structural dimensions"—which describe the possible variations of whole stratification systems.

Each of the above lines of thought is still being elaborated. Even so, as the situation stands today, stratification researchers have learned which content dimensions must be measured, and they now have the capacity to measure several—perhaps most—of the variables encompassed by them. Among these, the best understood are differences in social status and economic status, especially the former. There is widely shared consensus that people's social status may be validly and reliably measured by numerical scores assigned to their occupations, either in terms of prestige (the average relative evaluation of each occupation) or in terms of socioeconomic status (as determined by the average income, and often education, of the incumbents of each occupation). Effective measures of economic status, especially income, have lagged a bit, but are now more or less readily available. Power differentials have been much more difficult to measure. Dr. Pastore's book deals with occupational status, which is the main variable researchers consider when studying social status.

The structural dimensions of stratification are less widely understood, although by 1970 several had been identified. One is the average level of a variable which taps a content dimension. Another is the degree of dispersion of that variable around its own average, often called the degree of inequality. Still another consists of the rate of movement of persons from level to level of a given content variable over time. In general, this is called mobility, and movement from level to level within an occupational hierarchy is called "social mobility." The obverse of mobility would be immobility; the degree of immobility is sometimes called the "degree of status inheritance." A fourth structural dimension, called "crystallization," is the degree to which the variables measuring the different content dimensions are correlated with each other. Sometimes called the "rigidity of inequality," this measures the average degree to which the various statuses of each person are similar to each other within a given society. Other structural dimensions have been proposed but have received relatively little attention to date. Dr. Pastore's book is a study of social mobility in a society where the degree of inequality is unusually high.

Definitive empirical research on social mobility is of course a product of the last 20 or 30 years, especially the last decade. For reasons sketched above, only recently have the various capacities required for such work come into being. Such studies are still few in number. Most have been conducted in industrialized nations such as Australia, Canada, Great Britain, Hungary, Japan, West Germany, Poland, and the United States. They show the degree to which people rise and fall within their stratification systems. The portion of a society's mobility that is due to a general rise in the occupational structure of society may be called "structural mobility." The portion that is due to other factors may be called "circulation mobility." It is widely believed that industrialization promotes a high degree of upward structural mobility. One would think, then, that the most industrialized countries would have a high degree of social mobility, and indeed research has shown that a certain degree of such mobility does in fact exist. Whether this degree is "high" or not is something that will only be known after suitable comparisons have been made with less industrialized nations. For countries with a high degree of inequality, upward structural mobility would presumably offset most of the resentment that might otherwise be felt by or for those at the bottom of societies. This too remains to be seen. Presumably, too, more egalitarian societies would have especially high degrees of circulation mobility. Thus, one would think that industrialized socialist societies should show particularly high levels of upward structural mobility and circulation. This also remains to be seen.

The present book breaks new ground in the study of social mobility. It is a report of a massive study of the occupational mobility of Brazilian heads of families of 20 through 64 years of age. The data were collected by means of a multistage probability sample of households, in ways that permit generalization to Brazil as a whole and to its various regions (except for the remote, inaccessible, and sparsely settled lands in the Amazon valley). The data were collected and transferred to magnetic tape for computer analysis by the Brazilian Institute of Geography and Statistics, the nation's central statistical agency, an organization which has regularized its capacity to obtain and process large amounts of high quality data from standardized personal interviews in households selected by scientific sampling methods.

A few words about Brazil may be useful. The nation's territory occupies about one-half of South America, and is roughly the same size as Australia, Canada, China, or the United States. In 1970 its population was 95 million and by 1980 had increased to 121 million. In 1970 about 90% lived on the two-fifths of the land surface that, for about 400 miles inland, parallels the southern 2,500 miles of the Atlantic coast. The remaining 10% lived in the interior and northern three-fifths, mostly in and near half-a-dozen widely scattered cities. One-fifth of the population live in the northeastern part of the country, an area long noted for its widespread poverty and largely devoted to agriculture. The bulk of the people, about 60%, live in the South, where both agriculture and manufacturing are rather highly developed. For many years Brazil's rural-urban population balance has been shifting, and the industrial and commercial sectors of the economy have been expanding. For example, in 1950 only 36% of Brazil's 52 million people were classed as urban. Yet only 20 years later, 56% of the nation's 95 million people were so classed.

Since 1964 the nation has followed a development strategy that encourages rapid economic growth and in which questions about the distribution of income have mostly been ignored. So an income distribution which was already quite unequal by world standards has become even more unequal. This is not to say that most of the poor have become even poorer. Indeed there has been a long debate among Brazilian economists as to whether this is true. As of today, the general consensus seems to be that the economic standing of most of the poor is probably improving slightly while, at the same time, the degree of inequality is increasing. The present book has probably contributed to this opinion.

This book presents statistical data concerning the status of each male head of family as his standing is manifested in the average income of all the people employed in his occupation. Thus on the average, carpenters earn more than sharecroppers, and medical doctors earn more than store clerks. Index scores are used to describe the order of the average income differences among occupations. These differences are rather durable, despite effects of regional differences in pay scales, inflation, etc. So it is safe to assert that, on the average, medical doctors who are sons of store clerks are better off economically than their fathers. Similarly, most carpenters who are sons of sharecroppers are better off than their fathers. Thus while incomes may vary among individuals in the same occupation and for the same individual over time, the strategy followed herein provides a reasonably interpretable overview of the main patterns of upward and downward mobility. The book thus contributes to the debate on economic growth and the distribution of income in Brazil. In a few words it shows that Brazil's occupational structure has shifted upward as its economy has industrialized. Some have risen and others have fallen as this vast process of industrialization and urbanization has proceeded. While it is true that many have fallen and that only a relative few have risen dramatically, the great bulk have apparently experienced small but real increases in occupational status.

Before this book, the common wisdom of academic people held that there is no social mobility in developing societies—that immobility is part of a larger picture of inequality. Indeed, Brazil has one of the most unequal income distributions in the world. Hardly anybody would have thought that mobility could exist within such a sharply unequal system. This book shows beyond doubt that there is quite a substantial amount of mobility in Brazil. In numerical terms, of course, most of it could be described as small upward intergenerational mobility out of the lowest agricultural stratum into the urban working class. But there is a surprising rate of long-distance upward mobility as well. Some of it is from the bottom into the higher levels of the Brazilian elite stratum. The latter moves are especially interesting; while only about 1% of those at the bottom actually get to the very top, the elite stratum itself is rather heavily populated with people from the bottom. This top group is expanding as time passes. But its ranks are more than replenished, not only by the sons of the old elites, but also by those from all other strata, including the lowest. In addition to all this, a surprising number of sons of the older elites find themselves in lower positions than their fathers.

For quite a few years the South of Brazil—especially the states of São Paulo, Rio Grande do Sul, Rio de Janeiro, and Minas Gerais—has experienced a particularly fast economic growth rate. The growth of manufacturing and of a high technology agriculture whose products are sent to foreign markets are especially impressive. The notoriously poor Northeast has also gained economically, although it lags far behind the South. As a result, people are flooding out of agriculture everywhere and into manufacturing and services. Jobs are the magnets which draw them to the cities of the South.

In a few words, this book shows that Brazil's vigorous economic growth is transforming most of the population, generally if slowly raising the whole occupational structure.

The author of the book is Dr. José Pastore. A native of the City of São Paulo, he studied at the University of São Paulo and at the Foundation School of Sociology and Political Science before conducting his doctoral studies at the University of Wisconsin. He completed the Ph.D. degree in 1968. In the years since then, he advanced from Assistant Professor to Professor of Sociology at the University of São Paulo. Most of his present activity with the university is conducted through the Foundation Institute of Economic Research. From the beginning of his career he has been active in research and in policy formation. In the early 1970s he headed Brazil's Commission for Technology Transfer. During the mid-1970s he served as a key advisor to the Ministry of Agriculture and in this capacity designed the new organization of Brazil's federal agricultural research and extension services. At present he is a key advisor to the Ministry of Labor. Through all of this time he has carried on a vigorous program of research during which he has published several books dealing with research on education, income differentials, adaptation of migrants, and agricultural policy.

Results of his research activity have also appeared in technical journals in Brazil, Mexico, and the United States. A substantial portion of his research, including analyses performed as a part of the present book, has been conducted in collaboration with stratification researchers at the University of Wisconsin.

It is a special pleasure to introduce this book by José Pastore, a friend and collaborator of many years.

Archibald O. Haller

Madison, Wisconsin
June 1981

Acknowledgments

This study is the result of the good will and collective efforts of various people and institutions. The primary material—the data—was provided by the Fundação IBGE (IBGE Foundation) which is efficiently carrying out the Pesquisas Nacionais por Amostra de Domicílios—PNAD (National Household Research—PNAD). The PNAD is a huge task which is being carried out at an extremely high level of quality. The Fundação IBGE recently entered a very productive period in which it encourages researchers to use its scientific data. For this we wish to congratulate Drs. Isaac Kerstenesky and Speridião Faissol and express our gratitude for the support they provided. We also extend our gratitude to the technicians of the Grupo de Indicadores Sociais (Social Indicators Group) of the Fundação IBGE, who contributed a great deal to putting this project into operation.

New stimulus has also come from the Secretaria de Emprego e Salário do Ministério do Trabalho (Secretariat of Employment and Wages of the Ministry of Labor) which, also entering a new phase, has demonstrated a sincere interest in obtaining an objective view of what is happening in the Brazilian labor market. There is an obvious determination in that agency to base its programs on scientific analysis and accurate data. For this, in particular, Professor F. Menna Barreto deserves our sincere thanks.

A piece of work as difficult and controversial as this one demands several tests of its quality. We are grateful for the care and the competence of various colleagues of the University of São Paulo, of the FIPE—Fundação Instituto de Pesquisas Econômicas (Institute of Economic Research Foundation), and of other research institutions, who patiently offered their comments and suggestions at various stages of this work. Those who deserve explicit mention include Drs. Nelson do Valle Silva, Aparecida J. Gouveia, Adroaldo Moura da Silva, Archie O. Haller, Ramonaval A. Costa, Clovis de A. Peres, Gláucio A. D. Soares and Manoel Cabral de Castro. They have done all they could to purge this work of its gravest errors. If any persist, they do so only because of the author's stubbornness.

The author again thanks the FIPE—Fundação Instituto de Pesquisas Econômicas—and the National Science Foundation, grant number SOC 78–07414, for financial assistance given for this project, and he thanks the technicians in the processing and copying departments, especially Srta. Edna Buganza, for her patience and accuracy in typing the innumerable versions of this text. Thanks also to Daramea Godfrey for preparation of the index.

J. P.

Inequality and Social Mobility in Brazil

1

Inequality and
Social Mobility

This book represents one more study of social inequality. It is a new work
that deals with an old theme, for the debate about the question of inequality
among men is as old as humanity itself. From the most primitive communities
to the industrial societies of the contemporary world, social inequality has
always been present among people. No historical evidence exists of even one
human society that achieved conditions of full social equality.

Nevertheless, the fact that inequality has always existed is very far from
being accepted unanimously. In fact, men have always been divided on this
point. The varied interpretations of social disparities are as old as inequality
itself. On the one hand, there have always been men willing to explain and
justify the coexistence of rich and poor, strong and weak, oppressors and
oppressed. The modes of justifying it have assumed different forms, although
all of them have been variations on the same theme, that is, the determining
force has been said to be out of human control: the divine will, the natural
order, the necessity of complementarity. Such justifications carried and still
carry, at the gut level, an obvious basis in the status quo and form, in Lenski's
words, the *conservative thesis* (Lenski, 1966:5). From the conservative point
of view the differences in the distribution of wealth among men are absolutely
just, useful, and unchangeable.

Alongside this point of view the opposite position has always existed also—
that is, the position of those who have denounced and still denounce the system
of distribution of wealth as unjust, not useful, and changeable. This is the
radical antithesis. From the radical point of view, social differences are merely

3

the reflection of the distribution of wealth and of the abusive exercise of power by the stronger over the weaker in the process of the formation of human society itself.

The conservative thesis presupposes that the key factor in maintaining the social order and a minimum of social integration is consensus, while the radical antithesis defends the thesis that the social order and integration are maintained on the basis of tension and force. Consequently, the first point of view supposes that disparities among men and the system of social stratification itself originate in the specialization of labor, which is essential in any society; the second regards disparities and social stratification as the results of struggle and of power (Allardt, 1968:14).

The most competent advocates of the two points of view have followed each other throughout history, and, indeed, they have coexisted in the same societies and in the same times. Each society has and always has had vigorous proponents of the two currents of thought. Their interpretations and arguments have varied in time and space but the two positions have coincided in their markedly normative character. However, if we have a thesis and an antithesis, we should have a *synthesis*. In fact, modern sociology is demonstrating the emergence of a synthesis which is predominantly analytical and which is concerned primarily with empirical relations and with the determinants that influence social inequality.[1] While the conservative thesis and the radical antithesis based themselves upon deduction and upon isolated illustrations by way of validating their propositions, the modern synthesis bases itself upon inductive-deductive logic and upon the gathering of empirical data pertinent to the phenomenon of inequality. This is the position taken in the present study. Its basic concern is to understand how social inequality has behaved in Brazil, its nature, how it has varied in time and in space, and its consequences.

Although this study deliberately excludes the normative positions, it seems clear that the answers to the above questions are of undeniable relevance to the formulation of policies which are aimed at modifying Brazilian reality in the desired direction. That is, a maximum of social efficiency with a minimum of inequality. But first, we must know how the system of stratification is evolving. How does the present social structure distinguish itself from that of the past, with reference to the degree of internal disparities? What is the situation of the individuals who are in the work force today compared to that of their parents? And when compared among themselves? In other words, what has been the general state of social mobility in Brazil throughout the present century?

---

1. One of the most outstanding examples of this approach is the work of Lenski. The pioneering endeavors of this synthesis, however, are found in the following sociologists: Weber, 1947: Parts 3–5; Dahrendorf, 1962: Chaps. 3–4; Ossowski, 1964.

Mobility and Development

Social mobility is one of the central themes of the sociology of development. To know the scope and the nature of social mobility is to know much about the social dynamic. A society without mobility tends to be a stagnant society which simply reproduces its social structure ceaselessly. Such a society offers little in terms of human advancement and social progress. A human society develops to the extent that it raises its population's standard of living and provides opportunities of social mobility to large social segments. In this sense, mobility can be used as an indicator of social development.

The type of mobility which best functions as an indicator of social development is vertical mobility, which refers to the progress of an individual (or of a group) from one social level to another.

The study of vertical mobility relates the individual's present social position to that of the past, seeking to find out how individuals distribute themselves through time and the various levels of social structure, and how great are the influences of social inheritance, individual resources, and the socio-economic opportunities offered by the society in that period of time. Other than this, the study of mobility seeks to examine the impact of individual and group movement upon the social structure itself, paying special attention to the question of the decline and growth of the different social layers (Goldhamer, 1968:429–37).

Social mobility, therefore, refers to changes of *social status*. It may be upward or downward mobility. In the analysis of the social dynamic, studies of upward and downward movements are equally important. The two types of mobility coexist in dynamic societies and bear equal relevance to understanding social development. In the beginning stages of development, the movement from one position to another tends to depend predominantly upon the creation of new opportunities. In the later stages, when the society has already reached high levels of employment and social differentiation, mobility tends to depend upon an exchanging of positions, where some rise and others descend in the social structure.

Of course, mobility may occur through a leveling from above as well as from below. However, in the early stages of development in the capitalist societies of today, the paradigm sought is that in which upward vertical mobility is considered a *necessary* condition (although not sufficient by itself) for individual and social development. More precisely, the development of these societies is defined on the basis of shrinking as rapidly as possible the immense base of the social pyramid and upon expanding the middle classes (Smelser and Lipset, 1966).

What are the repercussions of social mobility upon the individual and upon the society? When an individual goes from an occupation of low status to an occupation of higher status—of middle class status, for example—such movement tends to be accompanied by various benefits in terms of economic, educational, and social opportunities, as well as by changes in values, in attitudes, and in the individual's cultural horizon.[2] The individual and his descendents feel these repercussions over both the short and long terms. Upward mobility functions as a mechanism of social advancement in these cases. Such advancement clearly can be attained also by individuals who remain in the same positions through an elevation in the material and cultural benefits of life. However, it happens that the systems of stratification are formed (as history progresses) on the basis of inequalities, within which different gratifications are associated with different social positions. In these cases, to improve one's life, for the great majority of people, depends upon a change of status and a rise in the social ladder. More precisely, to improve one's life depends upon a change of occupational status.[3]

The associate result of social mobility as time passes is a modification in the sizes of the different social classes and in the society itself. Depending on the nature and rhythm of social mobility, the result can be one of increasing equality or inequality. In both cases, however, mobility reflects the internal dynamic of a society. For example, when one analyzes intergenerational mobility (that which occurs from father to son) one finds very useful tools with which to compare today's society with the society of several decades before. This permits one to characterize the larger tendencies of the social structure and what has happened in the various strata and social classes. Such analysis offers a point of view relative to the diverse social layers and to social inequality itself through time. Many times the static position of a society is not what we want (comparison of absolutes); it is the examination of mobility through the passage of time that permits one to identify retreats or advances in relation to the point of departure (comparison of relatives).

Mobility and particularly upward mobility is associated intimately with

2. Beside the benefits pointed out, social mobility also tends to provoke certain personal frustrations that stem from a feeling of relative deprivation, from inconsistencies in status, and from other phenomena which will be examined here and again in Chapter 10. For a look at the whole of these phenomena, see Runciman, 1966. See also Section 2 of this chapter.

3. It is true that many times a better standard of living is acquired by individuals remaining in the same occupation who change only their position of responsibility (rank). Indeed, studies of salary determinants indicate that, given an occupation, changes of rank have had an enormous influence in determining individual remuneration. Nevertheless, occupations in the social structure are arranged as are the branches of a tree. The individual can better his salary traveling along the branch he is in, but he soon reaches an impassable limit. For additional raises he will have to pass to another branch and repeat the process. Social mobility is concentrated in this second type of movement, although the analysis is much more vigorous when movements of rank are combined with movements in occupations. See Pastore, 1973.

economic development. Mobility is (1) *effect* and (2) *condition* for economic development (Pampel, 1977). (1) The process of development, to the extent that it advances, provokes the social differentiation necessary for mobility. This occurs through a transformation of the economic sectors and especially through the shrinking of the agricultural labor market and the increase in opportunities in the sectors of industry, commerce, and services. (2) On the other hand, mobility in itself constitutes a stimulus and an important condition for the same economic development. Germani identifies two relevant roles played by mobility in this process. In the first place, he points out that modern society depends upon great mental plasticity to innovate and to accept innovations, which, for their part, go hand in hand with individual progress in the educational and professional spheres. In the second place, modern society depends upon geographical movement of manpower, and this movement is substantially increased to the extent that the individuals believe that migration means possibilities of upward movement. In this way, mobility and development nourish one another mutually (Germani, 1965:274–75).

Mobility and Political Change

Mobility also affects economic development in an indirect way—that is, through political changes. How does this occur? Sociological literature suggests that social mobility is linked to relative deprivation (Runciman, 1966: Chap. 10). According to such a theory, satisfaction or frustration on the part of individuals depends upon how they relate to their peer groups, upon what happens in these groups in terms of mobility, and upon the discrepancies between aspirations and the mobility actually achieved. Generally, when a society moves toward a new stage and social mobility begins (or accelerates), both satisfactions and dissatisfactions tend to arise. At the same time that it points out open pathways to some, mobility presents walls to others. Consequently, various kinds of social tension emerge which did not exist in the previous stage.

As it freezes certain individual plans, mobility brings about new aspirations; that is, as it opens new opportunities for some it brings a certain insecurity to others. This is a phenomenon, therefore, that creates varied effects at the individual level. Once it begins, mobility itself brings about greater diversification in the occupational structure. As people attain new positions, they individually begin to use their greater prestige, power, and contacts to make the inequalities even greater—clearly, in their own favor (Wrong, 1970). In this sense, we can say that mobility both mitigates and accentuates inequality. Keeping in mind the highly varied effects of mobility upon different groups and in different historical moments, it is delusive to think that it always eases social tensions. Indeed, under certain conditions, it reduces tensions, elevates the level of satisfaction, and contributes to a harmony of personal interests; under other conditions, however, it creates tensions, increases dissatisfactions, and contributes to the polarization of personal interests. Numerous sociological studies have tried to identify the respective conditions in which mobility reduces or increases social tension. Such works have focused upon the political consequences of both upward and downward mobility (Germani, 1965; Runciman, 1966).

Upward mobility functions to ease social tensions to the extent that it affects large groups of the lower class, elevating them to the middle class and smoothing out the effects of disparity. For those individuals who rise, this represents a personal solution to the problems stemming from low status. For the group that stays behind, it would represent a weakening of collective power to better the living conditions of the lower class as a whole. This kind of mobility would undermine the political base of the lower class because of the continual loss of its best leaders (Ratinoff, 1967).

The most recent studies have shown that this theory is exaggerated. In the first place, they point out that great masses of individuals rarely move toward the middle class, and that it remains to be proven that the lower class loses the greater part of its leadership even in the most dynamic societies. In the second place, there are no data which demonstrate a change in political orientation among individuals who move up to the middle class, precisely because most upward movement is of a short distance and does not place individuals in such highly contrasting levels of income. This being the case, the political base of the lower class is weakened, and the bourgeois values are strengthened in those who rise, only when the numbers and the social distances covered are truely large (Parkin, 1971: 50–52).

If such is the nature of this phenomenon, then we have to conclude that upward mobility of small groups should accentuate both the feeling of relative deprivation and the political radicalization among those who remain in the lower class. Indeed, such radicalization among those who could not rise is commonly found. However, this is only one of the ways in which groups react to relative deprivation. Another reaction, more common than the first, is resignation and an acceptance of their level of living. This is especially true when the social distance between the lower and middle classes is so great that the members of the former simply do not see those of the latter (Runciman, 1966).

On the other hand, the many social contacts and the mass communication of modern society act as counterforces to conformity. They tend to elevate the aspirations of all the social classes regardless of the distances that separate them. In this case, then, the acceptance of a level of living is less common; consequently, there is a greater probability of a political movement that questions the pattern of inequality and that demands upward mobility. This occurs most frequently among individuals with status inconsistency such as foremen who have the power of command over others without belonging to the dominant class. Sociological literature has shown that inconsistency of status constitutes one of the forces of non-conformity and political mobilization (Lenski, 1967).

Germani assumes the accuracy of the relationships analyzed above, and attempts to generalize. He argues that mobility causes ruptures of social stability (short- or long-lived) in the following situations: (1) when the mobility occurs in the midst of inconsistencies of status; (2) when there is a large gap between the expected and the real opportunities for social mobility. On the other hand, mobility contributes to a common acceptance of the social order when (1) the aspirations for social mobility are widely diffused throughout the population; (2) there is a certain equilibrium between the expected and the real mobility; (3) the mobility takes place within certain limits of status consistency (Germani, 1969:94–104).

It should not be surprising then that social and political outcries increase in the first stages of social mobility, especially when the minority moves a great deal. To the extent that this persists, the political and social movements become more and more organized until they are crystallized into constant forces of social integration. In sum, mobility coexists with both satisfactions and frustrations, past successes and new dreams, with redefinition of expectations and of values: in short, with a dynamic and restless society.

Studies of the consequences of mobility also show that the nature of social tensions changes to the extent that upward social movement reaches great masses of the population and that it is accompanied by improvements (both material and cultural) in the standard of living. Here we leave the situation of rupture and approach the conditions of consensus. But the tension does not disappear totally. Its nature changes: the questioning of the basic values of the political system is reduced, while we find increases in specific outcries in favor of concrete and immediate objectives such as better salaries, better working conditions, a higher standard of living, and individual rights (Cardoso, 1969: Chap. 9). The evolution of the union movement all over the world has followed such a pattern and has been related to the amount and nature of social mobility.[4] But the emergence and the systematic action of such movements constitutes an important and necessary feedback mechanism whose effect is an increasingly dynamic society. No society changes, and none develops, without social tensions.

4. Rodrigues, analyzing the workers in the automotive sector (who generally do ascend socially), found that 88% of his informants judged industrialization positively, as a creator of jobs, but they expressed demands for better salaries and more job security. See Rodrigues, 1967: 240.

Mobility and Social Stratification

In the study of social mobility, social status is a key concept. In the socio-logical literature, *status* is conventionally defined as the position occupied by a person in a social hierarchy of a given system of social stratification. The highest or the lowest social rank in the social pyramid is related primarily to the norms of the stratification system by which the individual is placed.

The norms or criteria of social stratification vary greatly from society to society, from epoch to epoch. In the most dynamic and industrialized societies, individual status tends to be based upon achieved criteria—that is, upon characteristics that the individual can acquire throughout his career, such as education, occupation, and information. In the more static and less industrialized societies individual status tends to be tied to ascribed criteria, such as heritage, race, religion, political affiliation. Within this framework, individuals in modern societies are valued by that which they are able to do; in the traditional societies, by that which they are.[5]

These criteria of status determination, however, are far from being mutually exclusive. Even in the highly industrialized societies, the coexistence of achieved and ascribed factors of determination is common, and it seems that this duality is more pronounced at the extremes of the social structure than in the middle class. Still, the achieved criteria clearly predominate in these so-cieties, since *occupation* and *job rank* (position of responsibility) clearly stand out in them. In other words, individuals position themselves socially, and then their styles of life evolve according to their occupations and, within the oc-cupations, according to the positions they hold. Excluding the rare cases of inheritance, the lottery, and other windfalls, passing from one status to another depends in great part upon changes in occupation or rank. These, in their turn, depend upon structural and individual changes. Although the models by which we interpret social mobility are specifically discussed in Chapter 2, it is ap-propriate at this point to distinguish between the structural and individual determinants on the one hand, and social mobility on the other.

The process of mobility in a given society depends upon structural and individual changes. Structurally, the forces of greatest impact upon social mobility are the transformations in the various sectors of the economy, the level of employment, and the emergence of new occupations. Individually, what especially stand out are education, experience, knowledge, and individual relationships. Mobility is the product of the two types of factors. The weight of each in determining the phenomenon varies according to the stage and the

5. This point of view is in contrast to the Marxist position, according to which individual status is determined by the person's position in the productive process. Such positioning places him in determined social classes, each with its own problems and which struggle among themselves. See, for example, Poulantzas, 1975: 11–44; Carchedi, 1975.

rhythm of the society's development. In the beginning stages of development, as in the case of Brazil, social mobility depends primarily upon structural transformations and secondarily upon the individual modifications. The data of the present research will show, for example, (Chapters 6 and 7) that several social groups have attained much vertical mobility in Brazil despite their meager formal schooling.[6] The market has accepted them as they are and, in one way or another, has allowed them to take advantage of new opportunities and upward movement.

Mobility depends upon occupation and job rank. Before anything else, though, mobility depends upon employment, particularly in societies whose population is growing rapidly. In these societies, not just any type of employment promotes mobility. If the society, for example, simply multiplies the number of jobs in the present structure to attend to the vegetative growth of the economically active population, it will attain full employment but will produce few possibilities for mobility. Mobility will be restricted to an exchanging of positions among individuals of different levels through death, retirement, and other forms of leaving the labor market. If the population is growing significantly, this type of mobility will provide few possibilities to advance a great number of individuals socially. Such possibilities will appear only if the society can create jobs which differ quantitatively and qualitatively from the present ones, jobs that bring about a differentiation of skills and permit the acquisition of new experiences and new positions in the productive structure.[7] In this case, movement is greater and upward movement can occur not only through exchange or substitution, but principally through the opening of new spaces. In other words, mobility depends upon the *number* and the *type* of available jobs. These, in their turn, depend upon numerous changes in the economic sectors and upon the nature and the dynamic of the labor market itself.

The changes in the economic sectors normally lead to social differentiation.[8] Social differentiation in modern societies is based largely on occupation and rank and attests to the fact that, in a determined system of stratification, in-

6. Schooling has a greater or lesser capacity to advance a person depending upon market conditions. In a market which is becoming more and more nearly balanced, education plays an enormous role in advancing people. In an extremely uneven and stagnant market, education can do little. The potential of schooling, therefore, depends upon the nature of the market, upon the style of development, upon the patterns of investing and allocating resources. See Pastore, "Recursos humanos e ensino superior": 35–36.

7. The position taken here admits the importance of the individual's positioning in the productive structure but does not consider it to be the exclusive criterion for defining status. Status is understood to follow from that positioning and from the individual's occupation. This question will be addressed again in Chapter 2.

8. In the classic concepts of sociology, social differentiation coincides with the notion of social development itself. See Durkheim, 1893.

dividuals with different characteristics slowly begin to occupy distinct positions, act out specific roles, and receive different rewards. Such positions are grouped and hierarchized and, as a whole, form the social structure. This being the case, in these societies the nature and the level of internal disparity in the social structure depend fundamentally upon the differentiation of occupations and of job ranks. Consequently, the strategy for studying the social dynamic is based largely upon analysis of the occupational differentiation, of the metamorphosis of occupations in the various sectors of the economy, of the access to new positions, and of the movement among hierarchized occupations—that is, among different levels of occupational status. Vertical mobility, in this conception, is understood as a change of social status occasioned by the individual's passing from one level of occupational status to another. Given the importance of occupational differentiation, one of the first tasks of the study of social mobility is to establish basic concepts by studying the changes that occur through time in the occupational structure.[9]

So far we have discussed the role of structural factors. The factors linked to individual resources also have different origins and characteristics. Some typically are achieved, such as education and experience. Others are ascribed, such as family background and race.[10] Any predominance of some criterion for the definition of status depends greatly upon the society and the period in question, and determines the general picture of equality or inequality in the society's opportunities. In other words, changes in the criteria can cause changes in the origin of social inequality. For example, improvements in education can act together to increase the importance of achieved criteria and to diminish the hegemony of ascribed criteria, so that disparities become more dependent upon the recent past than upon the remote past. Modifications in the quantitative and qualitative availability of jobs can generate new social opportunities and tend toward the same objective; that is, they make the occupational structure flexible and promote structural mobility.

According to the model outlined here, we see that in the beginning stages of development a large part of mobility depends upon changes in the occupational structure. But the sociologist is interested in knowing what is the net impact of such changes vis-a-vis the changes occurring in the individual factors. The analysis of this question will be pursued throughout this book but will be the specific object of Chapter 10.

Considering that social mobility reflects the degree of dynamism and flex-

9. An analysis of the evolutions of occupational structure will be the object of Chapter 4.

10. Until recently, sociological literature insisted that race was of little importance as a determining factor in relation to social disparities in Brazil. According to this point of view, the differences between whites and blacks were differences of class and not of race. A recent work shows that race in itself is a definite factor in social discrimination in Brazil. See Valle-Silva, 1978.

ibility in the social structure, we can conclude that mobility synthesizes a complex of changes that occur through time in the social system and in individuals as both a product and a determinant of development. Social mobility reveals the rhythm and the nature of the changes taking place in the social structure. In the case of Brazil, is the structure opening up or becoming more restricted as a result of social mobility? Internally, is Brazil becoming more flexible or more rigid? Who has risen in the social structure, and why? Who has descended, and why? And why is it that some have not moved at all? Finally, what is the general trend of the Brazilian social structure?

The study of mobility recounted in this book has sought to answer these questions, seeking the answers in the innumerable social changes that have taken place in Brazil throughout the twentieth century, relating them to the changes that have occurred at the individual level. The study seeks to insert itself within the structural-individual perspective summarized above and is based upon secondary data of various sorts (demographic, agricultural, and industrial censuses) and, above all, upon specific data about social mobility in reference to the entire Brazilian population and made available to the author by the IBGE Foundation.

2

Explanatory Models
of Social Mobility

Understanding the phenomenon of social mobility depends largely upon understanding the patterns of social stratification in the society in question. Thus, theories of social stratification form the groundwork for the study of social mobility. Such theories seek to explain the principal characteristics of social differentiation, taking into consideration the historical conditions that produced them, and also the current socio-economic factors that act as sources of disparity among people.

The basic question that the theories of stratification address is perhaps the central problem in all of society: why are people socially different? This question itself includes several other more specific questions which have been the object of sociological research into social stratification: how do people become part of a hierarchy? How do social differences become re-integrated? What is the basic criterion for social differentiation? To put these questions in contemporary jargon, we are seeking the explanatory models of social inequality and social mobility.

As we saw in Chapter 1, the stratification and mobility models are rooted in the two opposite positions which Lenski calls the conservative thesis and the radical antithesis. These positions have had a deep influence upon the development of sociological thinking to this day. In this chapter we shall present the contemporary stratification and mobility models and show that they continue to proceed from the conservative thesis and the radical antithesis. Specifically, this chapter provides a general picture of the models of social differentiation.

14

Mobility and Social Differentiation

Contemporary sociology has used two basic approaches to analyze social differentiation: the *functionalist* approach and the *conflict* approach. These approaches have been derived from the conservative and radical positions mentioned above.

The functional approach sees social differentiation as universal and necessary for societal efficiency. Davis and Moore advanced furthest in formalizing this approach. In their formulation, the tasks which must be carried out in a society differ in importance, difficulty, and prestige. Consequently, a society creates a structure of positions with differentiated rewards. Those individuals receive greater rewards who work in occupations of greater importance, difficulty, and prestige (Davis and Moore, 1945; Stinchombe, 1963). This being the case, social differentiation would arise from the fact that certain social positions are more difficult to fill than others. In modern times, according to this approach, such occupations are those which require more schooling and experience—in short, higher qualifications. In addition, these occupations are "more important" than others and, therefore, are differentiated as to the rewards that society offers. Consequently, occupational statuses become distributed in a hierarchy in the social structure.

The functionalist approach argues further that the differentiation of rewards given to incumbents with different occupational statuses stimulates them to prepare themselves to compete actively for ever higher and better-paid positions. As a result we would have individual progress and better manpower qualifications in the labor market. In other words, individual progress would be the functional basis of social efficiency. The functionalist approach represents the sociological version of the supply and demand approach of neoclassical economics.

Few sociological propositions provoke as much debate as do those presented above (Tumin, 1953; Davis, 1953; Wesotowiski, 1962; Grandjean, 1975). And no wonder. Besides their strong ideological content in support of the status quo, the proposals of Davis and Moore are difficult to prove or disprove. How can we decide whether differentiation is universal and necessary or universal and unnecessary? Empirical procedures to make such a decision do not exist (Svalastoga, 1964).

In contrast to the functionalist approach, and almost as a reaction to it, the conflict approach argues that differences in rewards and status have much more to do with the positioning of the individual in relation to capital in the productive process than they do with the individual's qualifications. Access to and command of strategic resources, especially capital, put individuals in positions of greater power. Therefore, the most relevant social differentiation is that which springs from power and not from individuals' occupations. In this formulation, the labor market is merely a locus where trajectories of power are determined and where competition and tension occur between the various interest groups (Giddens, 1973. See also Fernandes, 1968; Ianni, 1963; Cardoso, 1969; Cardoso and Falleto, 1970).

These two approaches have different implications in the explanation of social mobility phenomena. To the functionalist mind, rewards are directly proportional to the degree of specialty in an occupation and to the qualifications of the person in that occupation. Profession is a powerful determinant of social and economic rewards—that is, of individual status.

According to the conflict approach, rewards and status are functions of the positioning of the individual in the power structure. Mobility here depends upon a changing of professions. Proximity to or distance from the centers of power is what determines the pattern of social differentiation.[1] To undergo mobility depends fundamentally upon the individual's positioning in the power structure.

Thus, the most important implication of these two positions is that which relates to the definitions of status and of social structure. In the functionalist approach, the key element is occupation; in the conflict approach, it is power.

It is possible to visualize a combination of the two approaches, so that mobility becomes understood as stemming from a combination of occupation and power within the social space. The difficulties involved here are more of a methodological than of a theoretical character.[2] The ways to define and measure power are still obscure. The sources of power seem to go beyond the possession of capital and labor in modern society. Furthermore, the nature of the interaction between occupation and power in the various levels of the social structure is unknown. All these difficulties are methodological obstacles to using an eventual hybrid model of the determinants of social stratification and mobility. Theoretically, no greater incompatibilities exist than those in these two approaches. But on the contrary, we can see very promising aspects in this effort. We believe that it may significantly increase the effectiveness of existing theories. Above all, a hybrid model of this type could simultaneously take into account two of the principal dimensions of social structure.

Blau seems to have gone far in this direction. He discerns two types of parameters in social structure. Of the first type are the *nominal parameters*— that is, those which divide the population into subgroups with explicit boundaries. In these groups there is no inherent hierarchy, although empirically they may be connected by hierarchical criteria. Sex, religion, race, and profession

1. Recently, this position has been making its first advances toward the operational level. Social status is seen as the product of an individual's position relative to capital and labor. See Wright, 1976; Wright and Perrone, 1977.

2. Support for this synthesis can be found in R. Bendix's comparison of Marx and Weber (1974).

are examples of nominal parameters. Of the second type are the *graduated parameters,* which differentiate individuals in terms of a hierarchy or status. At first, this graduation is continuous, which means that the parameters in themselves do not constitute borders among the strata; but their actual distribution may reveal discontinuities which reflect hierarchies of status. Education, age, income, prestige, and power are examples of graduated parameters (Blau, 1975:222–224).

The nominal parameters produce a horizontal differentiation, or heterogeneity, while the graduated parameters produce a vertical differentiation, or inequality.

Connections between a nominal parameter and the graduated parameters denote status differences among groups, as is the case of differences in education, income, and prestige among religious groups. High correlations between the two types of parameters allow one to construct new parameters, *ordinal parameters,* which divide people into groups with distinct boundaries and which are ordered according to a hierarchy (Blau, 1975:225–226). Based on this principle, occupational status indices have been constructed which take into account the differences in education and income among the large occupational groups (Duncan, 1961; Bogue, 1963).

Within this same methodological strategy we see the possibility of combining professions and levels of power. With this procedure we could close in on an operating definition of social class. When we consider individual possession of produced goods, we are dealing with a nominal parameter (ownership), and the individuals become divided into two relatively distinct groups—capitalists and workers. When we introduce education and income, we are using graduated parameters to hierarchize people within each nominal category. And when we combine the two, we get a status hierarchy described by ordinal parameters, the product of combining the previous categories. Such efforts, however, are in the beginning stage.[3] It will be some time before we attain an adequate methodological level and before data become available that will turn this new approach into a viable project.

For now we must continue to use the models for social mobility analysis which are based upon occupational status, combining profession, education, and income. Such an approach sees social differentiation as a differentiation of occupational statuses that are defined by ordinal parameters, the product of combining a nominal parameter (profession) with two graduated parameters (education and income).[4] In the meantime, we already can add a great deal to conventional analysis of social mobility by inserting into the explanatory

3. Wright is coming very close to this method of operation and, we believe, within a few years we will be able to work at the empirical level with the hybrid model mentioned above. See Wright, 1977.

4. How occupational status operates will be discussed in Chapter 3.

models certain structural factors which act as intervening and, often, independent variables, and which precede individual factors. In other words, we shall analyze social mobility as a function of occupational structure differentiation and of modifications in individual resources (education, ability, job training, age). We see this type of approach as conforming to the empirical-analytical synthesis mentioned in Chapter 1.

Employment and Mobility

In order to understand how social mobility occurs, one must try to find the ruling logic behind the phenomenon. In this context, to discover the logic means to identify the key components of the phenomenon, their order of occurrence, and their mode of articulation. This and the next sections present an attempt to create an explanatory model of social mobility. This model will be used as a paradigm for analyzing all the empirical material of the present research.

In modern societies, the determination of occupational status and the movement of individuals to higher or lower status levels take place within a complex of labor market forces. These forces are basically of two natures. On the one hand are the market forces themselves, which are manifested in the demand for manpower and also in the specific demand for certain occupations. On the other hand are the forces connected to individuals, which are manifested in the quality of manpower offered on the market. New opportunities for work, and their attainment, arise simultaneously from a coming together of these two complexes of forces.[5] The emergence of opportunities has more to do with the characteristics of the economy. The attainment of these opportunities has more to do with the qualities, decisions, and possibilities of individuals. Therefore, to understand more precisely why individual A reached a higher status than did individual B, one must grasp in detail the dynamic of the process of *emergence* and *attainment* of opportunities; this implies a joint study of the characteristics of the labor market and of the individuals involved. This is especially true for developing societies, whose mobility depends greatly upon generating opportunities.

The most conventional sociological perspective, functionalism, tends to begin with the assumption that opportunities are pre-existing; thus, the question becomes: given these opportunities for work, what are the individual factors which determine the success or failure of the people involved in the process? Clearly, when the opportunities are many and diverse, the question of success or failure does in fact tend to restrict itself to individual performance and to

---

5. This integrated conception is being formalized by Sorensen and others in recent works. See Sorensen, 1977 and 1976; Schervish, 1977.

the abilities acquired by the individual in school or at work. But, when opportunities are few and not diversified, education, experience, and abilities can do little to create jobs and to promote mobility.[6] In these circumstances, the first step in the study of mobility seems to be to understand the conditions by which jobs are created.

Generally, jobs are made available by businesses.[7] Theoretically, the availability of employment is a consequence of the ability of businesses to sell their goods and services on the market. In this way, as the market expands, employment goes up. But the nature of the market expansion is more important than the generation of jobs itself. There are indications that in the beginning stages of development, expansion of the market toward mass consumer items tends to generate more employment than does an expansion in luxury items (Moura da Silva, n.d.: 91–98).

Thus, the nature of the goods produced and sold, and the nature of the productive process, end up influencing the level of employment and the types of jobs. This, in turn, determines the prestige, power, and income that the society can offer to the employed. In other words, society counts upon an initial level of inequality that stems from the types of jobs offered—this inequality being relatively independent of individuals' characteristics. In the beginning stages of development, societies which offer few jobs or jobs concentrated in certain places in the social structure tend to make social mobility difficult. Societies which supply many jobs and which diversify their occupational structure tend to facilitate social mobility. This is to emphasize the idea that the question of employment depends more upon the society than upon the individual, just as mobility in the beginning stages of development depends more upon market characteristics than upon the quality of the individuals involved.

Occupation and Mobility

Both intergenerational and intragenerational mobility depend fundamentally upon occupational changes. Occupational changes can be of three types: (a) the individual moves between *professions* of different levels; (b) the individual

6. Several studies have questioned this formulation of the role of education in social mobility. See Jencks, 1972; Bowles and Gintis, 1976.

7. It is true that in the informal markets, jobs are generated and made available under diverse circumstances (just as the streets and plazas make possible itinerant laborers, ticket sellers, shoeshiners, etc.), assuming the relevance of labor market segmentation for the study of social stratification and mobility phenomena. Nevertheless, given the nature of this book, the approach to this problem in terms of market dualism will remain for a later analysis. Velloso, using the same occupational scale used in this book (see Chapter 3), has studied the impact of market dualism in the economic attainment of people in Brazil. See Velloso, 1975.

stays in his profession but moves between *ranks* (jobs, or positions of responsibility); (c) the individual moves between professions and ranks of different
levels. These three movements are special dimensions of social mobility. In
the first case, mobility is determined by changes in profession; in the second,
by changes in rank; in the third, by changes in profession and rank.[8]

These three types of occupational movements reflect instances of mobility.
They come about through a combination of individual and market characteristics. On the individual side, sociological studies indicate that individuals
change professions, ranks, or both, keeping in mind the following benefits:
(a) *intrinsic* benefits, related to the profession and rank in themselves, referring
to the satisfaction or dissatisfaction of carrying out the tasks inherent to the
new occupation; (b) benefits of *convenience,* related to the comfort and security
involved in carrying out the new tasks; (c) *financial* benefits, having to do with
remuneration and profits (present and future); (d) *social* benefits, referring to
the community of colleagues, to the hierarchy, to the level of political organization in the occupation, to the strength of union activity; and (e) *career*
benefits, involving the possibilities for promotion.

The rewards handed out to the different occupational statuses are varied and
fall within a large spectrum, affecting not only the incumbents but also their
dependents (Bielby and Kalleberg, 1975). These rewards are material and non-
material, immediate or eventual, for the individual or for his offspring. The
importance of each of them obviously varies from person to person. Some are
inclined to sacrifice convenience for financial benefits; others prefer to sacrifice
social rewards in favor of their children's careers, and so on. In one way or
another, these factors are taken into consideration by the person who is con-
fronted by the process of changing professions, jobs, or both. Thus, changes
in occupational status reflect vast modifications which are far removed from
the changes revealed by common indicators (income, education, standard of
living).

On the societal side, economic studies indicate that people are limited in
their desires by the structural restrictions of the labor market; that is, the levels
of employment and unemployment and the distribution of opportunities affect
the individuals' possibilities for social mobility.

In the same manner, the value of an individual in the labor market is determined, on the one hand, by his own resources and, on the other, by characteristics of the market itself. As for the first aspect, it can be argued that, *ceteris
paribus,* the greater the individual's resources (education, experience, skills)
the greater will be his opportunities, and consequently, the greater will be his

---

8. When an individual changes jobs he eventually may undergo mobility of types *a, b,*
and *c*. The scales that take into account profession and rank clearly include the three types of
mobility.

possibility for mobility. Touching on the second aspect, individuals face different pressures of hiring and firing that stem from structural factors of the labor market, particularly the general level of employment.[9]

Structural and Circulation Mobility

In considering the structural variables, one must understand that opportunities open up in the labor market and that opportunities for changing professions, ranks, or both open up as a consequence of this. For the sake of simplicity, opportunities for changes in positions, ranks, or both will be considered as opportunities for new positions in new jobs.[10]

The positions or jobs generated in a society may be vacant or filled; individuals may be employed or unemployed. The vacant positions in the various levels of new jobs occur when individuals leave existing positions through death, retirement, sickness, etc. When the new positions become abundant, mobility tends to take place more or less independently of the individuals' characteristics. In the long run, these people adjust themselves to the requirements of the new positions (Sorenson, 1975). The mobility in this case is called *structural mobility*.

When the new positions are scarce or created slowly, personal characteristics tend to become more important and to determine who will be chosen from among the candidates to fill the few open spots. In this case, a person's rise in the occupational structure depends upon the fall or exit of another; the resulting mobility is called *circulation mobility*.[11]

9. These pressures obviously affect people's capacity to make decisions themselves—that is, voluntary mobility. The capacity to make decisions is a variable existing between structural and individual factors, so that decision-making autonomy is a proxy of the determinants of *a-*, *b-*, or *c*-type changes. When the individual has full autonomy, the changes will be determined by his resources—that is, by that which he has accumulated in the past. When the individual has no autonomy at all, changes will be determined by oscillations in the labor market. Keeping in mind that individuals always seek to maximize their prestige, power, and income in their moves, we can anticipate that mobility will reach a maximum point when the individuals have full autonomy. Conversely, when they have no autonomy, changes are involuntary, and because of this they tend to accept any job available, no matter what it may be; in these circumstances, we can anticipate a minimum level of mobility, depending, of course, on the point of departure.

10. Therefore, the possibilities for mobility are conditioned at this level by the possibilities for employment, since it is through employment that the individual is rewarded in terms of prestige, power, and income. The rewards stemming from an individual's performance in a certain job will be ignored for the sake of argument. The basic presupposition, although not realistic, is that different individuals in the same jobs receive the same rewards, and that equal individuals in different jobs receive different rewards.

11. For a more detailed discussion of the various types of social mobility, see Kahl, 1957: Chap. 9; Germani, 1965:278–283; Broom and Lancaster, 1977: Chap. 3. The differences in the scales of these two types of social mobility will be presented in Chapter 3.

Circulation mobility includes two types of movements. One type is the movement of individuals from filled positions to positions which had been vacant. In this case, mobility itself creates vacancies to be filled by individuals from other positions or by recruiting people who were not in the work force. The other type is movement of vacant positions in a direction opposite to people's mobility. When a person moves from a position at level y to fill a position at level $y + 1$, the vacancies move in the opposite direction; that is, a space at level $y + 1$ has been filled, and another has opened up at level y.

The creation of vacancies and entrance into the various positions of the social structure depend upon the level of the position in question. The higher the position, the greater the difficulty of access to the position. Thus, it is reasonable to expect more structural mobility at the base of the social pyramid than at the top and, conversely, more circulation mobility at the top than at the base. In the same way, one expects structural mobility to predominate in the beginning stages of development and circulation mobility in the more advanced stages.[12]

The dynamic of the generation and disappearance of vacancies depends largely upon the nature of the labor market: this brings about a mobility of positions and of individuals recruited from outside the work force.

Opportunity Attainment

People are exposed in different ways to the various occupational opportunities in the several levels of the social structure. They also differ in their ability to attain these opportunities, because of the inequalities in resources among them—particularly education, experience, skills, and contacts. The higher the level of the position in question, the greater must be the resources for attaining it. Generally, the majority of people enter the work force in pursuit of positions offering modest rewards. The greater the time spent in the labor market, the greater is the probability of mobility—that is, the greater the probability that professionals will adjust their individual characteristics to those required by the positions. If there are no structural barriers, this adjustment is a function simply of the time spent in the work force. But if barriers do exist, the adjustment comes about through the interaction of individual resources and the structural restrictions (Sorenson, 1972).

Individuals move within discrete positions in the labor market, so that competition for filling new positions occurs mainly within each level or among

12. Various authors deliberately restrict the study of social mobility to circulation mobility. They argue that structural mobility is induced by the social system and for this reason can not serve in an analysis of the tightening or loosening of the social structure; an analysis would be possible only if based upon circulation mobility. See McClendon, 1977.

contiguous levels. When one considers the various levels of the social structure it becomes clear that, once mobility starts, the next stages are determined by a complex of dependent probabilities which reflect the individual's possibility of moving from a level i position to another at level j. The higher the level, the more difficult is mobility. Putting it another way, we can say that the higher the status level reached by an individual, the fewer will be his chances to accumulate additional rewards.

In summary, social mobility is taken here to be the product of a combination of individual resources and structural restrictions (Sorensen, 1977). Thus, there is a function f which relates the individual resources X to the opportunities and structural inequalities Z, so that the level of attainment is given by

$$Y = f(Z)(X)$$

In fact, Z represents the structure itself of opportunities (or inequalities). The individual resources X are acted upon by the structure Z to determine Y. As we relate X to Y, it is obvious that the result differs from society to society owing to the intermediation of Z.

If we want a more realistic point of view, Z and X can be broken down into their various components. From the structural side Z, of special importance are the general levels of employment, occupational differentiation, regional development, urbanization, and industrialization. From the individual side X, of special relevance are formal education, age, experience in the labor market, and whether from a rural or urban background. The analysis adopted in this book follows precisely this logic. Mobility will be examined, first, as a function of structural characteristics and, second, as a function of the interaction among the individual and structural variables. We believe that this conception of the phenomenon has the advantage of keeping the individual's career within a more realistic framework. In addition, this formulation allows the idea that, for the same resources in limited opportunity conditions, careers tend to stabilize themselves rapidly. When opportunities are greater, careers tend to progress continuously (Sorensen, 1976). Let us suppose, for example, that we want to examine the impact of one of the individual resources, let us say education, upon the level of career attainment; let us suppose further that by analyzing the impact of education between two periods in the same society we observed a substantial increase in its power of determination. Does this mean that education has become more important than before in attaining the higher positions? Not necessarily, for the increase in determining power may have stemmed from changes in the structure of opportunities or inequalities. Thus, when the structure begins to open up, more opportunities emerge for change of status. Here, education has a strong impact upon mobility. However, when the structure opens up further and education becomes widespread, it tends to play a less relevant role in mobility. Even if such an interpretation is trivial from a statistical point of view, it is interesting to note that both the theory of human capital and stratification studies make very naive comparisons of the impact of education in different times and societies, omitting the role of the different opportunities in determining career and mobility.

3

Methodology of Social Mobility

Sociology already has a nearly fifty-year tradition of social mobility study. Early works from the end of the twenties and from the thirties were conceptual and descriptive in character. They established definitions and the basic types of horizontal and vertical mobility (Sorokin, 1927; Sorokin, 1930), as well as the first attempts to measure social status (Edwards, 1938; Sewell, 1940), and the first studies of social structure at the community level (Lynd and Lynd, 1937; Davidson and Dewey, 1937). The first attempts to formalize a theory of stratification and social mobility began to appear in the forties (Parsons, 1940; Davis and Moore, 1945; Lipset and Rogoff, 1954; Lipset and Bendix, 1959; Lenski, 1958; Boalt, 1954). The next fifteen years brought enormous efforts in methodological formulation and applications of existing tools for the study of specific societies. Studies from that period also sought to establish more precise relationships between social origin and individual attainment, as well as to explain the determining factors of individual successes and failures in the professional career.

Studies of intergenerational mobility were based upon occupational status change between fathers and sons; analyses of intragenerational mobility were based upon status change between the first and current jobs. These studies pioneered the development of various measurements of association for research into the relationships in the occupational status change matrices (Glass, 1954 a and b; Rogoff, 1953; Prais, 1955; Jaffe and Carleton, 1954; Carlsson, 1958; Deasy, 1955).

The studies of the past 20 years have introduced a new technical rigor, especially the techniques of regression studies and of path analysis; they aim at a higher level of explanation based on causal models, nearly all of them seeking to identify the net effects of the various determinants of social mobility. This type of methodological approach continued in the seventies and is still largely accepted today (Blau and Duncan, 1967; Duncan, Featherman, and Duncan, 1972; Sewell and Hauser, 1975; Hauser and Featherman, 1977). Recently, however, various studies have sought to rework the strategy of status change, combining it with regression models or, more precisely, using log-linear regression models in mobility tables (Featherman and Hauser, 1978).

In Brazil, early empirical studies began in the second half of the fifties and maintained the current methodological orientation; that is, they used primarily the change matrices and indices of association.[1] The most eminent study in that period was Glass, et al., 1954, which analyzed social mobility between generations in England and introduced various new procedures for detecting the basic types of mobility and their determinants. Less than a year after publication of that study, the same methodology was brought to Brazil by Hutchinson, who in 1955 carried out a now classic study of mobility in São Paulo (Hutchinson, 1960). Although this work was limited in scope to the citizens of the city of São Paulo, it represents a methodological landmark in the field of social mobility. Hutchinson and his collaborators established for the first time in Brazil an occupational status scale based on professional prestige (Hutchinson and Castaldi, in Hutchinson, 1960; Hutchinson, 1957). They were also the first to carry out in Brazil a study of intergenerational social mobility by age groups (Hutchinson, "Mudanças . . ." in Hutchinson, 1960). Finally, the work introduced into Brazil an approximate notion of structural and circulation mobility.[2]

Hutchinson's work suffers from several problems. The most serious is an inadequate sampling for comparison of the inhabitants of the city of São Paulo with the social structure in England, Italy, France, and the United States. Apart from this, one must recognize in this work an innovative leap, especially in the use of change matrices, association indices, and various other methods for the study of social mobility, which had been developed recently in Europe.

After this work, Hutchinson expanded his studies into the comparative area

1. Before the fifties various studies were carried out at the local level which also dealt with the questions of socio-economic level, occupations and social status, but rarely with social mobility. For the record, we must mention the following works: Lowrie, 1938a and 1938b; Araujo, 1947; Hermann, 1948.

2. Hutchinson was referring to social mobility "due to structural change and mobility due to exchange of positions." Comparing the Brazilian situation with that of England, Hutchinson pointed out that in the latter country most mobility occurred through "exchange of positions" within a very stable structure, while in São Paulo mobility was due basically to the "creation of new opportunities" and to economic development (Hutchinson, 1960:218–22).

(1962) and even into analysis of the effects of particular variables, especially education and migration (1958; 1961; 1962). Almost simultaneously, but using secondary data, Havighurst carried out a series of comparative studies on social mobility, in which Brazil was compared to the United States, England, and Australia (Havighurst, 1957). Working for UNESCO, both Hutchinson and Havighurst emphasized the role of education as a force for social mobility in Brazil. They eventually influenced various other projects of educational sociology, in which the theoretical focus upon stratification and the methodology for measuring social status were further developed. Such is the case for Moreira, 1960; Gouveia, 1965; and Kahl, 1965 and 1969.[3] But in reality, the methodological innovations introduced by *Mobilidade e trabalho* (*Mobility and work* [Hutchinson, 1960]) were not continued through either the sixties or the seventies. Even the theme of social mobility seems to have been put aside in the sociology taught and practiced in Brazil, even though sociologists, almost without exception, have been concerned with the question of inequality, of relationships between social classes, and of the interactions of class and race.[4]

In this sense, this study represents a return to the methodology introduced by Hutchinson, incorporating, of course, the advances of the last twenty years which have brought about better tools for explaining social mobility. This study uses data from the first national sample on social mobility in Brazil.[5]

Orientation of This Study

In this study, occupational mobility is used as a proxy for social mobility. As we shall see, the empirical material supplied by the PNAD/73 (National Household Research, 1973) permitted us to hierarchize the occupations of heads of family according to education and income, thus obtaining an occupational status scale. These statuses were grouped beforehand in six social strata based upon the degree of homogeneity of the occupations.

Occupational status as a proxy for social status has been used extensively in sociology, although with reservations. Many specialists in mobility question the unidimensionality of occupational classifications, the legitimacy of grouping occupations in social strata, and the establishment of the strata. However, most specialists recognize occupational status as the most stable and synthetic indicator for revealing the social condition of an individual and his family. Occupation in itself is a powerful indicator of an individual's positioning in

3. One of the few recent attempts to study the structure of social inequalities in Brazil, at the aggregate level and based upon census data, is Araujo, 1976.

4. Brazil has produced a number of studies in the area of class-race relationships: Cardoso and Ianni, 1960; Fernandes, 1965; Ianni, 1966.

5. These same data have already permitted three preliminary studies to be carried out on the subject: Pastore, 1977a; Costa, 1977; Pastore, 1978.

the social structure. When we meet a person for the first time, our most immediate question is, "What do you do?" Knowing what the person does provides a basis for classifying him in social space. But this positioning is not always consistent. To get a better idea we need to know more: How much does he earn? What is his education level? These are the steps by which one constructs an occupational status index (Hall, 1975; Treiman, 1978).

Many contemporary sociologists agree that measurements of mobility based upon occupational status provide a reliable base from which the flexibility or the rigidity of a society may be calculated through time. Mobility today is seen as stemming from a series of events which govern access to social positions; access in itself brings together many of these events. In this sense, understanding the entries into and departures from occupations of different statuses becomes a key for understanding the social dynamic, the changes in the social structure—or, as Featherman and Hauser (1978:20) would have it, the "social metabolism."[6]

Sociologists have come to attribute great importance to the study of occupations. They see occupation as the most stable (and theoretically the richest) indicator for comparing generations and social groups through time. Attempts to use only income over long periods of time, besides being theoretically poorer, have faced insuperable difficulties stemming from a differentiated participation of non-monetary income from inflation, from differences in procedure (hourly wages, monthly incomes), etc.[7]

Besides the above reasons, occupations are an early basis for social differentiation in modern society; the level of differentiation is the starting point which enables one to estimate the possibilities of structural and circulation mobility within a society.

This study has adopted the strategy of status change matrices and of regression analysis. The option to analyze status matrices was based upon numerous advantages considered to be of special relevance to the case of Brazil: (a) the lack of basic, descriptive studies in Brazil seems to recommend a certain caution as to entering directly into more sophisticated analytical models, such as those of regression and path analysis; (b) examining occupational matrices is what permits us to visualize and to locate more easily the changes in social structure. It is important to know if the greater amount of mobility occurred

6. For a complete discussion of the various methods of measuring mobility, see Bibby, 1975.

7. It is true that the significance of an occupation today may be different from the significance of the same occupation 30 or 40 years ago. But, although occupations may interchange positions, rarely do they cross the boundaries of strata or social classes. One of the instances generally cited is that of the primary school teacher. This occupation, which today is commonly classified within the middle-middle stratum, apparently belonged to higher social strata in the past. (This has not affected this study, since the sample is made up only of men, with a low incidence of primary school teachers.)

in the base, in the top, or in the middle of the social pyramid; (c) analysis of mobility from occupational matrices facilitates the identification of the predominant type of mobility in the system.[8]

Although nearly all of this analysis has been based upon status change matrices, the final chapter concentrates upon developing more analytical models, in which the relative weights of each of the determinants of social mobility in Brazil are established.

Status Change Matrices and Types of Mobility

Table 3.1 is a status change matrix which relates social origin to social destination. It may take as origin the father's status or the individual's first job. It may take as destination the individual's first or his current job. Analysis of the rows of data provides an idea of origin-destination; that is, we learn to what extent individuals born or beginning in the various status levels finally reach different levels. Analysis of the columns of data can show whence come the individuals who compose the various status levels of destination.

TABLE 3.1. Matrix for Change in Social Status

Status of Origin	Status of Destination								
	1	2	3	4	5	6		r	Total
1	n_{11}	n_{12}	n_{13}	. . . .				n_{1r}	$n_{1\cdot}$
2	n_{21}	n_{22}	n_{23}	. . . .				n_{2r}	$n_{2\cdot}$
3	n_{31}	n_{32}	n_{33}	. . . .				n_{3r}	$n_{3\cdot}$
4	.	.	.	. . . .				.	.
5	.	.	.	. . . .				.	.
6	.	.	.	. . . .				.	.
.	.	.	.	. . . .				.	.
.	.	.	.	. . . .				.	.
.	.	.	.	. . . .				.	.
r	n_{r1}	n_{r2}	n_{r3}	. . . .				n_{rr}	$n_{r\cdot}$
Total	$n_{\cdot1}$	$n_{\cdot2}$	$n_{\cdot3}$	. . . .				$n_{\cdot r}$	N

Total mobility refers to the percentage of people who depart from the principal diagonal, falling or rising in the social structure. Total mobility reflects the degree of flexibility in the social structure. A flexible society tends to place people in statuses different from those of origin. In a rigid society, people tend

8. The author recognizes the dangers and the caution necessary for validating the results of these matrices. The principal concern in interpreting these results is shown by the fact that when one speaks of a 1% probability of a person reaching a certain social stratum, this has a different significance when that stratum constitutes 1% of the population than it has when the stratum constitutes 5% of the population. Other proposals to improve the use of mobility matrices are presented by McCann, 1977.

to remain in their original status (along the principal diagonal), and the social structure reproduces itself through time.

A flexible structure may show various types of mobility. Part of the people may achieve *upward mobility,* eventually occupying statuses hierarchically superior to those of origin. Another part of the people may suffer *downward mobility,* shifting to status levels lower than those of origin.

Social mobility itself may have diverse origins. Most important is the mobility stemming from changes in the distributions of origin and of destination, such as from fathers to sons. In this case, individuals move in the direction of new spots and positions which appear in the market, from fathers to sons. In their turn, differences between the fathers' social structures and those of the sons normally are due to changes in the society's occupational structure. It is common for agricultural occupations to diminish with time, while opportunities in the secondary and tertiary urban sectors increase. The differences between fathers and sons stemming from this change "force" a mobility defined in Chapter 2 as *structural mobility* or *induced mobility.*[9]

One must also consider the mobility that is the result of individual improvement and successes, which do not depend upon what happens with the marginal distributions of origin and destination. For example, a hypothetical society in which the spots available to the sons were exactly the same as those available to the fathers might still exhibit a high degree of social mobility. This would depend upon competition among individuals, upon exchange of positions, or upon departure of people from the work force, thus opening up places for others. This type of mobility has less impact than does structural mobility upon any change in the social structure format. It was defined in Chapter 2 as *circulation mobility* or *pure mobility* (Featherman and Hauser, 1978: 70–73; Yassuda, 1964).

Many sociologists argue that studies which seek to identify flexibility of social structure and the degree of openness of a society should control for structural mobility and try to discover the net effects of circulation mobility— that is, to focus only upon mobility which does not stem from differences between the distributions of origin and of destination (McClendon, 1977; Collins, 1975: Chap. 8). Others argue that the structural dimension is particularly important for finding a society's capacity to generate new occupational opportunities, and, therefore, for the labor market to differentiate socially. Consequently, they propose that total mobility be decomposed into structural and circulation mobility in order to estimate the percentage of each and to situate them on the pattern of development of the society (Rogoff, 1953; Lipset and Bendix, 1959: Chap. 10; Marsh, 1963).

The present study aligns itself with more recent sociological thought ac-

9. For criteria for measuring and analyzing structural mobility, see: Boudon, 1973; Matras, 1975: Chap. 10; Yassuda, 1964.

cording to which structural changes are considered important propelling forces of social mobility. This orientation was recommended explicitly by Miller (1971) when he said that "future studies should concentrate upon factors that produce or retard the mobility of strata or particular groups. This will force sociologists to analyze more carefully the role of economic changes in social mobility." Goldthrope (1966), in the same line, had already argued that circulation mobility has remained at the same level in the last decades in numerous societies, suggesting that the determinants of the fluctuations of total mobility should be sought in structural mobility. Hauser (1975a, 1975b), Payne, Ford, and Robertson (1974), and various Eastern European sociologists (Zagorski, 1976; Andorka and Zagorski, 1978; Szymanski, 1978) are dedicating special attention to structural mobility.

Various authors use the model of perfect mobility as a paradigm for the study of deviations of the real situation from the theoretical situation. With this model as a base, it is possible to estimate structural and circulation mobility and to contrast them with the (perfect) theoretical situation. Formulas proposed for putting this strategy into practice have been more varied. The formula proposed by Yassuda is one of the most frequently used, and has shown itself to be relatively insensitive to the impact of marginals. In this study we have followed Yassuda's model to estimate the three types of mobility described above. Table 3.1, for example, row by row, makes possible a disaggregated estimate of the following types of social mobility:

Total Mobility $= n_i. - n_{ii}$

Structural Mobility $= n_i - \bar{n}_{ii}{}^{10}$

Circulation Mobility = Total Mobility − Structural Mobility $= (n_i. - n_{ii}) - (n_i - \bar{n}_{ii}) = n_i. - n_{ii}$

For the matrix as a whole (Table 3.1) we can estimate the three types of mobility in a similar manner.[11]

Total Mobility $= N - \sum_{i=1}^{r} n_{ii}$

Structural Mobility[12] $= \sum_{i=1}^{r} n_i - \sum_{i=1}^{r} \bar{n}_{ii} = N - \sum_{i=1}^{r} \bar{n}_{ii}$

Circulation Mobility[13] $= (N - \sum_{i=1}^{r} n_{ii}) - (N - \sum_{i=1}^{r} \bar{n}_{ii}) = \sum_{i=1}^{r} \bar{n}_{ii} - \sum_{i=1}^{r} n_{ii}$

10. N_{ii} is the minimum of the two marginal values $n_i.$ and $n._i$.

11. When one wants to express these measurements in percentages, as will be done in the body of this study, it suffices to divide them by N and to multiply them by 100.

12. Structural mobility reflects the proportion of individuals who are mobile due to the differences of the marginal distributions of the rows and of the columns.

13. Circulation mobility refers to the proportion of individuals who are mobile through various causes of structural mobility.

With these three formulas, Yassuda proposed a synthetic index of social mobility, also called mobility index or *openness coefficient,* which actually measures the degree of flexibility in the social structure. This index is defined as

$$Y = \frac{\sum\limits_{i=1}^{r} \bar{n}_{ii} - \sum\limits_{i=1}^{r} n_{ii}}{\sum\limits_{i=1}^{r} \bar{n}_i - \sum\limits_{i=1}^{r} \frac{n_{i\cdot} \times n_{\cdot i}}{N}}$$

The numerator indicates circulation mobility and the denominator reflects a structural mobility compared with the theoretical situation ($\sum \frac{n_{i\cdot} \times n_{ii}}{N}$).[14]

Let us look at an example based upon a real matrix of fathers-to-sons mobility (Table 3.2), which will be analyzed in detail in the next chapters:

$$\text{Total Mobility} = \frac{\sum\limits_{i=1}^{6} n_{ii}}{N} = \frac{25908}{44307} = 0.58$$

$$\text{Structural Mobility} = 1 - \frac{\sum\limits_{i=1}^{6} \bar{n}_{ii}}{N} = 1 - \frac{29,792}{44,307} = 1 - 0.67 = 0.33$$

Circulation Mobility = Total Mobility − Structural Mobility = 0.58 − 0.33 = 0.25

Mobility Index:

$$Y = \frac{\sum\limits_{i=1}^{6} \bar{n}_{ii} - \sum\limits_{i=1}^{6} n_{ii}}{\sum\limits_{i=1}^{6} \bar{n}_{ii} - \frac{n_{i\cdot} \times n_{\cdot i}}{N}} = \frac{11,393}{17,896} = 0.64$$

One concludes, then, that in Brazil there was 58% total mobility between fathers and sons. This mobility can be decomposed into two components. Structural (or induced) mobility, due to differences in the distributions of fathers and of sons, was 0.33; circulation mobility, due to exchanges and sub-

---

14. The Yassuda index shows the proportion of circulation mobility in relation to structural mobility (in its turn compared with a situation of perfect mobility or independence). See Yassuda, 1964. Featherman and Hauser (1978:71) used the *Y* mobility index as an indicator of the proportion of circulation mobility (in relation to the sum of structural mobility) given by the percentage of individuals who would have been mobile if there had been independence between origin and destination.

TABLE 3.2. Intergenerational Mobility Matrix

Father's Status*	Individual's Status in 1973							Total Fathers (%)
	1	2	3	4	5	6	Total	
1. Upper	270	204	245	113	45	28	905	
(%)	(29.8)	(22.5)	(27.1)	(12.5)	(5.0)	(3.1)	(100.0)	2.0
2. Upper-middle	211	399	397	214	84	80	1,385	
(%)	(15.2)	(28.8)	(28.7)	(15.5)	(6.1)	(5.8)	(100.0)	3.1
3. Middle-middle	525	879	2,221	1,157	647	704	6,133	
(%)	(8.6)	(14.3)	(36.2)	(18.9)	(10.5)	(11.5)	(100.0)	13.8
4. Lower-middle	156	360	890	1,904	613	195	4,118	
(%)	(3.8)	(8.7)	(21.6)	(46.2)	(14.9)	(4.7)	(100.0)	9.3
5. Upper-lower	97	227	637	1,092	732	293	3,078	
(%)	(3.2)	(7.4)	(20.7)	(35.5)	(23.8)	(9.5)	(100.0)	6.9
6. Lower-lower	284	719	3,775	6,046	4,991	12,873	28,688	
(%)	(1.0)	(2.5)	(13.2)	(21.1)	(17.4)	(44.9)	(100.0)	64.7
Total individuals in 1973	1,543	2,788	8,165	10,526	7,112	14,173	44,307	
	(3.5)	(6.3)	(18.4)	(23.8)	(16.1)	(32.0)	(100.0)	100.0

Source: PNAD/73. Fundação IBGE. Author's tabulation.
*The classification of occupations into six levels of status will be explained in section 3 of this chapter.

stitutions, was 0.25. Putting them in relative terms, we can say that 57% of the total mobility was structural and 43% was circulation.

Developing societies tend to show relatively high percentages of structural mobility. The distributions between point of origin and point of destination are due in large part to the increase in employment opportunities and to changes in the occupational structure stemming from the diminishing of rural occupations and the increase of urban occupations. Advanced societies tend to show a small population growth (or even a negative growth) and a stable number of jobs and professions. In these conditions, mobility comes to depend upon success in the ceaseless competition that establishes itself in the labor market. For example, in the United States, social mobility of the remote past was primarily structural, but that of the recent past has been predominantly circulation. In 1973 the United States showed nearly 60% total mobility—close to that of Brazil. However, 40% was due to circulation mobility and 20% to structural mobility (Featherman and Hauser, 1978:70).

The Yassuda index, Y, provides a net measurement of social mobility, giving structural and circulation mobility simultaneously. Y is, in fact, an *openness coefficient* which indicates the degree of flexibility of the social structure between the point of origin and the point of destiny. Y has a value of 1 when the values of the instances in the change matrix reflect a situation of perfect mobility; it has a value of 0 when there is no circulation mobility. The value 0.64 found in the example indicates a medium degree of social mobility, but with clear tendencies toward flexibility. This flexibility will tend to increase even further to the extent that the weight of structural mobility (57%) decreases and the weight of circulation mobility (43%) increases.

Hutchinson, in his study of mobility in São Paulo in 1955, also calculated a structural mobility index and another for circulation mobility. He used a procedure different from that of Yassuda. Although he considered structural mobility as movement between positions that did not involve exchanges, and circulation mobility as that which is based upon exchanges of positions, he used a different calculation. Hutchinson calculated initially the difference between the numbers of ascending and descending individuals. This difference he considered as referring to individuals who rose without exchange. The percentage of these people in relation to the total of mobile individuals was called structural mobility (without exchanges), while its complement was called mobility through exchange. To avoid confusion we will call the Hutchinson measurements *mobility without exchange* and *mobility with exchange*. In Table 3.1 these measurements may be calculated (for every row) thus:

$$\text{Mobility without Exchange} = \frac{\sum_{i=1}^{r} n_{1i} - \sum_{i=1}^{r} n_{i1}}{N - \sum_{i=1}^{r} n_{ii}} = 0.76$$

$$\text{Mobility with Exchange} = 1 - \frac{\sum_{i=1}^{r} n_{1i} - \sum_{i=1}^{r} n_{i1}}{N - \sum_{i=1}^{r} n_{ii}} = 0.24$$

The Hutchinson measurements give less information than do those of Yassuda. They do not find internal changes in the social structure. For example, great changes in the base of the structure in one direction tend to generate a high volume of mobility without exchange, not easily balanced by movements from the top of the pyramid. On the other hand, mobility through exchange, which generally occurs at the top, is totally neutralized by intense movements at the base. But Hutchinson's measurements have the advantage of permitting an immediate evaluation of the volume of structural mobility that stems from expansion of employment positions. They are useful particularly when used for examining upward social mobility. Besides this, they permit us to situate

TABLE 3.3. Changes between Fathers and Sons (%)

Social Stratum	Total Sample		Northeast		Rio de Janeiro		São Paulo	
	Father	Son	Father	Son	Father	Son	Father	Son
Upper	2.0	3.5	0.7	1.3	3.7	5.9	2.7	4.5
Upper-middle	3.1	6.3	1.7	3.0	4.8	8.6	3.0	7.8
Middle-middle	13.8	18.4	11.3	16.2	20.1	20.7	14.1	18.6
Lower-middle	9.3	23.8	4.6	13.5	18.0	33.2	13.7	33.2
Upper-lower	6.9	16.0	5.0	13.2	12.8	22.9	10.2	18.3
Lower-lower	64.9	32.0	77.6	52.8	40.6	8.7	56.3	17.6
Total	100.0	100.0	100.0	100.0	100.0	100.0	100.0	100.0
Index of dissimilarity between father and son	32.9		24.0		32.0		38.8	

Source: PNAD/73. Fundação IBGE. Author's tabulation.

the point in the social structure at which mobility without exchange is transformed into mobility with exchange. In this study we shall seek always to contrast upward mobility with mobility without exchange, so as to know how much of the upward social movement was due to the creation of new positions in the labor market.

Rogoff, in a classic work, also proposes a simple methodological strategy for finding structural mobility and differentiating it from circulation mobility. Her proposal seeks to estimate an index of dissimilarity between the occupational structures of fathers and sons. This index is based upon a calculation of the percentage of individuals of one generation who must change occupational status so that the two distributions (fathers and sons) would be equal.[15] Table 3.3 portrays an original example from the sample of his study which will be elaborated in detail in the next two chapters. For illustrative purposes we have reproduced the occupational structures of fathers and of sons in the total sample and in a few selected regions. For each pair, the index of dissimilarity (ID) between fathers and sons was calculated. As we see, the size of each of the

15. Rogoff in Smelser and Lipset, 1966. This type of comparison, however, involves methodological problems for which sociologists have only partial solutions (see the section on methodological problems in this chapter).

lower strata is always greater among the fathers. The index of dissimilarity is always given by the difference occurring in each stratum between fathers and sons. It shows that in the fathers' time the job profile was heavily based upon rural activities, which no longer is true today. Meanwhile, we discover that the dissimilarity is proportional to the level of urbanization and industrialization in the region considered. São Paulo is positioned well above the mean, and the Northeast well below. One sees also that the level of change is a function of the point of departure—that is, of the size of the father's stratum in relation to that of the son. One notes that the regions considered differ in their points of departure. In spite of this, the tendency in the three regions was clearly a diminishing of rural occupations and an increase of urban ones.

These changes in the occupational profiles establish, in a certain way, a step towards social mobility. When such an accentuated diminishing of rural occupations occurs, it becomes practically impossible for the sons to remain in the same positions as their fathers (although such immobility is possible theoretically). *Net mobility* commonly refers to the smaller percentage of sons who would have been able to move in relation to their fathers given the change of profiles between the two generations. *Gross mobility* is the total percentage of people whose status differed from that of their fathers. From these two types of mobility, Rogoff estimated circulation mobility—that is, mobility through exchange. Taking the previous example, we can construct Table 3.4. This table shows clearly that circulation mobility is more prevalent in the more urbanized regions. Mobility in these regions involves a certain rearrangement of the sons within a structure that is a bit more stable. Unquestionably, however, in all regions the impact of structural mobility is accentuated.

The above considerations serve only to illustrate the methodology to be followed in the subsequent chapters. Most of our efforts will be to distinguish types of mobility by region, by group, and by level in the social structure. We must do this because a high rate of mobility may have varying meanings. For example, it may indicate external changes occurring in the occupational struc-

TABLE 3.4. Gross, Net, and Circulation Mobility

Sample Considered	(1) Gross Mobility	(2) Net Mobility	(1)–(2) Circulation Mobility
Total	58.5	32.9	25.6
Northeast	42.3	24.0	18.3
Rio de Janeiro	72.2	32.0	40.2
São Paulo	69.2	38.8	30.4

(1) = 100.0 = Percentage of mobile individuals in relation to their fathers (independent of direction).

Source: PNAD/73. Fundação IBGE. Author's tabulation.

ture as a consequence of migration, industrialization or urbanization. It may also reflect improvements in individual resources (education, training, experience), so that people come to adjust themselves better to existing jobs. In short, identifying the types of mobility has greater theoretical relevance than simply detecting the sums of total mobility.

The analysis presented in the following chapters refers to movements detected in the occupational status change matrices. Chapter 10, more analytical, goes further and seeks to identify the determinants of mobility on the basis of regression models.

Measurement of Occupational Status

Inter- and intragenerational mobility will be analyzed through comparisons of occupational statuses. The key variables for this analysis are the father's occupational status (measured at the time when the son began to work), the respondant's occupational status at the beginning of his career, and his current status—that is, his status in 1973. These three statuses were measured by one scale of the social positions of occupations (Valle Silva, 1974) so as to assure comparability between fathers and sons, and also between the individual's first job and his current job. This scale combines occupation, education, and income. To construct it, Valle Silva used a sample of 25% of the 1970 census and hierarchized the 259 occupational titles, following these methodological steps:[16] (1) in the first place, he estimated the mean income for 18 educational levels, using equations of regression between education and salary for age groups of five-year intervals; (2) in the second place, he estimated the mean income for each occupational title, thus obtaining a mean for each occupation and for each age group; (3) next, he used the mean of the means as the value of each occupation's status; (4) he then standardized these values so that they varied from 0 to 100 points; (5) finally, he grouped and hierarchized the scores into six occupational groups which, in this study, we shall treat as six social strata.[17] Table 3.5 presents a summary of the different occupations which form each social stratum, as well as the mean value obtained for each stratum

16. This procedure has been quite conventional in modern sociology. See Bogue, 1969:428–62; Duncan, 1961. Valle Silva obtained high and significant correlations between his scale and others already used in Brazil and based upon prestige of professions. It is important to note that Valle Silva's scale is not a scale of prestige; on the contrary, it is more a measure of individuals' socio-economic status. For the reader interested in other measurements of social status we recommend consulting the following works: Warner, 1960; Reiss; Featherman and Hauser, 1978: Chap. 2; Treiman, 1978.

17. This last step seems to have been adopted by technicians of the Fundação IBGE in the work, "Classificação dos Grupos de Ocupação Considerando Documento Elaborado por Nelson do Valle Silva" (1974).

TABLE 3.5. Social Strata, Mean Values, and Sample Occupations*

Social Stratum	Mean Value	Sample Occupations
Upper	63.71	Industrialists, large farmers and ranchers, high banking administrators, doctors, lawyers, engineers
Upper-middle	30.84	Public service administrators, comptrollers, administrators, medium-sized landlords, business representatives
Middle-middle	17.01	Draftsmen, musicians, broadcasters, buyers, office workers, small landlords, construction foremen
Lower-middle	9.47	Electricians, masons, plumbers, carpenters, carpet sellers, drivers, barbers
Upper-lower	5.84	Urban manual workers, deliverymen, shoeshiners, janitors
Lower-lower	4.70	Rural manual workers, fishermen, rubberworkers

*The designation of strata used here shows traces of arbitrariness, as would any other. An alternative designation could be: upper, upper-middle, lower-middle, upper-lower, urban lower-lower and rural lower-lower. The latter classification has the advantage of describing the lower strata better and the disadvantage of denying a middle-class status, even if at its lowest level, to the more skilled manual professions.

according to Valle Silva's method.[18] We must emphasize at this point that the social strata are not equidistant in the scale used. In fact, the distances increase to the extent that the strata are small. The principal difference between the two rests in the fact that the lower one consists of low qualification, rural zone jobs, while the upper one consists of occupations of a similar level in the urban zone.

The sample used in this study included the 259 occupations of the census, although the frequencies for some of them are quite low because they relate to predominantly feminine occupations such as elementary school teachers, seamstresses, domestic servants, etc. Thus, the selected sample tended to eliminate the low-status occupations generally carried out by women and children. In reality, though, it appears that society "reserves" the better occupations for the heads of family and leaves for women and children the activities characteristic of the lower tertiary sector of the urban zones, as well as the lower-lower stratum occupations in the rural zone. Thus the explosion of the lower tertiary in Brazil in the last thirty years would have to have a differentiated effect upon the work force—that is, a greater impact among women and chil-

18. For a complete view of all the occupations covered, as well as their absolute frequencies in the 1970 census, the reader is invited to inspect the appendix.

dren and a lesser one among male heads of family. In view of this it seems convenient to reformulate the hypothesis that the lower tertiary is an inhibiting factor for general social mobility. It seems to have a lesser effect on the heads of family—who account for the families' mobility—and more of an effect on the other members of the family unit.

Control Variables

As we have seen, the first stage of the analysis of social mobility will be based upon occupational matrices. Mobility is indicated always by movements from a point of origin to a point of destination. This mobility can occur in three stages: (a) from paternal social origin to the individual's entry into the labor market; (b) from this point to the current position; (c) from paternal social origin to the current position, thus covering all the space between the two generations considered.[19]

Analysis of mobility via occupational matrices will be performed also by means of a control by age group. As we know, almost by definition, social mobility is related to age. Mobility is a phenomenon which occurs over time in societies and over the years for individuals. In fact, it is the product of a process of accumulation of experiences in the labor market.

On the other hand, the social structures are affected by the age composition of the population, as well as by people's ages upon entering the labor market. Generally, very young structures tend to show a concentration at the pyramid base: very early entrance into the labor market tends to limit the social distance to be covered by individuals. In addition, the various age groups tend to have different educational and employment opportunities. Finally, division of individuals into age groups permits us to standardize most of the ages of the fathers, and, therefore, it helps us to get closer to an idea of generations.

In view of these methodological advantages, the individuals from the sample were grouped in four age brackets: 20–30 years; 31–40; 41–50; 51–64. These brackets, besides permitting the control mentioned above, indicate both the different points in the respondents' careers and the different historical moments in Brazilian development. They group together people who were exposed to different opportunities for employment and education during a period of approximately 50 years. When we take into account the respondents' fathers, we then cover a period of practically 80 years—that is, the entire twentieth century. This permits us to treat the data from a longitudinal perspective and to detect changes that have occurred over several decades.

19. Normally, studies of mobility concentrate upon groups *b* and *c*—that is, upon intra-generational mobility and intergenerational mobility.

Besides the control by age, the analysis of mobility will be done by region and by migratory status. The control by region seeks to identify the intermediary power of this structural variable in determining social mobility. Regional inequalities in Brazil are accompanied by profound social differences in terms of occupational opportunities. Thus, we expect to find mobility patterns that differ from one region to another.

Finally, the control by migratory experience seeks to test the rather conventional hypothesis according to which social mobility is generally associated with geographical mobility. Migrants tend to achieve much social mobility; in fact, migration promotes upward movement of both migrants and non-migrants.

For the regional analysis we shall use the classifications of the PNAD/73 itself, which divides Brazil into eight geo-economic regions: Brasília, Rio de Janeiro, São Paulo, South, East, Northeast, North, and Central-West (Fundação IBGE, 1974). The last two regions will be excluded in many cases from the analysis due to the lack of representation of rural occupations (see details in the next section of this chapter).

As for migratory experience, the PNAD/73 permits us to work only with individuals who in 1973 were in their native state and those who were in other states (migrants). Unfortunately, the data do not tell us when the individual moved, where he reached social maturity, or where he began his professional career.

The Sample

The analysis presented in the study is based upon a random national sample of 92,700 households carried out by the Fundação IBGE in the fourth quarter of 1973. A special questionnaire for collecting data on mobility was used in all regions, and included people of ten years and older who lived in the selected households (Fundação IBGE, 1974: Appendix). This questionnaire collected conventional demographic data from the dwellers, as well as information about the person's current occupation (in 1973), his first occupation, and his father's occupation (when the son entered the labor force). This was the first time that the data of this nature were collected on a national level. The first studies of social mobility in Brazil as a whole and by regions came out of these data (Pastore, 1977a; Costa, 1977), and the present study represents a further development of these works.

The first results from the PNAD/73 were released by the Fundação IBGE in May, 1975. The great innovation of this PNAD was the inclusion of the urban areas of the North and the Central-West regions (Acre, Amazonas, Pará, Rondonia, Roraima, Amapá, Mato Grosso, and Goiás). However, the rural areas are still not being adequately sampled in the North region and in part of

TABLE 3.6. Positions of Persons of Ten Years or More in Relation to the Work Force (in thousands)

Sex and Position in the Work Force	Age Groups						Total
	10–19	20–29	30–39	40–49	50–59	60 & up	
Employed men	5,488	6,871	5,297	4,026	1,436	1,436	25,488
(%)	(21.6)	(27.0)	(20.8)	(15.8)	(9.2)	(5.6)	(100.0)
Employed women	3,099	3,285	2,181	1,530	787	401	11,283
(%)	(27.5)	(29.1)	(19.3)	(13.6)	(7.0)	(3.5)	(100.0)

Source: PNAD/73. Fundação IBGE, p. 14. Author's adaptation.

the Central-West for practical reasons—principally, the enormous difficulties of access into the interior of Amazonia. If, on the one hand, the inclusion of these regions was a definite benefit in the attempt to cover the households fully, on the other hand it accented the urban bias which one notes in all the PNADs.[20] However, the Fundação IBGE itself is making numerous efforts to provide the researcher with a clear picture of the consequences of sampling problems which normally occur in samplings as gigantic as the PNADs. Specifically, concerning the problem of a lack of coverage in the rural zones of the North and Central-West regions, the Fundação IBGE informs us: "These two regions represent about 9% of the total national population, with an urban concentration of 43.6%. This indicates that the national sample represents about 95% of the total population" (Fundação IBGE, 1975:48).

To study social mobility in Brazil, we have selected from the PNAD/73 a subsample of male heads of family between 20 and 64 years of age, to whom relates the basic information concerning the respondent's occupation (in 1973 and originally) and that of his father. Before describing this sample in detail and presenting its theoretical justification, we must look at the sample which it represents, the PNAD/73.

The PNAD/73 identified about 69 million people of ten years or more in Brazil in 1973. Of these, about 38 million were in the work force. Thus, about 55% of Brazilians ten years old or older were in the work force; that is, they made up the economically active population. Table 3.6 shows the distribution of this employed population by sex and age.

The percentage of employed men of 10–19 years (21.6%) is smaller than that of the women (27.5%). The same thing occurs in the next age group of 20-29 years. From there on the pattern reverses. The PNAD/73 confirms, then, that women begin to work earlier than do the men, and that they stop working earlier. As we shall see later in this study, most women who enter the market before age 20 do so into occupations of low qualification and remuneration.

20. For the purposes of this study, the mentioned bias brought about an underestimate of rural occupations and an overestimate of urban occupations of the respondents.

TABLE 3.7. Distribution of Heads of Family (%)

Position in Work Force	Men	Women	Total	N
Employed, working	91.4	8.6	100.0	(15,834,782)
Employable, but not working	87.8	12.2	100.0	(776,575)

Source: PNAD/73. Fundação IBGE, p. 18. Author's adaptation.

The PNAD/73 permits us to identify also the individual's position within the family structure. This is useful for social mobility studies, because the heads of family are especially relevant. Table 3.7 shows the distribution of the heads of family who were working and to whom relate the occupational data necessary for the study of mobility. The data show that in 91% of the Brazilian families whose head was working, the head was a man; in 8.6% of the cases, it was a woman.[21] The data from Table 3.6 indicate that the group which covers men older than 20 years of age contains 78% of all employed, male manpower. Based on this we can say that in the majority of cases, the Brazilian family is a social group whose head is a man more than 20 years old.[22] Among these heads of family, legally married individuals predominate; there were also, however, unmarried men, widowers, and relatives. All of them were responsible for a woman and/or children (who may or may not have been working). Thus, the male heads of family, from 20 to 64 years of age, continue to be the principal element in determining status and the standard of living of the great majority of Brazilian families. This was one of the basic reasons for the choice of this sample. We must point out also that 20–64 year-old men constitute the empirical base of practically all recent studies of social mobility in other countries; this opens up (with due caution) the first possibilities of international comparisons based upon the Brazilian national sample.

Nevertheless, the choice of this sample also has a theoretical justification which, in fact, is a more fundamental reason for its selection. Studies of social mobility have ignored the fact that the family, and not the individual, is the most relevant social unit for the study of the stratification system of a given society; within the family the head stands out, and the head is normally a man. Although the family is a basic unit, the members of the family unit have different significance and importance in determining the unit's status.[23] The

21. The data from the 1970 census indicate that 87% of the Brazilian heads of family (working or not) were men. See *Censo Demográfico, Brasil*, Brasília: Fundação IBGE, p. 211.

22. According to the data from the sample, 92% of the families had a male head who was between 20 and 64 years old.

23. One of the sources of inspiration for working with the family unit was a recent work by Kuznets, who said: "In the analysis of income distributions (. . .) the recipient unit should

woman, for example, tends to be affected by a series of disadvantages in social life when compared to the man, these disadvantages manifesting themselves particularly in the areas of employment, occupational opportunities, the possession of goods, etc.[24] In fact, for the great majority of women, the distribution of economic and social rewards is determined basically by the positions of their families, and, in particular, of their fathers or husbands. Given that the major determinant of the distribution of economic and social rewards is the family, including wives and daughters in samples for the study of mobility, introduces a masking of the phenomenon. Using the same argument, one questions whether adolescents and children have the same significance as the head in determining status. They also undergo the social disadvantages mentioned. Their status stems equally from the position of the family, and of the head in particular. In sum, we believe that the social dynamic is highly dependent upon changes of status which occur in families, and that these changes, in their turn, depend upon changes in the status of the heads of the family units (Parkin, 1971).

The sample thus described included 58,286 individuals.[25] To get this number, however, there were some exclusions from the original sample. In the first place, we excluded the unemployed individuals because of the impossibility of analyzing their current occupational status. This applied to 2,011 people. In the second place, people were excluded who made defective responses for the item relating to current occupation. This applied to 1,308 individuals.[26] In the third place, we were forced to eliminate, in certain cases, individuals whose fathers' occupations were imperfectly described or were impossible to codify.[27] This occurred only in the analyses which compared the fathers' statuses with those of the sons. These exclusions did not reach a point of marring the sample. The distributions of age, occupation, and education remained unaltered. For those who are accustomed to this type of study, the losses are minimal. We can say without doubt that the empirical material of the PNAD/73 which refers to social mobility is most precise.

---

be the family or the household and not the person (. . .) We have adopted the family or the household as the basic unit for the study of personal distribution of income because it is more clearly identifiable, more inclusive and more independent than are individuals." See Kuznets, 1976; see also Rainwater, 1978.

24. Various studies have pointed out a strong discrimination against the woman in the Brazilian labor market, including her very modest participation in relation to that of the man. See Salm, 1970; Blay, 1978.

25. The work of Blau and Duncan (1967:1) was based upon a sample of 20–65 year-old men which included 21,700 individuals.

26. About a third of them were sons of peasants.

27. In this case the sample used was of 44,307 individuals, not of 58,286.

To analyze the net effects of each variable presented in Chapter 10, we used the sample of 58,286 as well as another of 10%, chosen at random, which included 5,820 individuals.

With a sample of 10%, obviously, statistical tests require a great deal of care; thus, their significance is indicated for each model examined. The sample of 58,286 provided practically all the tests with a significance equal to or greater than 95%. Thus, we shall indicate in the test only those few cases in which the tests utilized did not reach that level of significance.

Methodological Problems

The study of social mobility is certainly one of the most fascinating and problematic studies in sociology. The methodological difficulties are of all orders; some can be overcome, but others, perhaps the majority, can only be bypassed. In fact, the specialized literature is full of studies of methodological problems.[28] A monograph such as this one has no room for detailed discussion of the diverse methodological questions. However, it is important to point out the principal difficulties involved in these studies. In brief, the following problems stand out: (1) data for the occupation of an individual and of his father are based upon the informant's response, and there are certainly differences in reliability of response in the two cases; (2) when fathers are compared to sons, we are contrasting people of different ages and not of two generations absolutely separated in time (Broom and Lancaster, 1977); (3) mobility involves numerous successions of individuals in the work force, and when only two or three points in a career are compared in time, it is difficult to know who replaced whom in the work force; (4) not all members of the past generation produced offspring who were still living at the time of the study; (5) people who produced surviving children have different probabilities of being represented in the sample due to differences in fertility (Hope, 1972; Matras, 1975:351–55; Schnore, 1961); (6) inter-regional or international comparisons involve past generations who were on different plateaus in the social structure (Rogoff, 1953); (7) the social distances between strata may vary a great deal from one generation to another due to peculiarities of hierarchizing occupations in each of them (MacDonald, 1972); (8) comparisons between fathers and sons tend to be affected by the size of each strata in the two generations, producing effects which, many times, are more the product of statistics than of reality (Yassuda, 1964).

The problems listed above are well known among specialists today. The indicated bibliography contains solutions or attenuations for each of them. In

---

28. For an ample account of the methodological problems see Duncan, in Smelser and Lipset, 1966.

most cases controls are introduced by age, by time of entrance into the market, and by estimate of different types of social mobility. These are precisely the procedures that were used in this study. These procedures attenuate the difficulties but, in most cases, they do not resolve them totally. Even so, comparisons of the respective statuses of fathers and sons or of beginning and current career positions constitute the most adequate strategy for analysis of the social metabolism. All additional methodological refinement implies much more fully detailed studies at incalculable costs.

A problem that deserves special attention is that of the fertility differential. Many scholars argue that the greater fertility of the lower classes induces social mobility (Matras, 1975:351–55), while others allege that mobility has differentiated impacts upon fertility and family size, and consequently, that it has differentiated effects upon subsequent mobility (Hope, 1972:89–99). These arguments have provoked lengthy debates among sociologists and demographers. The fact is that including one characteristic of the populational dynamic in the analysis of mobility (fertility) requires the inclusion of various others. If, on the one hand, it is true that there is a difference in fertility among the classes, then on the other, it is not less true that there are important differences in mortality, in life span, in family structure, and in migration. Thus, to know the net effect of all these phenomena is an extremely complex task which goes far beyond the data available for the study of mobility. Blau and Duncan (1967:14), in a methodological effort to capture these nuances in past generations, reached the conclusion that the association between mobility and fertility is not sufficient to explain the differences in fertility and mobility among the social classes. A whole series of conditions can be attributed to fertility and to mobility simultaneously.[29]

The situation in underdeveloped societies, however, would be different. Differences in fertility are more accentuated, and apart from the behavior of other factors (mortality, life span, etc.), families who achieve upward social movement and who come from the lower stratum tend to reduce in size and to accelerate subsequent mobility. If this occurs, then, there would be a greater number of people who enter into the labor market in high status occupations, which consequently would elevate the general level of mobility. At this point,

29. For example, people who live in cities and whose fathers were peasants and farmers show a higher fertility level than do those who are two generations removed from the rural zone. Couples who marry young have more children than do those in which the woman is older at marriage. But if the couple married early, the occupational status of the husband or his education does not retain any relationship to the couple's fertility, although income relates negatively. Couples who marry later tend to have more children when they have a high income, and less children when they have a low income. In short, the relationship between fertility and social position is mixed with a series of other variables; it is rarely possible to detect net effects of mobility upon fertility, and then upon subsequent mobility. See Blau and Duncan (1967:410–18).

the polemic is transformed into an empirical question. In other words, we want to know the nature of the differences between fathers' and sons' social structures when these effects of mobility upon fertility and family size are "discounted." The research of the PNAD/73 did not provide the necessary data for a rigorous test of this hypothesis, but our future plans include an examination of this aspect of the problem.

4

Occupational Opportunities in Brazil

Development and Occupational Differentiation[1]

The study of mobility requires an initial effort to identify the fluctuations in the labor market and, more specifically, the differentiation of the occupational structure through time. We know that in the beginning stages of any society's development, structural mobility tends to predominate, and that this is a reflection of changes in the labor market. Numerous theories have insisted that mobility increases to the extent that a society industrializes and subsequently enters into the service phase. The decisive step for mobility would be the movement of people from manual to nonmanual occupations; this would be facilitated by industrialization and the growth of the commercial and service sectors (Lipset and Bendix, 1959: Chap. 2; Lipset and Zetterberg, 1956). This point of view carries with it the classical conception of the labor market dynamic, according to which modern societies would tend to reduce employment in the primary sector, in order to gradually transfer its energy and dynamism to industry and, finally, to the tertiary sector.

Simply moving in the direction of industry, commerce and service is often taken as a sign of economic development, a facilitator of social mobility and a promoter of openness of class structure. Marx, for example, related the expansion of capitalism to a relative shrinking of the proportion of agricultural workers which, in its turn, would stem from the increase in the amount of

---

1. Much of this section is based upon a paper by Soares (1978).

capital in the industrial sector and from limitations of physical space and of land. The changes in the composition of the work force and in the differentiation of the occupational structure, for Marx, would be consequences of capitalist growth (Marx, 1968:1306–08).

Clark returned to this concept and transformed it into a necessary condition for economic development, going so far as to use it as its principal indicator (Clark, 1957:496–97). In economic theory, this point of view has gained wide acceptance; until recently, the proportions of manpower in the various sectors were used as basic indicators of development (Rostow, 1964; Fisher, 1945:6–7).

From a sociological point of view, this vision has had important implications. Specialists in stratification and social mobility hold that mobility would result from the withdrawal of people from the primary sector and their entry into the other two. The secondary and tertiary sectors would absorb excess rural manpower into a more diversified occupational structure; they would offer jobs which required more education and which enjoyed sufficient levels of prestige for reaching higher levels of social status. Thus, industrialization and the tertiarization of the labor market would be the surest road to social mobility (Rogoff, 1953; Marsh, 1963; Treiman, 1970; Hutchinson, 1960).

Comparative analysis of the labor markets in various societies, however, has shown that diversification of the occupational structure of the secondary and tertiary sectors varies with the stage of economic development. In advanced economies, in fact, many jobs created in these sectors demand high qualification and distribute the income and prestige, which permits a permanent social mobility (Baurer and Yamey, 1951). In slowly developing societies, however, the acceleration of economic growth seems not to provoke the same expansion of employment and the same differentiation of the occupational structure. In the tertiary sector of these societies at least two segments, the upper and the lower tertiary, stand out; they include occupations of high and low social status.[2] The various studies of labor market behavior in Brazil show also that economic growth since the war has induced employment increases in the two subsectors, greater in the secondary than in the primary, generating more jobs of low than of high qualification. They indicate also that this growth was accompanied by an increasing concentration of income, making the society more unequal from the economic standpoint. The reason for this could rest in the emergence of a small, upper-tertiary segment which has permitted the upward movement of people in the liberal professions, administration, and other technical categories. These professionals, although reduced in number,

2. Even this proposition is being questioned by more recent comparative studies. Hazelrigg and Garnier, looking at the situation of 17 countries at different levels of industrialization, were not able to identify significant differences in terms of social mobility. See Hazelrigg and Garnier, 1976.

come to take advantage of high incomes, prestige, and mobility, all this facilitated by the better educations they had the privilege to obtain throughout the
process (Langoni, 1973). Simultaneously, an increase in lower-tertiary employment was observed, concentrated in urban areas; these jobs required low
qualification and gave small rewards and social prestige, as in the cases of
deliverymen, office boys, sidewalk salesmen and the entire gamut of the informal sector (Bressan, 1971; Soares, 1969:93; Sant'Ana, 1976; Ekerman,
1976; Cunha, 1976; Calabi and Zaghen, 1978). However, the tertiary sector
is far from being a direct indicator of social development in Brazil. On the
other hand, accelerated urbanization came to exert even greater pressures for
the creation of jobs in the lower-tertiary, which would have limited even more
the possibilities of social mobility.

But there is also the argument that industrialization in itself induces differentiation through the generation of jobs in the upper-tertiary which gravitate
around the industries themselves. From this perspective, industrialization
would increase, first of all, the bureaucratic jobs of business itself. Secondly,
it would stimulate an enormous service sector outside of but dependent upon
business, as in the case of banks, the financial system in general, commerce,
and the various specialized activities which serve industry.

Some data available for Brazil show that, in fact, industrialization has
brought about employment outside the industrial sector, but most of these jobs
have been created in lower-tertiary, which tends to limit social mobility
(Soares, 1969:20–25). The data show also that the correlation between industrialization and industrial employment is decreasing, and that the association
between industrialization and lower-tertiary employment is increasing.[3]

There is no doubt that the tertiary sector in developing societies is far from
being an image of the past tertiary experienced by countries that are developed
today. On the other hand, it is difficult to deny that the demand of specialized
services is increasing in these societies, where there is clear growth in three
types of occupations: (1) nonmanual, at the technical level; (2) routine non-
manual (secretaries, typists, office workers, salesmen); (3) low qualification
occupations linked to services.

Routine manual occupations have increased (in absolute terms) more than
have technical level occupations, while those of lower qualification have passed
both of these, as in the case of intinerants, deliverymen, janitors, laborers,
ticket takers, etc. (Ekerman, 1976; Almeida and Silva, 1973). Contrasting

3. This general pattern holds true for various other Latin American countries, including a
few even more extreme cases. For example, in Argentina during the fifties, industrial production grew at annual rates of 5%; however, industrial employment fell at annual rates of more
than 2%. During the same decade in Mexico, industrial production grew at an annual rate of
6.5%, while industrial employment remained the same. See Soares, 1978:20–21; Almeida,
1976.

these categories, the first two types are more closely related to industrial expansion, while the low qualification occupations relate more strictly to urbanization: they are professions which attend to the necessities brought about by urban expansion.

It is clear that this heterogeneity of the occupational structure has different implications for structural mobility. From jobs linked to the technical occupations come greater prestige, higher income, and greater probability of mobility (unless all recruiting is done within the highest classes, which is practically impossible). Jobs linked to the routine nonmanual occupations also generate numerous opportunities for mobility, although it would be correct to expect their incumbents to travel shorter distances in the social structure. And those of the third group? On the one hand, these jobs are potentially more limited in terms of structural mobility. On the other, it is necessary to remember that mobility here will depend highly upon the individuals' point of departure. Migrants from the rural zone might find in the urban lower-tertiary an opportunity for upward social movement. Thus, the lower-tertiary would act against mobility for people in the urban zone, and would facilitate mobility for those who have come from the rural zone; this hypothesis is tested and confirmed in Chapter 9.

General Tendencies of the Labor Market

It should remain clear that we are seeing structural mobility as *initially* determined by the behavior of various economic sectors, and especially by the differentiation of occupational structures. The next step is to examine the evolution of labor markets as to job opportunities and occupational differentiation. This will be the objective of this section. The ideal in this type of study is to have a detailed picture of the modifications of the occupational structure covering the entire period considered in the mobility analysis. In practice, however, this is rarely attained.[4] In this study, in which we analyze inter- and intragenerational mobility, we intended to map the development of the Brazilian occupational structure throughout the twentieth century. This would be a rigorous method of identifying the structural determinants which influenced the actual situations of individuals and their fathers. The ideal, then, would be to have available various census results dealing with the Brazilian occupational structure since 1900. However, these data do not exist in Brazil. Available censuses were not patterned so as to permit rigorous comparisons of occupational structure. Thus, we pass from the ideal to the real situation; that is, we

---

4. Statistics do permit this type of study in more advanced countries. Bancroft, in the United States, was able to reproduce faithfully the development of the American labor market from 1890 to 1955, leaving for other authors the simpler task of a post-1955 analysis. See Bancroft, 1958.

look at what the data permit. For this, we made extensive use of data already treated and adjusted for the analysis of general tendencies of the occupational structure. In this sense, the work of Faria (1976) is of great value. He covers the period from 1920 to 1970, seeking to identify the principal economic changes that occurred and to relate them to the labor market. This section summarizes Faria's study in that which is pertinent to the study of social mobility.

At the beginning of the century, Brazil was still predominantly rural; rural-urban migration was modest, and the incipient industrialization was just taking its first steps. The few industrial jobs were related to traditional sub-sectors such as textiles and agribusiness.

The twenties, however, were marked by an increase in productive capacity in various areas, particularly in energy, cement, and steel; the importation of capital goods also increased. This decade did not register important structural changes (except those stemming from the 1929 crisis), but it did provide the bases for subsequent industrialization in the replacement of imported goods.

Generally, Brazil's economic performance in the next decade was quite reasonable in spite of the crisis of 1929–1932. The replacements of imports increased substantially and the economy began to come back with more attention paid to the internal sector. At the beginning of the period, industrialization was experiencing a certain inertia accumulated in the end of the twenties; but then the industrial base began to expand, and new sectors emerged, such as those of metallurgy and chemistry (Baer, 1975). During the thirties, then, structural changes of utmost relevancy began to occur. Alongside the new industrial sectors, commerce expanded, means of transportation were improved, and there was a certain redirectioning of the economy from outward to inward.

In the forties, this process accelerated rapidly, especially during and after the Second World War. Difficulties of importation had the effect of protecting numerous sectors of national industry. The economy began to grow at high rates (4.8% per year), with the industrial sector standing out with an annual growth rate of 7.2% (Simonsen, 1972:37).

This growth continued in the fifties, until, at the end of the decade, most of the internal market was supplied with goods produced in Brazil; the replacement of imported consumer goods was completed and the increased production of commodities was begun. The fifties also saw foreign capital entering Brazil on a massive scale to support industrialization. Table 4.1 contrasts the growth rates of this decade with previous ones.

In spite of the high growth rates, the speed with which new industrial jobs were generated fell in relation to the period before (see Table 4.2). Signs of the institutional crisis of the sixties already were beginning to appear in the form of runaway inflation, general discontent, and economic instability. The

TABLE 4.1. Annual Growth Rates of Production by Sectors (%)

Sectors	Periods					
	1921/30	1931/40	1941/50	1951/60	1961/70	1971/72
Agriculture	3.4	4.3	2.8	4.3	4.3	5.5
Industry	3.3	5.2	7.2	8.5	6.7	10.3
Transportation and communication	8.1	5.1	4.9	8.2	7.0	9.5
Commerce	3.4	4.6	5.2	5.7	5.5	9.3
GNP Total	3.7	4.6	4.8	6.6	5.8	8.6

Source: Faria, 1976:148,170.

sixties were marked by profound political and institutional changes, with the approach of military power toward nearly all public and private activities in the country. In the middle of the decade, numerous measures were taken to reestablish a minimum of socio-economic stability and to create confidence in the new administration. Improvements were made in the tax and finance structures, in incentives for exportation, in the encouragement of savings; all this brought about, in the second half of the decade, a return to the high growth rates observed previously. In the next decade, especially after 1973, the steep foreign debt, the renewed inflation, and the exhaustion of the governmental bureaucracy again caused collective dissatisfaction, although this did not affect the growth.

What were the general tendencies of the labor market in this period? In what measure was society capable of creating new jobs in the five decades we have examined?

The data to answer these questions are rather precarious, especially those which refer to the twenties and thirties. Comparison by sectors of created jobs involves numerous problems of a conceptual nature, and difficulties in collection and interpretation of data.

Nevertheless, this area of inquiry is not untouched. Faria's study is very useful for carrying out the intended analysis. A summary of the comparisons of decades is presented in Table 4.2.

The interpretation of these results cannot be free of errors, due to the uncertainty of the data, especially those from the remote past.[5] Data referring to the twenties and thirties indicate that job generation was heavily concentrated in the primary sector, particularly in agriculture. Faria himself emphasizes that these data should be used with caution.

Data from the forties and fifties are much more dependable. In his study, Faria demonstrates that during that period Brazil was able to create 7.5 million

5. Several authors believe, for example, that the 1920 census underestimated tertiary sector employment, especially employment in repair and restoration. See Singer, 1971.

TABLE 4.2. New Jobs Created and Annual Growth Rates of Employment (%)

Sectors	1920/30		1940/50		1950/60		1960/70	
	New Jobs	Annual Growth Rate	New Jobs	Annual Growth Rate	New Jobs	Annual Growth Rate	New Jobs	Annual Growth Rate
Primary	*59.5*	1.7	*41.1*	1.4	*34.2*	1.7	*13.4*	0.7
Secondary	*6.3*	1.0	*27.9*	4.7	*9.6*	2.0	*33.8*	6.0
Crafts	—	—	15.9	3.9	7.1	2.2	17.9	4.9
Construction	—	—	10.1	8.3	3.6	3.0	13.5	8.2
Others	—	—	1.9	3.1	−1.1	0.0	2.4	6.8
Tertiary	*34.2*	2.9	*31.0*	2.6	*56.2*	5.5	*52.8*	4.0
Distribution	12.1	2.7	15.5	3.3	20.1	5.0	15.2	3.1
Social	9.7	5.2	8.9	3.7	10.5	5.0	19.6	6.5
Others	12.3	2.3	6.6	1.3	25.6	6.4	18.0	3.4
Total	*100.0*	1.9	*100.0*	2.1	*100.0*	2.9	*100.0*	2.7

Source: Faria, 1976:156, 174.

new work opportunities, the general level of employment growing at an annual rate of 1.9. He emphasizes, however, that about 40% of the new jobs were still created in the primary sector—in spite of an already accelerating rural-urban migration (Faria, 1976:157). The secondary and tertiary sectors created 30% of the new jobs, the annual growth rates of each (4.7 and 2.6) being higher than that of the primary sector (1.4).

The changes of the last two decades, entered in Table 4.2, deepened the structural changes established in the fifties. The primary sector created 34.2% of the new jobs, the secondary 9.6% and the tertiary 56.2%. During the sixties, the pattern became classic; that is, the primary sector created only 13.4% of the new jobs, the secondary 33.8% (more than triple the rate of the previous decade) and the tertiary 52.8%.

Contradicting the hypothesis of excessive tertiarization in the labor market, the data show that the secondary sector participated in an important way in new job creation in the recent past.[6] In fact, one third of the new jobs generated in the sixties were secondary sector jobs, while in the fifties most individuals had to be absorbed by the tertiary. The general tendency shown by Table 4.2 is a noticeable shrinking of the primary sector and a strong expansion of the secondary and tertiary sectors.

Occupational Developments

What is the impact of this general tendency upon social mobility? According to existing theories (Lipset and Zetterberg, 1956; Jaffe and Stewart, 1951: Chap. 12), expansion of employment in the secondary and tertiary sectors should have provoked a general positive effect upon structural mobility. However, for a more rigorous analysis of this phenomenon, we need more detailed data that refer to changes in the occupational structure. This analysis is restricted to only two points in time because of the lack of better data. Thus, this section is limited to the study of occupational transformations between 1950 and 1970.

Apart from the obvious losses that this limitation imposes, this analysis still finds a certain theoretical support. In the first place, we can say that the census of 1950 reflects and synthesizes the numerous transformations of the labor market that took place throughout the forties. In the second place, the period studied (1950–1970) is itself a time of accelerated economic growth with a strong emphasis upon industrialization, the desire being to identify the eventual effects which it had upon the diversification of the occupational structure and upon social mobility.

6. New jobs, however, should be added to existing ones in the sector to obtain an idea of the aggregate demand in each period. We have presented these data in Table 4.4 for the period 1950 to 1970.

In the third place, it is necessary to note that about 55% of the manpower examined in the study entered into the market during the period 1950–1970, and another 25% entered during the period 1940–1950. If we assume that the 1950 census captured the transformations of the forties, and that the 1970 census did the same for its period, then we can conclude that 80% of the work force examined in this study began to work between 1940 and 1970.

The examination of occupational differentiation can be carried out beginning with the already-filled positions. It is true that there may be significant differences between open spots and filled positions. However, the limitations of data with respect to open spots induce us to construct a picture of occupational opportunities starting with the filled positions. On this basis it will be possible to detect variations in the levels of occupational differentiation for the period considered. There are three types of variations of special interest for the study of mobility: (1) the emergence of new occupations; (2) the expansion of already-existing occupations; (3) disappearances of occupations. Knowing these three types of variations constitutes the point of departure for the study of social mobility.

The following information is derived from the results of the demographic censuses of 1950 and 1970 put out by the Fundação IBGE.[7] There were some differences in the two censuses in the way occupations were grouped; these differences were overcome and the occupations standardized by regrouping them according to occupational titles included in both censuses.[8]

In 1950, the Brazilian population totaled about 52 million inhabitants; the economically active population (EAP) was 17 million. In 1970, the population had risen to 92 million and the EAP to 29 million. The population grew approximately 77% and the EAP 71%. This relative decline of the EAP is usually attributed to an increase in schooling and in the number of the retired, which, in fact, is suggested by Table 4.3 in the extreme age groups. Looking closer, we discover also that the behavior of the EAP varied a great deal according to sex. The female EAP grew by about 5% (going from approximately 13% in 1950 to 18% in 1970), and the male EAP shrank by 9%. It is relevant to note also that the participation of women in the labor market grew in practically all the age groups (see Table 4.3).

How does the greater participation of women in the labor market relate to the social mobility of men? The entrance of large contingents of female labor power into the labor market could have affected the social mobility of men in two ways. On the one hand, it could have facilitated male mobility in that the

7. Much of this section is based upon a paper by Gouveia (1977).

8. The reader should note that in 20 years the occupations themselves may change. For example, the attributions of a bookkeeper in 1950 were much different than they are today. Unfortunately, these changes could not be identified in this study, and, *ipso facto*, they were ignored.

TABLE 4.3. Economically Active Population by Age Group (%)

Age Group	Males		Females	
	1950	1970	1950	1970
10–14	31.0	19.2	8.6	6.4
15–19	80.6	61.9	23.4	24.2
20–24	95.4	87.4	18.9	28.3
25–29	96.4	95.2	13.5	23.2
30–39	97.1	96.2	11.4	20.8
40–49	96.3	94.0	10.6	19.8
50–59	92.8	85.2	9.4	15.4
60–69	56.6	40.3	7.7	10.1
70 and over	56.6	40.3	4.6	4.7
Total	80.7	71.8	13.6	18.5

Source: *Recenseamentos demográficos do Brasil, 1950 e 1970*, Fundação IBGE.

women had entered at the base of the social pyramid, occupying jobs of low status and propelling the men upward in their trajectory. On the other hand, it could have reduced the possibilities of male mobility in that the women had come to compete with the men for the same positions.[9]

Data available from the census and the more detailed data from the PNAD/73 suggest that the reality seems to have followed the first hypothesis. Examining the census evidence of Table 4.3, one notes that the age groups which experienced the largest increments of womanpower were those that included people from 20 to 49 years of age. This is a population whose access to education still must have been limited, suggesting that this contingent of labor had entered into the lowest levels of the market, especially in the category of domestic servants and similar occupations. The massive entrance of women must have contributed to more than it prejudiced the mobility of men.[10]

Table 4.3 shows also an increase in inactive men, especially in the groups lower than 20 years and higher than 70. This is a first indication, to be confirmed by the PNAD/73 data, that men were showing a tendency to begin to work later and to stop earlier in their lives. This tendency in itself favors male mobility (especially upward mobility), since a later entry into the labor market generally is due to a longer sojourn in school, and, therefore, a better education.[11] Education, as is known, not only promotes upward social movement—

9. The possibility must be considered of a certain independence between the entrance of women into the labor market and men's mobility. This would have happened if job expansion and differentiation for men and women had been much greater than the supply of labor power.

10. The data of the PNAD/73, compiled by the author, show that 72% of women working during that year held jobs in the lower-lower and upper-lower strata, while the participation of men in these strata was 48%.

11. The later entry is due also to the increase in the proportions of urban manpower in the labor market in the last decades.

ceteris paribus—but also permits the traveling of longer distances in the social structure.

But Table 4.3 shows a certain reduction of the proportion of active men also in the intermediate age groups. This phenomenon can be interpreted as stemming from the reduction in the proportion of the rural population in the period considered, and the passing of these people to the urban zones. The family business disappears rapidly in the urban zones, so that the individual enters into the labor market only when he gets a job; this also favors social mobility.[12] To this we should add the fact that educational opportunities expanded more rapidly in the urban zones, which retarded the entrance into the labor market but facilitated upward movement.

This is groundwork against which we should analyze social mobility. Summarizing the structural picture described above, we can say that the expansion of the female EAP in low status positions, the relative reduction of active members, urbanization and the increase in schooling must have acted as facilitating factors of social mobility for men. But, social mobility depends also upon changes in the levels of occupational differentiation that occurred in the period.

When we analyze the generation of new jobs (Table 4.2), we discover that the period 1950–1970 showed a relative reduction of new rural positions and an expansion of urban positions of the tertiary sector. As for the secondary sector, the period showed two movements: one relatively modest generation of new industrial jobs during the beginnings of industrialization (1950–1960), and another, more substantial, during the period 1960–1970. At this point we must add the new to the existing positions to obtain a measurement of the aggregated demand for manpower in each sector. An approximation of this demand is given directly by the EAP distributions in the three sectors of the 1950 and the 1970 censuses.

Examination of the occupational structure in this period shows that the Brazilian labor market exhibited a tendency close to Clark's predictions; that is, we observe the classic, relative reduction of primary sector jobs, a marked growth of the tertiary sector, and a modest expansion of industrial employment. Table 4.4 shows the new positions generated in the tertiary sector added to existing ones, making commerce and services the greatest absorbers of manpower, leaving industry well below them.

What is the impact of these movements upon social mobility? First, we can say that the relative reduction of people in the primary sector should have meant fewer people of low status. But, establishing the extent of this reduction requires a detailed analysis of the occupational differentiation within the sector which absorbed most of the manpower—that is, the tertiary. Table 4.5 indicates

---

12. This favoring of mobility is a product of statistics, for more people are formally employed in the urban zones than in the rural.

TABLE 4.4. Economically Active Population by Sectors (%)

Sectors	1950	1970
Primary	60.0	44.3
Secondary	14.5	18.0
Tertiary	25.5	37.7
Total	100.0	100.0

Source: *Recenseamentos demográficos do Brasil, 1950 e 1970*, Fundação IBGE.

that the economically active population of this sector was distributed among various subsectors. The most numerous, in order, are the subsectors of "commerce," remunerated domestic activities," "transportation, communications, and warehousing," and "public administration, defense, and national security." Note that included in the subsector "remunerated domestic activities" are domestic servants, who went from 680,525 in 1950 to 1,806, 656 in 1970. Given these high absolute numbers, this increment tends to neutralize the expansion in more highly qualified occupations such as those in "finance" and the "liberal professions" (Almeida and Silva, 1973).

The data show at first glance that there was little change in the number of higher status positions and an increase in the number of lower status positions, verifying the accentuated tendency towards a swelling of the urban lower-

TABLE 4.5. Economically Active Population of the Tertiary Sector (%)

Subsectors	1950	1970
Commerce	21.9	20.3
Transportation, communications and warehousing	15.9	11.1
Finance	2.7	3.9
Industrial services	13.3	9.2
Hotel and restaurant services	4.2	3.7
Personal hygiene services	1.4	1.3
Liberal professions	1.8	2.4
Public administration, defense and national security	11.7	10.3
Public and private instruction	4.9	8.1
Medical-hospital assistance, public and private	1.6	2.4
Social work	2.2	2.6
Entertainment, radio and television	0.9	0.9
Other services	1.9	7.6
Paid domestic work, including building superintendence and janitorial	15.6	16.2
Total	100.0	100.0

Source: Adapted from Almeida, 1974:74.

tertiary. But, it is still too early to conclude that this has inhibited mobility, for mobility depends also upon the individual's point of departure. If there was mobility, however, it must have been of short distance. No matter how people educate themselves and gain experience in the market, with these types of employment opportunities, mobility takes people only from one level to the level immediately above it. We can say, then, that the question of employment must have been settled more quickly than that of mobility. Perhaps this is the evolutionary pattern to be expected in a late-developing society. Employment asserts itself before mobility. Nevertheless, to affirm categorically that the flooding of the urban lower tertiary has blocked social mobility presupposes that the population has begun its occupational trajectory in the same position it is in now. This is not the case in Brazil. The point of departure for men has been extremely low. This compensates for the negative effects of the flooding of the lower tertiary, as we shall see in Chapters 6 and 7.

Occupational Differentiation and Regional Development

It is necessary to point out the role of structural forces linked to the differences in the various regions of Brazil. We know that the inequalities in Brazil are of individual, sectoral, and regional natures. If mobility depends upon occupational differentiation, then it is clear that one of its determinants is the differences in regional development.

Analysis of the behavior of the three sectors in the various regions of Brazil shows some similarities and some differences. The data from Table 4.6 show that, in nearly all regions, a certain increase in secondary participation corresponded to the relative decrease of the primary sector, but that the tertiary registered the greatest increments. Even in the Southeast, where the secondary employed more than one third of the EAP, the growth of this sector in 1970 had not removed the tertiary from its position. In that year, the tertiary was absorbing nearly half of the region's workers. Even in São Paulo, where close to 25% of the EAP were in industry, personal services represented, in 1970, a relatively high proportion—nearly one third of the people occupied in the tertiary.

What is the impact of this combination of region and filling up of the tertiary upon social mobility? Again, we can only speculate. But we can introduce the idea here that social mobility tends to be in high correlation with spacial mobility (Batchelder, 1965; Blau and Duncan, 1967: Chap. 7: Pastore, 1972; Martine and Peliano, 1978: Chaps. 2–3). In fact, migration in Brazil tends to free the rural zones of a manpower that is disadvantaged in terms of education, health, and employment opportunities. Most rural workers live under conditions of extreme poverty. All of them are engaged in occupations of the lowest status, which, according to the classification presented in Chapter 3, are those

TABLE 4.6. Economically Active Population by Region and Sector (%)

| | Sectors | | | | | |
| | Primary | | Secondary | | Tertiary | |
Regions	1950	1970	1950	1970	1950	1970
North	69.0	58.0	7.2	11.3	23.8	30.7
Central-west	77.1	54.0	7.6	11.6	15.3	34.4
Northeast	73.7	62.2	8.0	11.0	19.2	26.8
Southeast	47.0	27.2	19.0	25.2	34.0	47.6
South	63.3	54.4	12.6	14.3	24.1	31.3
Brazil	60.0	44.3	14.5	18.0	25.5	37.7

Source: Almeida and Silva, 1973:134.

of the lower-lower stratum (farm workers, fishermen, rubberworkers). These people, migrating to the cities and entering into the formal labor market, do experience some type of mobility, even though they enter into the lower tertiary. Often it is not so much the adult man who benefits from the move, but subsequent generations who enjoy services of the urban world (especially education) and the greater employment opportunities. In fact, the few studies upon this question show that spacial mobility for migrants, who, although they have come only short social distances, find in this mobility a decisive factor for elevating their standard of living and that of their children (Pastore, 1972).

We shall attempt to speculate upon this question, focusing upon three themes: social mobility, migration, and the regional dynamic. Table 4.7 presents the EAP fluctuations by sector in the various regions of Brazil. These data permit simple analyses clear enough for understanding of the social picture within which mobility took place. First we inspect the decreases and increases in manpower as shown in Table 4.7.

The Brazilian primary sector shrank (relative to the EAP) about 16% during the period. The two regions which showed the greatest decreases were the

TABLE 4.7. EAP Fluctuations by Sectors and Regions: 1950–1970* (%)

| | Sectors | | |
Regions	Primary	Secondary	Tertiary
North	− 11.0	+ 4.1	+ 6.9
Central-west	− 23.1	+ 4.0	+ 19.1
Northeast	− 11.5	+ 3.0	+ 7.6
Southeast	− 19.8	+ 6.2	+ 13.6
South	− 8.9	+ 1.7	+ 12.2
Brazil	− 15.7	+ 3.5	+ 12.2

Source: Adapted from Almeida and Silva, 1974:134.
*Differences between 1950 and 1970.

Central-West (23.1%), because of Brasília, and the Southeast (19.8%), because of the accelerated mechanization of the agricultural sector (combined with the employment increases in and the attraction exerted by other sectors). The North and the Northeast also lost (in relative terms) significant portions of their agricultural manpower, not because of an increase in productivity of labor via mechanization (as in the Southeast), but, on the contrary, because of severe restrictions of access to lands and other imperfections of the agricultural market. In other words, and in relative terms, the Southeast lost manpower, increased the productivity of the primary sector, and increased its capacity to export food and fibers. The North and the Northeast lost manpower with the stagnation of their productivity levels, going from exporters to importers of primary products, especially foodstuffs. However, it is dangerous to interpret these relative losses of manpower in the primary sector as an impediment to social mobility. On the contrary, in many regions, especially in those which have modernized agriculture, new occupations were created within the regions themselves, thus facilitating mobility.[13]

The secondary sector in Brazil expanded employment in a modest way (3.5%), although, it increased the most in terms of productive capacity (see Table 4.1). The increase in industrial employment was shared by all the regions, but the largest increase was in the Southeast. It is interesting to remember that the Southeast was also the region with the greatest absorption of capital-intensive technologies, which are highly automated and demand little direct manpower for accumulating capital. Apart from this, the sector created more jobs. Everything indicates that the volume of employment is associated more with a high degree of dynamism in the sector than with the choice of technology by industry (Alves, 1978: Chaps 2–3).

However, more important than the volume of industrial employment is the intensity of the demand for new occupations. The industrial sector of the Southeast region, particularly São Paulo, constituted a social niche very favorable to mobility because it had created so many new occupational opportunities related directly or indirectly to industry. As we shall see in Chapters 8 and 9, mobility over great distances was most frequent in this niche, favoring the Paulistas as much as Brazilians from other regions who migrated there.

The explosion of the tertiary sector has already been mentioned. In fact, this sector generated more jobs in Brazil during this period than did any other sector. Among the regions, the Central-West stands out, with an increase of approximately 19%, along with the Southeast, with 14%. These regions showed the greatest expansion of commercial and service activities, the

13. The data of Chapters 6 and 7 show a reasonable proportion of upward mobility within the rural zone, due to the status differentiation between laborers and fishermen on the one hand, and surveyors, agricultural and animal technicians, agronomists, veterinarians, etc., on the other.

Central-West because of Brasília and the Southeast due to industrialization and urbanization. Considering that industrialization and public administration tend to create jobs in the upper tertiary and that urbanization generates more lower-tertiary jobs, we conclude that despite having registered an expansion four times greater than the secondary, the tertiary sector must have contributed less to social mobility (in relative terms). That is, given the same level of initial status, industrial jobs provided more opportunities for mobility than did lower-tertiary jobs.

Here we can introduce the distinction between *employment effect* and *mobility effect*. Multiplication of opportunities for work has the effect of producing jobs and of employing workers. Occupational differentiation has the effect of creating new opportunities and of facilitating structural mobility. In this sense, we can say that, given the same initial statuses, expansion of the tertiary sector should have shown an effect predominantly of employment, while the growth of industrial employment should have contributed more to social mobility (Pastore, 1976). This hypothesis will be tested in detail in the next chapters. At this general level of analysis though, we can consider this tendency by examining the behavior of occupations between 1950 and 1970.

Table 4.8 shows the EAP distribution, the grouping of occupations being based upon the relative homogeneity of the occupational strata.[14] The differences in indicated growth are simply the differences between the occupational strata percentages in the two census years. It is important to appraise them keeping in mind the size of the EAP in the two years under consideration. For example, the stratum of occupations linked to services, which represented 5.3% of the EAP in 1950, became 7.8% in 1970, with an increase of 2.5%. In absolute terms, however, the picture is more lively and clearly shows the flooding of the tertiary. In 1950, 5.3% of the EAP meant approximately 900,000 people in the service sector; in 1970, 7.8% meant almost 3 million. Many of the jobs created were of low status, which established narrow limits for long distance mobility.

The last column in Table 4.8 indicates that most of the groups increased at an annual rate higher than the demographic expansion *per se*. Professions, for example, grew at the rate of 6.5% per year; the services presented an annual growth of 4.7%.

An internal inspection of the services stratum indicates that most of the 2.5% increment was due to an increase in numbers of domestic servants and similarly employed workers. Domestic servants, who totaled almost 700,000 in 1950, formed an enormous army of more than 1,800,000 in 1970. Certainly, this is

---

14. The reader should note that each stratum is still internally heterogeneous. The object here was to obtain a snapshot of the behavior of the occupational structure during the period. More refined aggregations based on the PNAD/73 are presented in Chapters 6 and 7.

TABLE 4.8. EAP Fluctuations by Occupational Strata* (%)

Occupational Strata	Difference (1950–1970)	Annual Rate of Growth**
1. Services	+ 2.5	4.7
2. Crafts and construction industry	+ 2.4	3.6
3. Office administrators and personnel	+ 2.2	4.0
4. Professions	+ 1.9	6.4
5. Commerce	+ 1.1	4.1
6. Transportation and communications	+ 0.8	3.9
7. Defense and security	+ 0.4	4.3
8. Mining	− 0.1	1.9
9. Farming and harvesting of natural plant products	− 13.0	1.3

Source: Adapted from the *Recenseamentos demográficos do Brasil, 1950 e 1970,* Fundação
IBGE.
*Excluded from table: + 2% for other and undeclared occupations.
**Geometric rate of growth.

not an occupational niche for long distance mobility, although for many young migrant women these occupations have represented a reasonable form of employment and a higher standard of living, not to mention the potential mobility reserved for their children to the extent that they took advantage of work opportunities in the urban centers. In terms of growth, the domestic servants added 4.9% of new workers in the labor force annually. This is what is shown in the last column of Table 4.9.

The next two categories in Table 4.8 are more heterogeneous than the preceding one. The stratum of civil construction includes occupations which show different possibilities of social mobility. The same occurs with the stratum of administrators and office personnel. Thus, we must analyze each one of them in detail.

Table 4.10 shows the behavior of the principal industrial branches as far as employment is concerned. The greatest increment is in the civil construction

TABLE 4.9. EAP Fluctuations in Service Occupations (%)

Occupational Strata	Difference (1950–1970)	Annual Rate of Growth*
Domestic and food services	+ 2.2	4.9
Personal hygiene services	+ 0.2	3.8
Professional athletes	+ 0.1	7.2

Source: Adapted from the *Recenseamentos demográficos do Brasil, 1950 e 1970,* Fundação
IBGE.
*Geometric rate of growth.

sector. The sector grew at the rate of close to 5.0% a year (see last column in Table 4.10). But, within civil construction there is a heterogeneity of occupations. Most employment created in this subsector was in manual occupations of low qualification, which leads us to conclude that the expansion of civil construction had to have more of an employment effect than a mobility effect, still keeping in mind the possibilities for upward movement opened up for migrants of low social origin.

The subsector of mechanics, with a more modest expansion but the same annual growth, perhaps contributed more to mobility (in relative terms) than did civil construction itself. This may be true because the contingent of non-qualified positions is relatively small in that subsector. Most of the opportunities that open up in the subsector of mechanics tend to demand qualified professionals, and this puts them into an upward trajectory.

It is interesting to note that almost all of the other cetegories of Table 4.10 showed a relative decline in employment between 1950 and 1970, although in absolute terms, of course, they all showed growth. For instance, the category of electricians grew at the rate of 6.5% per year; crafts, 8.4% per year (see last column Table 4.10). This seems to have resulted basically from the technological modernization undergone by the industrial sectors. This same modernization, however, induced an occupational differentiation which finally facilitated mobility for the few who participated in it.

Table 4.11 analyzes the same data referring to another heterogeneous stratum, the "administrators and office personnel." Here, too, most of the increase

TABLE 4.10. EAP Fluctuations in Industrial Occupations (%)

Industrial Occupations	Difference (1950–1970)	Annual Rate of Growth*
1. Civil construction	+1.6	4.9
2. Mechanics	+0.8	4.8
3. Crafts in general	+0.7	8.4
4. Electricians	+0.3	6.5
5. Food and beverages	0.0	3.0
6. Graphics	0.0	4.9
7. Metallurgy	0.0	2.9
8. Leather	−0.1	−0.6
9. Lumber and furniture	−0.1	2.5
10. Ceramics and glass	−0.1	1.8
11. Clothing	−0.3	2.0
12. Textiles	−0.6	−0.2

Source: Adapted from the *Recenseamentos demográficos do Brasil, 1950 e 1970*, Fundação IBGE.

*Geometric rate of growth.

TABLE 4.11. EAP Fluctuations in Clerical Occupations (%)

Occupations	Difference (1950–1970)	Annual Rate of Growth*
Office workers	+ 2.2	5.9
Administrators in general	+ 0.5	5.2
Proprietors in general	− 0.5	2.1

Source: Adapted from the *Recenseamentos demográficos do Brasil, 1950 e 1970*, Fundação IBGE.
*Geometric rate of growth.

is found among the office workers. These are nonmanual professions of middle qualification, as is the case with bookkeepers, typists, and secretaries. This category showed much opportunity for mobility, especially for individuals of low social origin whose fathers were laborers or something similar. Some of them were even able to move great social distances (see Chapter 8), beginning their career trajectory in a family of laborers and reaching an upper-middle class position, for example, that of a bank director. This area of the occupational structure deserves to be observed with care in the analysis of social mobility, since it has attracted to itself a large number of migrants from a fairly low social origin.

Another subsector of occupations whose behavior favored mobility is that of the technical-scientific and the artistic professions, the number of whose positions grew on the order of 1.9% (Table 4.8). This subsector is also heterogeneous and deserves a detailed treatment. Table 4.12 presents ten groups of occupations which compose this subsector. Within them, the category whose number of employees increased the most was that of teachers and their auxiliaries, with an increase of 1.6%. This category grew up at the rate of 7.7% annually. This indicates also social mobility possibilities for many people whose origin was from the rural, lower-lower stratum. However, we must mention that the case of the teacher is typically characterized by a status inconsistency where the social prestige of the occupation tends to be higher than its monetary rewards. In any case, no matter how small the distance covered, for people of very low origin, this always represents a reasonable intergenerational mobility.

The case of doctors and engineers is different. On the one hand, growth was small because of the group's small basis at the beginning of the period (0.4% and 0.2%), not enough to change the social structure substantially. But the annual rate of growth of these professions was close to 7%. Yet these professions continue to be relatively out of reach for individuals of low social origin, suggesting that self-recruitment and recruitment from strata neighboring those

TABLE 4.12. EAP Fluctuations in Professional Occupations (%)

Occupational Strata	Difference (1950–1970)	Annual Rate of Growth*
1. Teachers and assistants	1.6	7.7
2. Physicians, dentists, and assistants	0.4	5.5
3. Engineers and assistants	0.2	6.9
4. Mathematicians, sociologists and other sciences	0.1	—
5. Artists and assistants	0.1	—
6. Judges, lawyers and assistants	0.1	4.4
7. Clergy and assistants	0.0	8.1
8. Writers and journalists	0.0	3.1
9. Agronomists and veterinarians	0.0	5.1
10. Chemists, pharmacists, etc.	−0.1	−0.8

Source: Adapted from the *Recenseamentos demográficos do Brasil, 1950 e 1970*, Fundação IBGE.

*Geometric rate of growth.

of the fathers is more frequent than it is in the case of teachers. This being the case, one expects less mobility among doctors and engineers than among teachers, as well as a smaller status inconsistency and a higher standard of living.

How can we summarize the general tendencies of the Brazilian occupational structure, and how can we assess the various changes as either facilitating or inhibiting social mobility?

From the data presented, we discover that the changes in the occupational structure generally followed the known pattern of a draining of primary-sector occupations and a flooding of tertiary. Apart from this, we identify here and there a series of changes in certain industrial sub-sectors, suggesting the emergence of numerous new occupations.

At this point it is difficult to establish a unified vision with respect to the impact of these changes upon social mobility. The changes produced structural inducers and inhibitors of social mobility. Apart from this, many parts of the commentary are hypotheses, and are based upon the conclusions of other works which focused with different purposes upon the occupational categories. But, despite these limitations, a summary of these tendencies is necessary. Thus we can identify the principal structural inducers and inhibitors of social mobility as follows:

(1) Economic growth in Brazil during the period from 1950 to 1970 created a substantial number of new jobs. The EAP incorporated large contingents of women. This massive entrance of women seems to have followed various patterns, but the main ones were the following: (a) some women took men's

places in low-status jobs, allowing the men short-distance upward mobility; (b) most women entered into low-tertiary positions which were multiplying rapidly and which were filled by workers 20 to 49 years old with low education; (c) a few women, better educated, filled new positions in the secondary and upper-tertiary sectors (education and health), many of them coming to compete with men, making social mobility difficult for them. It seems that most of the female labor power entered into low-status jobs.

(2) With respect to regional differences, we discover that the greatest changes took place in the Central-West and the Southeast of Brazil. The greatest expansions of the tertiary were observed there, and the Southeast also had the highest growth rate for the secondary sector. There are strong indications that these changes generally promoted mobility. They also functioned as points of attraction for workers of a low social origin, and this in itself guarantees a certain upward mobility. These same regions, however, were urbanized rapidly, and, as we saw, the lower-tertiary jobs created by urbanization offer only limited possibilities of long-distance mobility. Thus, the Central-West and the Southeast experienced a combination of positive and negative forces in the promotion of mobility, but analysis indicates a favorable balance; further, these two regions apparently were very propitious niches of mobility. In other regions, the emergence of new occupations in the secondary and in the tertiary seems not to have overcome the negative effects of lower tertiarization. Consequently, their mobility structures were less favorable.

(3) Comparatively, the changes in the Brazilian occupational structure during the period seem to have followed employment and mobility, although with more emphasis upon the former. For certain occupations the amount of employment in absolute terms was reduced. However, in relative terms and in terms of impact upon social mobility, these occupations were of great importance. This mobility is of small groups (as in the case of qualified workers in agriculture, of professionals in civil aviation, and others of a like genre). There are indications, however, of a more voluminous mobility for teachers, administrators, qualified technicians of the industrial sector, and public administrators.

5

The Career Beginning
in Brazil

The entry into the labor market is one of the more critical moments in individual careers in advanced societies. In these societies, the impact of labor force entry is not limited to an individual's passing from economic dependence to economic activity. It manifests itself also as rites of passage from one phase of life to another: as the end of certain stages (schooling) and the beginning of the next (work), as the individual's departure from his original family and his entering into another one, or as plans for a new family. For this reason, social mobility studies in highly developed countries tend to consider the status of labor market entry as one of the principal determinants in the individual career (Pikes, 1968; Muller and Mayer, 1973:270–311).

In less developed societies, however, labor market entry seems to be quite different. The career beginning occurs at an earlier age. Many more children assume active roles in terms of both working for society and working for the family unit. Consequently, the entry into the market can further establish an individual's permanency in the family structure, so that he remains far from the phase of forming a new family. Many people, especially in the urban zones, find ways to work and to study at the same time.[1] In this sense there is no marked passage from one phase to another, and each career beginning seems to follow its own peculiar pattern. For this reason we have devoted a chapter

1. As an illustration of this contrast one is accustomed to hear in developed societies that "a person enters the work force when he stops being a full-time student and participates in the labor market for a certain period (generally 16 months) without returning to fulltime schooling." See Ornstein, 1976:24.

specifically to identifying the principal social characteristics of the phenomenon in Brazil. Analysis of labor market entry conditions will help also to understand intergenerational and (mainly) intragenerational mobility. To what point is social mobility affected by the early entry? How important is the point of departure in determining the career? How much does the precocity of the labor market entry perpetuate social inequalities?

Social Conditions in Entry

Table 5.1 presents the approximate time of labor market entry for the different age groups which composed the male work force of heads of family in Brazil, at the time of the PNAD/73. Most people who, in 1973, were 51–64 years old began to work during the twenties and early thirties. Their fathers must have entered the labor force at the end of the nineteenth century. At the other extreme are those who, in 1973, were 20–30 years old and who began to work during the sixties; their fathers must have entered the work force before the Second World War. Thus, the PNAD/73 sample covers practically the entire twentieth century, and makes possible a study of people who began to work and who established their careers in quite different social situations. The various age groups had to take advantage of quite varied structural conditions. As we know, Brazil changed profoundly in the eighty years covered in this study. Reducing Chapter 4 to its basic information, we can say that at the beginning of the century Brazilian society was predominantly rural, that rural-urban migration was slow, that industrialization was only incipient, and that most new job opportunities had to do with agriculture and agribusiness. These were the basic characteristics of the economy and of the labor market for those who entered the work force during the twenties and the early thirties.

Those who began to work during the forties found a Brazil that was taking more decisive steps in the direction of aggressive policies for the replacement of imports and for internal industrialization. Rural jobs were beginning to show

TABLE 5.1. Age of Entry into the Labor Market*

Age Groups	Period of Birth	Mean Age of Entry into the Labor Market	Period of Entry into the Labor Market
51–64	1909–1922	14	1923–1936
41–50	1923–1932	15	1938–1947
31–40	1933–1942	16	1949–1958
20–30	1943–1953	17	1960–1970

*Estimates based upon EAP patterns from the PNAD/73.

clear signs of decline. Rural-urban migration was speeding up, especially at the end of the period. New occupations were gradually arising in the cities, the results of industrialization. The educational system, still of low quality, remained restricted to the few.

People who entered the market during the fifties began to work in a climate in which industrialization was becoming the basic strategy of Brazilian development. With the increase in participation of foreign capital came numerous new industries which generated much indirect employment as well as direct opportunities for qualified personnel. A feeling of euphoria dominated the period, especially after the inauguration of President Juscelino Kubitschek in 1955. Migration and urbanization were speeding up still more. The sectors of civil construction and of lower-tertiary services expanded very quickly in the large cities. New occupations arose as a consequence, and there was an increase in the number of low-qualification professions which until that time were only incipient in that sector.

The educational system began to expand with greater impetus, although the quality of education remained low. This climate lasted all through the sixties, which, as we know, were marked by accelerated growth, inflation, and the tertiarization of the labor market.

People who entered the labor market between 1960 and 1970 are still establishing themselves in their positions. Urbanization, industrialization, and education, all accelerated, were the hallmarks of that period. From the mid-sixties until the present, Brazil has also been experiencing profound political and institutional changes. The high rates of growth and the expansion of employment must have influenced markedly the careers of many (especially of those who entered the market in the late sixties). At that point Brazil was already more urban than rural. Its population was concentrated in a few capitals, where employment and educational opportunities were growing most quickly.

The combination of all these factors suggests that each age group must have entered the labor market in social conditions that differed substantially from the previous ones. The general tendency was a growth in urban and a reduction in rural employment. Thus, the analysis of mobility by age group is a method of longitudinal analysis based on cross-section-type data. A comparative study of these groups thus corresponds to an approximate analysis of what happened in mobility not only in 1973 but also in the various decades mentioned. Among other things, the data allow us to explore the hypothesis that people who entered the labor market more recently enjoyed better employment opportunities and a more differentiated occupational structure, and that, reaching higher statuses, they achieved more vertical mobility than did older individuals. Studies which have focused upon the question of social inequality in Brazil have concentrated upon short and recent periods. It should not be surprising, therefore, that the results of these studies do not correspond to those of this research.

Mobility depends not only upon market opportunities, but also upon the situation at the point of departure. At the individual level, this situation refers to age at the career beginning, to initial occupational status, to social origin, and to educational background. At what age do most Brazilians begin to work? At what level do they start their careers? What is the role of education in all of this?

Age and the Career Beginning

Table 5.2 indicates that in Brazil entry into the labor market occurs early. About 70% of the heads of family began to work at 14 years of age or less.[2] This is an impressive proportion which reflects simultaneously difficulties within families and within the educational system.[3] Family and school seem to be unable to maintain most of the school-age population exclusively in schools.[4]

TABLE 5.2. Age of Entry into the Labor Market

Age	%
14 years or less	70.2
15–17	17.7
18–20	8.8
21–25	2.8
26 or more	0.5
Total	100.0
N = 53,609	

To what extent was this situation aggravated or improved with the passage of time? Analysis by age groups suggests that the problem was more serious

2. The reader will note an incongruity between the data of this section and those presented in Table 4.3 in Chapter 4. Here, we see that 70% of the heads of family began to work during the fifties at age 14 or younger; in Table 4.3 the data of the 1950 census indicated 31% of the men were between 10 and 14 years of age. However, the census reports the economically active population, which is defined as persons who worked in the 12 months prior to the date of the census. The PNAD, on the other hand, reports the first occupation of an individual, as well as his age, but without the 12-month restriction. As we know, the work of Brazilian children tends to be concentrated in the informal sector and may be carried out intermittently.

3. It is important to note that approximately 18% of the individuals entered between 15 and 17 years of age, it being reasonable to assume that many of them had not finished their education. The others, about 11.5%, started to work at ages more compatible with the completion of education.

4. In advanced societies the participation of children aged 14 or younger is substantially less. The same occurs in relation to career beginning. Kreps, studying the situation in more than 80 countries, shows that in the highly industrialized societies only 4% of the people begin working at age 14 or less. See Kreps, 1971:44.

TABLE 5.3. Age of Entry into the Labor Market by Age Groups (%)

Age of Entry	Age Groups			
	(51–64)	(41–50)	(31–40)	(20–30)
14 or less	74.7	71.7	69.0	66.5
15–17	15.3	16.5	18.2	20.2
18–20	7.0	8.4	9.3	10.4
21–25	2.3	2.9	3.0	2.8
26 or more	0.7	0.5	0.5	0.1
Total	100.0	100.0	100.0	100.0
N = 53,609	12,790	17,069	13,890	9,860

in the past. In fact, Table 5.3 shows that among individuals 51–64 years old (who thus entered the labor market during the twenties), almost 75% began to work at age 14 or less.

This proportion falls slightly with age, reaching a value of about 66% for the youngest in the sample (who began to work during the sixties). This decline, however, did not change the general pattern of the phenomenon; entry into the labor market continues to be extremely early and determined by the general problem of rural and urban poverty. In the rural zones, as we know, the family is the principal productive unit, and is remunerated generally according to the number of its members effectively engaged in work. For this reason, it is common to find a large number of children between the ages of 8 and 10 in the work force.[5] But in the urban centers children also help with the family income in numerous informal ways (carwashers, shoeshiners, errand boys). Thus, early entry continues to be a function of poverty. The data suggest, however, that the situation was more serious in the remote past than in the recent past.

Status at Career Beginning

Informal work with little security and low remuneration is common among 8- to 18-year-old youths. On the other hand, many 18-year-old men are interrupted in their careers by military service. These men begin their careers again at age 19–20. The sample studied here includes only individuals of from 20 to 64 years. This is a group, then, which has already passed through the phases of informal work and of military service.

5. The data of the Agricultural Census of 1975 showed a 10% annual increase of children under 14 in agriculture, which is higher than the population growth rate and contradicts the tendency reflected by the data of the PNAD/73. This incongruity deserves more detailed study. Could it be a belated effect of implementation of the Rural Worker's Law (Estatuto do Trabalhador Rural) in the countryside? See *Sinopse preliminar do censo agropecuário*, Brasília: Fundação IBGE, 1978.

The individuals included in the sample began to work in various occupations and at various ages. The PNAD/73 supplies data with respect to initial occupation, and allows us to identify where Brazilians begin their careers. Table 5.4 shows that the earlier the beginning, the lower is the individual's occupational status. In fact, about 72% of those who began to work at age 14 or less did so in occupations of the lowest social status—lower-lower stratum occupations in the agricultural sector. This is well above the total for the population, which, as the table shows, is about 58%. Among those who began at age 15–17, this proportion falls drastically to about 37%. In the next age group the decline is even further (12%), while it stabilizes at about 7% in the two remaining groups.

The career beginning in occupations of the urban lower class (upper-lower stratum) increases in the group of individuals who began to work at age 15–17, while it falls thereafter. Everything indicates, therefore, that among very young children in the rural zone the pressure to help the family is enormous, with the question of remuneration passing to a secondary level. Adolescents distribute themselves in a more or less equal way in terms of rural and urban employment. Adults, however, begin in jobs of much higher status, especially in the middle strata. Early entry is a bad beginning to a career. The later the entry, the better the start.

What is the significance of the early entry for the final social destiny? The data of the PNAD/73 allow us to examine the occupational status of individuals in 1973, controlled by age of entry into the market (Table 5.5).

Comparing Table 5.5 with 5.4, one sees much mobility between current and initial statuses. This is revealed particularly by the "Totals" columns of the two tables. The tendency between age and status, however, is still the same; that is, early entry into the labor market has a limiting effect upon individuals'

TABLE 5.4. Age of Entry into the Labor Market and Initial Occupational Status (%)

| Initial Occupational Status | Age of Entry into the Labor Market | | | | | |
	14 or less	15–17	18–20	21–26	26 or more	Total
Upper	0.0	0.1	1.2	10.7	30.8	0.6
Upper-middle	0.0	0.6	3.3	9.1	9.8	0.7
Middle-middle	1.3	11.2	34.0	38.3	21.9	7.0
Lower-middle	4.4	12.3	19.5	15.5	11.3	7.4
Upper-lower	22.3	39.1	29.7	19.0	19.0	25.8
Lower-lower	72.0	36.7	12.3	7.4	7.2	58.5
Total	100.0	100.0	100.0	100.0	100.0	100.0
N = 55,801						

TABLE 5.5. Age of Entry into the Labor Market and Current Occupational Status (%)

Current Occupational Status	Age of Entry into the Labor Market					
	14 or less	15–17	18–20	21–25	26 or more	Total
Upper	1.8	4.1	9.7	21.7	36.9	3.7
Upper-middle	4.5	8.5	14.8	19.8	17.8	6.7
Middle-middle	16.4	22.4	28.7	27.3	14.7	18.9
Lower-middle	23.6	29.2	26.2	19.1	13.6	24.6
Upper-lower	17.0	17.8	14.4	8.7	12.0	16.6
Lower-lower	36.7	18.0	6.2	3.4	5.0	29.5
Total	100.0	100.0	100.0	100.0	100.0	100.0
N = 53,609						

social destination. The earlier they begin to work, the greater the probability that they occupy and remain in a low-status position in the base of the social pyramid. More than one third of those individuals who began to work at age 14 or less remained in the lower-lower stratum, and 17% in the upper-lower. For those who began at age 15–17, this percentage falls to about 18%. This pattern maintains itself for the other age groups. In the oldest group, however, there is a slight increase in the lowest levels and a substantial increase in the upper stratum.

The general tendency in Table 5.5 reaffirms the hypothesis that early entry is a detriment to the individual. Early entry constitutes a limiting inheritance.[6] It is a poor beginning and makes access to higher positions difficult. Conversely, late entry is associated with a good beginning and facilitates the upward trajectory. Generally, we can say that for every year the individual puts off his entry into the market (and continues in school), he increases by 10 to 15% his probability of entry into the middle class or of going higher. But, clearly, years in themselves cannot guarantee a good future. The age of labor market entry must be related to social origin and to educational background.[7]

The Role of Social Origin

Much of the problem of an early entry into the labor market is associated with individuals' social origins. The age upon entry is a function of family background.

6. This point was made in a different way by Morley (1978); Simonsen, 1978.

7. However, it would be hasty to conclude that education by itself could reverse the limiting effect of early entry. Several studies show that adaptation of individual qualifications to job requirements have the desired result upon mobility only when social differentiation is high. See Sorensen and Kalleberg, 1977; Bowles and Gintis, 1976.

Table 5.6 relates social origin (given as the fathers' statuses) and the age of entry into the labor market. The lower the origin, the earlier an individual begins to work. For example, among individuals originating in the lower-lower stratum, 82% began to work at age 14 or less. Among the sons of the upper-lower stratum, 65% began to work early. This percentage decreases as the individual rises in the social structure. It is interesting to note, however, that even among the sons of the upper class this percentage is still 32%. Early entry, in Brazil, is a phenomenon that occurs with a certain frequency in all the social classes.

The percentages of people who began to work at age 15 or over decrease substantially in all the classes. But here also the percentages are distributed homogenously, with the exception of the lower-lower stratum.

Early entry seems to reflect difficulties that strike families and the educational system itself. Brazilian society, with the exception of its highest layers, has experienced chronic problems in adequately educating its population and permitting its members good career beginnings.

How has this phenomenon behaved through time? To what extent can one say that individuals today enter *later* and *higher* on the social scale? The data of Table 5.3 showed that men are delaying their entry into the labor market. Table 5.4 indicates that an early entry is a bad career beginning. There are, however, signs of change.

Table 5.7 lists the beginning occupational statuses of the different age groups considered so far, and permits an answer to the question above. The data show that individuals generally enter very much near the bottom of the social structure. However, the situation was worse in the remote past than in the recent past. Let us consider the two lowest status levels as forming the lower social stratum. We then discover that almost 90% of the oldest individuals began to

TABLE 5.6. Social Origin and Age of Entry into the Labor Market (%)

Father's Status	Age of Entry into the Labor Market					
	14 or less	15–17	18–20	21–25	26 or more	Total
Upper	32.3	23.1	26.1	16.4	2.1	100.0
Upper-middle	40.2	25.9	22.6	9.0	2.3	100.0
Middle-middle	54.7	22.3	15.9	6.2	0.9	100.0
Lower-middle	58.8	27.3	11.6	2.1	0.2	100.0
Upper-lower	64.6	23.4	9.7	2.1	0.2	100.0
Lower-lower	82.3	12.6	3.9	1.0	0.2	100.0
Total	72.6	16.8	7.7	2.5	0.4	100.0
N = 45,892						

TABLE 5.7. Occupational Status upon Entry into the Labor Market (%)

Initial Social Status	Age Groups			
	(51–64)	(41–50)	(31–40)	(20–30)
Upper	*0.6*	*0.6*	*0.6*	*0.5*
Middle	*11.4*	*14.0*	*16.7*	*17.8*
Upper-middle	0.6	0.7	0.7	0.9
Middle-middle	5.3	6.8	7.7	8.0
Lower-middle	5.5	6.5	8.3	8.9
Lower	*88.0*	*85.4*	*82.7*	*81.7*
Upper-lower	20.8	24.3	27.4	29.6
Lower-lower	67.2	61.1	55.3	52.1
Total	*100.0*	*100.0*	*100.0*	*100.0*
N = 45,892				

work in the lower stratum; this percentage falls to about 82% for the youngest individuals, although it clearly continues to be very large in absolute terms.

A great part of this tendency toward change was due to an inversion in participation by men in the rural and the urban labor markets. Most of the oldest individuals entered as farmhands, woodcutters, fishermen, rubber workers, etc. The proportion of people who entered these occupations falls substantially with age. On the other hand, the tendency was toward an increased number from the younger groups beginning their careers in occupations of low status in the urban zone. However, this increase was less accentuated than the reduction of entry into low status occupations in the rural zone. We conclude, then, that many younger individuals entered into the labor market at higher levels.

In short, entry into the Brazilian labor market continues to take place at a low level and in a groping manner. However, there are already clear signs of change, due mainly to a decrease in rural occupations and to direct entry into middle class occupations (which, in the two groups studied, jumped from about 11% to about 18%). This is a reasonable increase and reflects not only the later entry but also a certain level of occupational differentiation and of expansion in education.

Education and Early Entry

So far we have seen that a good part of the Brazilian work force enters the market when it still should be in school. It would be wrong to conclude, though, that this entry means a definitive interruption in the Brazilian individ-

TABLE 5.8. Percentages of Individuals who were in School upon Entry into the Labor Market

Age Groups	Individuals in School	%
51–64	11,637	23.0
41–50	14,992	28.5
31–40	18,115	36.0
20–30	13,542	41.8
Total and average	58,286	32.8

ual's preparation. In the first place, one must consider that a great part of the individual's professional preparation takes place in the market itself, just as in various other societies. In the second place, we must emphasize the frequent and growing coexistence of school and work in Brazilian life. The PNAD/73 data (Table 5.8) show that about one third of the heads of family were taking some kind of course when they began to work.[8] Analysis of this phenomenon by age group suggests that the percentage of people who are experiencing this coexistence is growing in the recent period. Only 23% of the people 51–64 years of age were in school when they began to work. For the 20- and 30-year-olds, this percentage almost doubles. Everything indicates that those who entered the labor force yesterday, despite the general precocity, were further away from school than they are today. The worker-student and the student-worker are phenomena from recent decades in Brazil.[9]

There are various indications that the youngest groups are enjoying a better level of education, although, as the data indicate, the Brazilian work force continues to have a rather precarious standard of formal education. Table 5.13 tells the story: almost 63% of the heads of family never even finished grade school.

The general tendency shown in Table 5.9 is that the percentage of the unschooled increases with age, suggesting greater educational restrictions yesterday than today. The difference between the youngest and the eldest is 16% in favor of the former. However, this is not the case between those who have finished and those who have not finished grade school. The difference between these two groups is small (5.4% and 3.4%, respectively).

Although we are dealing with different bases in the distribution of the totals of the rows, a better marker exists for people who finished junior high school

8. The study, unfortunately, does not permit us to differentiate the individuals who left school to begin work from those who continued to study.

9. Pastore and Perosa, 1971. Gouveia mentions a series of studies of students' social origins, including the origins of those who work. See Gouveia, 1971.

TABLE 5.9. Age and Educational Attainment (%)

Age Groups	No School	Grade School Incomplete	Grade School Complete	Jr. High School	High School	University	Total
51–64	37.5	40.0	16.2	4.7	2.2	3.0	100.0
41–50	24.7	41.5	19.0	6.7	3.4	4.7	100.0
31–40	19.2	39.7	21.3	9.6	5.0	5.4	100.0
20–30	17.6	36.8	21.6	12.9	6.6	4.5	100.0
Total N = 46,129	23.1	39.5	19.8	8.7	4.4	4.5	100.0

and high school. From the oldest group to the youngest, the percentages of those who finished junior high and high school almost tripled.

These educational distortions reflect not only the limitations of the Brazilian educational system; they also reflect the problems of low social origin that plague most Brazilians. A deep social discrimination still exists in Brazil in terms of educational attainment.[10] Table 5.10 shows that the sons of the lower class (lower-lower and upper-lower strata) do not often complete their primary education. Middle class sons more frequently complete primary and junior high school levels. Upper class sons find themselves in high school and in the university. Here again a low social origin (which holds for most of the population) has a limiting effect upon educational attainment.

Education is one of the main individual resources for taking advantage of employment opportunities, and, therefore, for upward mobility.[11] In other words, given certain occupational opportunities, getting a job and going on to higher status occupations are highly associated with an individual's education level.

We have already said that age upon entry into the labor market is indeed an indication of an individual's education. In fact, Table 5.11 shows that the higher the individual's level of education, the better his career beginning.[12] For example, almost 90% of unschooled people began their careers in low-status occupations linked to the rural zone. This percentage reduces to 73% for those who attended part of grade school, and it is only a little more than

10. Several other studies show this discrimination in Brazil. See, for example, Pastore and Owen, 1968; Moreira, 1960.

11. This suggests that the weight of social inheritance in determining individual status acts indirectly through education, and not directly. This hypothesis will be examined in Chapter 10.

12. We must note that Table 5.11 relates the individual's formal education as of 1973 with the social status of his first job. The table suggests that much of an individual's formal education was acquired as he worked.

40% for those who finished grade school. But for those who finished junior high school, these increases were not so impressive in terms of career beginnings. It is true that the percentage of those who began as laborers fell quite a bit, reaching 17%; however, 48% still entered into low-status occupations, although in the urban zone. Among those who finished high school, this percentage was still high, about 40%; the same can be said of the 24% who finished college who took low-status jobs. In order to clarify this apparent paradox, Table 5.12 relates these same educational levels to the individuals' occupational statuses in 1973.

TABLE 5.10. Social Origin and Educational Attainment (%)

Father's Status	Educational Attainment						
	University	High School	Jr. High	Grade School Complete	Grade School Incomplete	No School	Total
Upper	40.0	18.7	18.3	11.5	10.2	1.3	100.0
Upper-middle	23.7	17.2	19.4	21.2	15.2	3.3	100.0
Middle-middle	13.3	12.5	17.4	21.9	26.7	8.2	100.0
Lower-middle	4.2	7.5	20.1	34.9	27.6	5.7	100.0
Upper-lower	3.5	5.3	14.4	33.3	32.3	11.2	100.0
Lower-lower	0.6	1.0	3.7	15.8	47.1	31.8	100.0
Total	4.5	4.4	8.7	19.8	39.5	23.1	100.0
N = 46,686							

TABLE 5.11. Educational and Initial Occupational Status (%)

Levels of Education	Initial Social Status						
	Upper	Upper-middle	Middle-middle	Lower-middle	Upper-lower	Lower-lower	Total
University	11.1	9.3	47.6	3.9	24.0	4.1	100.0
High school	1.3	2.4	40.3	9.2	39.8	7.0	100.0
Jr. high school	0.3	1.2	18.0	15.6	48.0	16.9	100.0
Grade school complete	0.1	0.2	4.6	14.4	40.5	40.2	100.0
Grade school incomplete	0.0	0.1	0.9	5.7	20.3	73.0	100.0
No school	0.0	0.0	0.2	1.3	9.8	88.7	100.0
Total	0.6	0.7	7.0	7.8	25.6	58.3	100.0
N = 56,909							

TABLE 5.12. Education and Current Occupational Status (%)

Levels of Education		Social Status of Individuals in 1973					
	Upper	Upper-middle	Middle-middle	Lower-middle	Upper-lower	Lower-lower	Total
University	42.6	33.7	21.8	1.2	0.5	0.2	100.0
High school	12.7	26.8	47.4	8.7	4.1	0.3	100.0
Jr. high school	3.3	14.5	41.4	27.3	11.7	1.8	100.0
Grade school complete	1.7	6.2	23.2	40.3	17.8	10.8	100.0
Grade school incomplete	0.7	2.5	13.8	28.9	20.1	34.0	100.0
No school	0.3	0.6	7.3	10.9	18.0	62.9	100.0
Total	3.6	6.6	18.8	24.7	16.6	29.7	100.0
N = 54,950							

Although they do not refer directly to career beginnings, these data shed light upon the paradox of the preceding results. Generally, the association between education and current status is closer than it is in the case of beginning status. The higher levels of education tend to put people in higher statuses. In particular, the percentages fall sharply of individuals who finished junior high school or more and who remained in the upper-lower status jobs. The differences between these two tables with relation to this particular point suggest that, in fact, much schooling is attained after work has begun. This corroborates the hypothesis already put forward in Table 5.8, that a coexistence of work and study in Brazil is common.

Although education and social status are highly associated, it is too early to conclude that social attainment can be explained totally by an individual's level of education. As we saw, social attainment depends first upon the existence of jobs and upon a certain level of occupational differentiation. Second, it depends upon an acquisition of experience in the labor market.[13] The data show that there are still a large number of individuals well-placed in the social structure whose level of formal education is relatively rudimentary. For example, about 20% of the upper stratum individuals in 1973 had finished only grade school or less. Among the members of the upper-middle stratum, this percentage reached about 36%. In other words, the association between social inequality and educational inequality is high, but it is not perfect.

What kind of social structure would be formed by the heads of family if it were based strictly upon criteria of merit? Table 5.13 shows that about 63% of

13. Recent studies have sought to emphasize the importance of personal contacts established in the labor market. These contacts are powerful promotors of upward mobility. See Granovetter, 1974; Tinker, 1977.

TABLE 5.13. Social Structure and Educational Structure (%)

Social Status in 1973	%	Level of Education	%
Upper	3.6	University	4.5
Upper-middle	6.6	High school	4.4
Middle-middle	18.8	Jr. high school	8.7
Lower-middle	24.7	Grade school complete	19.8
Upper-lower	16.6	Grade school incomplete	39.5
Lower-lower	29.7	No school	23.1
Total	100.0	Total	100.0

the heads of family have not finished or even been exposed to grade school. If we put together the two lowest social strata, we would have a "lower class" of a little more than 46%. However, many people moved on the social scale, in spite of a meager formal education.[14] If we compare the size of the middle class strata and the percentage of people who have finished grade school or more, we again see that the social structure tends to be more "open" than does the educational structure. Such comparisons are rudimentary, of course, but they do seem to suggest that if we were to "construct" a social structure based exclusively upon education, then we certainly would have a level of inequality even more brutal than that which occurs in reality.

In conclusion, the career beginning in Brazil carries numerous social problems stemming from a greater problem, which is that of a still unequal society. Most Brazilian families are unable to educate their children adequately and to postpone their entry into the labor market. The early entry of the children of the lower social classes is in itself a strong indicator of social inequality which historically has permeated the Brazilian social system. This phenomenon is as old as Brazilian society, but has slowly been disappearing in recent years. But it is clear that we are far from a situation of full equality in matters touching upon entry into the labor market. The poorest families are "forced" to throw their unprepared children into the work force, where they must compete in extremely unequal situations with the children of the middle and upper classes, classes which are able to educate their children before sending them out to work.

Social origin, although not a direct determinant of the individual's status, plays a large, indirect role in that it limits education and, therefore, occupation and upward mobility. However, all this is not sufficient to cause social stagnation. In spite of low social inheritance and low education, Brazilians have

14. Previous studies have shown that "rank" as a variable is important in determining salaries and status and that it is not always closely associated with education. See Pastore, 1977b; Pastore and Ceotto, 1974; Kannappan, 1977:157–70; Pastore, 1975.

traveled far socially in the last three or four decades. This is a journey induced by the dynamism of structural forces, of a rural society becoming urban, of a growth in urban employment opportunities. In short, this is a mobility that is predominantly structural and which has overcome almost all individual deficiencies such as low social origin, early entry, and low education.

6

Intergenerational Mobility in Brazil

Table 6.1 is an intergenerational mobility matrix relating the status of the father (at the time the son began to work) to that of the son in 1973. The percentages in the rows represent the shifts from social origin to destination. Using more liberal terminology, we can say that the matrix presents the shifts from the social class of origin to the social class of destination. The totals at the ends of the columns and rows indicate, respectively, the proportions of the various social classes of origin and of destination. They reflect the changes that have taken place in the social structure of the generations under consideration.[1]

The percentages in the principal diagonal are still relatively high, indicating the persistence of a certain immobility; they reveal the relative weight of social inheritance. This pattern, however, is far from being homogenous in the various social strata. In some strata the immobility from fathers to sons is very low, indicating a high degree of social mobility. This is the case, for example, for the sons in the lower-lower stratum. About 66% of the people born into that stratum had already achieved upward social mobility in 1973, having progressed in relation to their fathers. The same occurred in the upper-lower stratum. Most people are better off than their fathers. But, before beginning

---

1. It is important to note that studies of intergenerational mobility (including this one) highlight populations which do not represent two perfectly isolated generations—that is, one work force from the past and one which is current. The sample for this research is a cross-section of the labor force in 1973. Within this population were fathers of young respondents who were themselves still young and still working, as well as old fathers (working and retired), deceased fathers, etc.

TABLE 6.1. Occupational Matrix of Intergenerational Mobility (%)

Father's Status	Individual's Status in 1973							Total for Fathers
	1	2	3	4	5	6	Total	
1. Upper	29.8	22.5	27.1	12.5	5.0	3.1	100.0	100.0
2. Upper-middle	15.2	28.7	28.7	15.5	6.1	5.8	100.0	100.0
3. Middle-middle	8.6	14.3	36.2	18.9	10.5	11.5	100.0	100.0
4. Lower-middle	3.8	8.7	21.6	46.3	14.9	4.7	100.0	100.0
5. Upper-lower	3.2	7.4	20.7	35.4	23.8	9.5	100.0	100.0
6. Lower-lower	1.0	2.5	13.1	21.1	17.4	44.9	100.0	100.0
Total for Individuals N = 44,307	3.5	6.3	18.4	23.8	16.0	32.0	100.0	100.0

a detailed analysis of what happened in each social stratum, it seems appropriate to present a general picture of the principal social mobility tendencies among Brazilian families.

General Tendencies of Intergenerational Mobility

Looking at the whole of the data in Table 6.1, we can say that the Brazilian social structure has shown high intergenerational mobility rates throughout the past 80 years, especially in the lower strata. As we have seen, the majority of the sons of the two lowest strata already have higher statuses than do their fathers. The proportion of individuals who remain in their fathers' positions is relatively small. The proportion for downward mobility is smaller still.[2]

Taken together, the two lower strata show more upward mobility than the others, reaffirming the fact that the great social movement is located at the base of the pyramid. This phenomenon is common in various societies, especially those which are beginning or intensifying their process of social mobility. But even in the most advanced societies, the amount of upward social movement at the base of the pyramid is considerable (Blau and Duncan, 1967:37).

Taking into account the fact that practically all of the fathers of the lower-lower stratum held rural occupations, it is important to mention immediately

2. Clearly, these strata had very little space in which to descend in the social structure. However, they might have remained immobile, and for the majority of individuals in these strata, this did not happen.

that the high degree of vertical mobility identified in the pyramid base is closely associated with changes in the agricultural labor market and with the great rural-urban migration that has taken place in Brazil in the last decades. These structural changes have created a large number of job opportunities especially in the lower tertiary in the large cities—that is, in occupations of low qualifications and low remuneration (Pastore, 1977: Chap. 1). In the study referred to, we raised the hypothesis that the rapid expansion of these occupations had done little to favor social mobility. However, the data referring to the heads of family in this research show the contrary. The great masses of individuals who entered into lower tertiary occupations in the urban zones did achieve intergenerational mobility. The majority traveled only short social distances, and others traveled far in the social structure.

It is pertinent to clarify this new discovery in relation to previous results. Given the lack of specific data for heads of family and their fathers, previous studies had to take into account the entire EAP—that is, men and women, children and adults, as well as all family members, without distinction. With that empirical base, only insignificant changes in the Brazilian social structure were observed, suggesting a small occupational differentiation and a timid social mobility (Pastore, 1976). The heads of family now being analyzed (men 20–64 years old) present a picture of great dynamism, especially at the base of the social structure. How do we explain this "paradox"?

In the first place, we are dealing with two different data bases. The 1976 study included the entire EAP and did not deal with data for the analysis of inter- and intragenerational mobility. In the second place, the 1977 study did include data about mobility, but it focused upon men and women over ten years old, independently of their position in the family structure. This research, on the other hand, focuses only upon the "heads" in the majority of Brazilian families—that is, the men 20–64 years old.

The occupational opportunities unquestionably are differentiating for this group; in addition, in one way or another, the individuals of this group are seizing the new job opportunities and the new occupations emerging in the secondary and tertiary sectors. How does one explain, then, that upon examining the entire EAP one discovers a massive entrance of individuals into occupations which are only slightly differentiated, of low status and income? The distinction identified suggests that the opportunities of less prestige and income are left for the remainder of the EAP—that is, for women and children.[3]

3. Data from this same source (PNAD/73) show that 72% of the women 20–64 years old are distributed between the lower-lower and the upper-lower strata; among young and adolescent girls 10–19 years old this percentage rises to 89%! Among young and adolescent boys this percentage is 87%. This shows that the work opportunities generated by development of the industrial, commercial, and service sectors (as presented in Chapter 4) were "distributed" in a quite differentiated way among male heads of family, women, and children.

The "best" positions fall to the heads of family and the "worst" to the other members. As a consequence of this fact, and given the large number of women and children who enter annually into the work force, there seems to be a certain regressivity of mobility for the social structure as a whole.[4]

On the other hand, it is necessary to admit that inter- and intragenerational mobility is studied best in terms of heads of family, especially in countries such as Brazil, where a good portion of single people continue to live with their parents, integrating themselves simultaneously with the labor market and with the family structure. Thus, fixing the sample in terms of male heads of family, 20–64 years old, made it possible to focus on the kernel of the work force for mobility purposes, as well as to facilitate some comparisons with other countries which, as is known, systematically analyze individuals with these characteristics.[5]

Examining the two totals in Table 6.1, we discover large differences between the social structures formed by fathers and by their sons. The data show a marked decline in the lower class strata and a corresponding increase in the middle class strata. This coincides with the shrinking of the agricultural labor market and the expansion of the others, as pointed out in Chapter 4. If we use the conventional hierarchization in terms of three social classes, we see by Table 6.2 that, from fathers to sons, the lower class was reduced by one half. The middle class more than doubled. The upper class almost doubled.[6] The three classes, each in its own way, were quite changed from one generation to the next.

The occupational differentiation that has occurred between fathers and sons, especially in the last 40 years, has been striking. As we have seen, a large change took place in the rural sector. In the fathers' generation, the rural sector employed close to 65% of the heads of family. Today, this proportion has been reduced to one half. Those who have left primary sector occupations and a large number of the new members of the work force have become situated in the more varied occupations of the middle class, which were nonexistent in their fathers' time.

When comparisons are made between generations, this question often arises:

4. Discrimination against women in the social mobility trajectory persists even in the advanced societies. Recent studies show that 85% of the salary differences among men and women in the United States was a monetary effect of discrimination. See Featherman and Hauser, 1975:481; Chase, 1975. Certain works show that the principal avenue of social mobility for women in developed societies is still marriage—an avenue, that is, that depends upon the man's status. See Chase, 1975; Treiman and Terell, 1975.

5. Parkin, 1971:11–17, gives one of the clearest justifications for studying social mobility among male heads of family.

6. Again, we caution the reader as to the great proportional differences in the class bases.

TABLE 6.2. Changes in the Brazilian Social Structure (%)

Classes and Social Strata	Fathers' Positions	Sons' Positions in 1973
Upper class	*2.0*	*3.5*
Upper stratum	2.0	3.5
Middle class	*26.2*	*48.5*
Upper-middle stratum	3.1	6.3
Middle-middle stratum	13.8	18.4
Lower-middle stratum	9.3	23.8
Lower class	*71.8*	*48.0*
Upper-lower stratum	6.9	16.0
Lower-lower stratum	64.9	32.0
Total	*100.0*	*100.0*
N = 44,307		

doesn't an occupation today have the same significance as the same occupation in the past? This question is pertinent to the study of social mobility and was touched upon lightly in Chapter 3. Let us return to it here in the light of the data.

Behind the question is the fact that, owing to eventual changes in the social positioning of occupations through time, the middle class, for example, might have seemed larger in the past simply because we have taken a more highly differentiated (current) occupational structure as our point of departure. In other words, low-status occupations today might have been middle-status in times past.[7] Several solid arguments counter this view. In this case, let us look at an empirical one. Table 6.2 shows that, for ten jobs available to the fathers of the respondents, almost seven were related to occupations of low qualification, education, prestige, and income—that is, farm hands, fishermen, rubber workers. On the other hand, for each ten jobs available to the heads of family interviewed in 1973, six or seven were in occupations which required more qualification and experience and which enjoyed greater prestige, education, and income. This was the basic transformation that took place in the occupational structure in Brazil. Today, there are more opportunities for occupational choice than in the past. Without a doubt, the number of alternatives has increased in almost all the different levels, although especially in the lower-middle and middle-middle strata.

The structural change pointed out above was responsible for generating new

7. This point is raised in Jaffe and Carleton, 1954, where the authors show ways to bypass the problem, based upon analyses by age group, upon discountings of mortality by social level, upon transformations of the occupational structure, etc.

TABLE 6.3. General Patterns of Intergenerational Mobility (%)

Types of Mobility	%
Upward	47.1
Immobility	41.6
Downward	11.3
Total	100.0

and better vacancies, so that those who entered the work force were situating themselves in higher levels than those of their fathers, without having to displace or force out other individuals of higher status. In other words, the structural mobility opportunities surpassed opportunities for circular mobility.[8] Although the analysis of this phenomenon is carried out in more detail in the following section, it is appropriate at this point to look at the behavior of the large groups.

Table 6.3 shows great dynamism in the Brazilian social structure. Most people occupy positions different from those of their fathers. It shows also that nearly half of the heads of family studied in 1973 were in positions higher than those of their fathers. About 42% remained like their fathers and a little more than 10% descended in the social structure. This is in large part the result of the changes in the occupational structure pointed out above.[9]

The general tendency of mobility, therefore, was clearly upward, which means that, socially, the majority of the heads of family today are better off than their fathers. When only the mobile individuals are analyzed, this fact is even more prominent. Table 6.4 gives the proportions for upward- and downward-moving individuals over the total of mobile individuals. Thus, for each ten people who were mobile in relation to their fathers, eight were better off (that is, went upward in the social structure) and close to two were worse off and went downward. But, did all of those who ascended benefit equally? Did everyone rise the same number of degrees in the social scale? Finally, what happened to each of the social strata in terms of inter-regional mobility?

To answer these questions it is necessary to alert the reader again to the fact that, by definition, people of different social strata have different probabilities of rising or falling in the social structure. Generally, people of the lower strata

8. The various studies which highlight this distinction show the same pattern in numerous societies, especially during the initial phases of development. See Jaffe, 1959: Chap. 1; Miller, 1960; Tumin and Feldman, 1961: Chaps. 2–5.

9. Again, we must emphasize that this description is for male heads of family in particular. Among women 20–64 years old, for example, the situation is less favorable. Upward mobility for them is about 42%; immobility, 40%; downward mobility, 18%. Among young and adolescent girls 10–19 years old, 28% ascended, 52% remained immobile, and 20% descended on the social scale.

TABLE 6.4. Types of Mobility for Mobile Individuals (%)

Types of Mobility	%
Upward	80.6
Downward	19.4
Total	100.00

have much more space in which to move up socially than do those who have already situated themselves in the highest levels. To go up, for the former, depends upon new spots opening up at high levels, upon personal qualifications, contacts, influence, etc. People of the highest strata have little space for upward movement and a great deal of space for downward movement. For them, downward movement might result from positions passing out of existence or from exchanges with other individuals (substitution), which in turn stem from problems of professional obsolescence or loss of power and prestige. In some cases, individuals lose power and prestige within an organization, with the most frequent result being a change of jobs. When they change, they change their occupation, their job rank, or both. In some cases, the profession itself loses power and prestige with the passage of time, and its occupants fall with it (a grade-school teacher in Brazil, for example).

However, those who do have the space to climb on the social scale confront different levels of difficulty. Generally, upward movement is more difficult the higher the status level under consideration. Everything depends upon how well one's resources interact with the rigidity of the structure. As in a mountain climb, the steeper the face, the more difficult it is to scale the peak. And those who are better prepared physically can go a little further than the improvisors. For this reason, room for access does not signify effective conditions for access.[10] When people climb from the lower social strata, they tend to travel only short distances during the first generation.[11]

Mobility in the Different Social Strata

What has been the behavior of each social stratum in Brazil? Table 6.5 shows the proportions of upward and downward mobility and of immobility in each social stratum. One can see that upward mobility is inversely proportional to

10. This pattern has been observed in all societies in the beginning stages of development. See Crevenna, 1950–52; Beals, 1959; Siegel, 1955; Miller, 1960.

11. The situation is more or less the same for downward movement. When employment suddenly goes down (due to recession, social upheaval, etc.), the falling of status is also rapid and pronounced. When the loss is due, for example, to demographic factors, controlling the downfall and reducing its impacts still depend upon individual resources (education, contacts, experience, etc.).

TABLE 6.5. Intergenerational Mobility by Social Strata (%)

Types of Mobility	Social Strata						
	Upper	Upper-middle	Middle-middle	Lower-middle	Upper-lower	Lower-lower	Total
Upward	—	15.2	22.9	34.1	66.7	55.1	47.1
Immobility	29.8	28.7	36.2	46.3	23.8	44.9	41.6
Downward	70.2	56.1	40.9	19.6	9.5	—	11.3
Total	100.0	100.0	100.0	100.0	100.0	100.0	100.0

the stratum level being considered. The higher the level, the smaller the upward social movement. Two facts must be explained at this point. First, the two lowest strata show a much greater volume of upward mobility than the others, which in large part is due to their inferior placement in the social structure. Second, within these two strata, the upper-lower stratum, which is made up of primarily lower-tertiary fathers with urban occupations, was the stratum which provided the most upward mobility to its sons. There is, therefore, an inversion of proportions in these two social strata. The effective probability of climbing was greater for a son of the upper-lower stratum than for a son of the lower-lower. Remember that the two strata are lower class and that they include occupations without professional qualification, with low education and income, and whose social values, on Valle Silva's scale, are very close. The major difference is the father's presence or absence in the urban zone. Everything indicates, then, that a son of the urban lower class has more social prospects than does a son of the rural lower class. This is understandable, since the great occupational differentiation discussed previously occurred in the urban zones and not in the rural. We are dealing with two different worlds which, in a more advanced study, perhaps deserve to be treated separately in terms of social mobility.

These comments, however, should not obfuscate the upward mobility of the sons of the lower-lower stratum. This stratum experienced great changes from one generation to the next. In fact, more than half of its sons climbed on the social scale, and, as we shall see, a reasonable portion of them covered great distances.

Upward social movement of people who originate in the middle strata is much more reduced than in the two previous cases, but it still is substantial when we consider the fact that less space is left for them to move upward in the social structure. Among those who were born into the lower-middle stratum, nearly 34% climbed. Most people remained in their fathers' positions and less than 20% descended. We are dealing with people whose fathers worked in manual occupations, generally in industry, but of a qualification level that was relatively low and acquired on the job, as in the case of bricklayers, plumbers, glassworkers, carpenters, painters, printers, bookbinders, and drivers. We can say, therefore, that the majority of people born into the "lower-middle class" are equal to or better off than their fathers.

In the two other strata of the middle class, obstacles to upward mobility persist. A new difficulty also begins to appear—that is, the tendency of a son to remain in his father's position. In fact, the majority of people in these two strata descended in relation to their fathers. How do we interpret this within a dynamic structure?

We have already mentioned that the number of available positions tends to be inversely proportional to the level of the positions in the social structure. The higher the level, the fewer the available positions. This is one dimension of social inequality. The greater the contrast, the greater the inequality. The decrease of upward social movement in the two highest strata of the middle class may be interpreted, then, as a reflection of the unequal structure which still persists in Brazil.[12]

On the other hand, social mobility in any country tends to be closely associated with the question of age. Age is a variable which brings together a series of individual characteristics relevant to mobility. From the labor market perspective, age tends to reflect experience, familiarity with business procedures, accuracy of information, etc. From the cultural perspective, societies tend to reward more highly the "mature" individuals—those who have already passed through their career apprenticeship (18–25 years of age), and especially those who have married. Age, marriage, and promotion are closely related. Marriage in itself seems to arouse in business and in society in general a recognition of higher responsibility in the person who has married and decided to form a new family (Parkin, 1971:17). This attitude seems to induce and to facilitate the advancement of married men in business or in the labor market in general.

In the sample for this study, all the individuals are heads of family and, legally or not, all are married. The only factor that varies is age. In the light of age, then, how can we interpret the apparently modest volume of upward mobility which we observe in the middle strata? Table 6.6 shows the proportions of mobile individuals who were upwardly mobile, by social stratum and by age group.

The data show, in the first place, that the direction of the proportions of upward social movement has a character that is consistent in all the age groups.

---

12. The data presented in Chapter 4 show that, in absolute terms, the number of jobs created at the middle-middle and the upper-middle levels was substantially less than it was in the lower strata.

TABLE 6.6. Upward Social Movement for Mobile Individuals by Age Group (%)

Social Strata		Age Groups			
	Total	(51–64)	(41–50)	(31–40)	(20–30)
Upper	—	—	—	—	—
Upper-middle	21.4	23.7	21.5	22.0	18.7
Middle-middle	35.9	36.8	38.7	37.3	30.2
Lower-middle	63.5	57.4	65.3	67.6	60.1
Upper-lower	87.5	77.9	87.9	90.4	89.8
Lower-lower	100.0	100.0	100.0	100.0	100.0

In the second place, the consistency among strata is notable, also. As for age, we can say that the data generally follow the hypothesis that upward social movement stands out most in the intermediate age groups. The extremes rise less. The oldest probably lack new opportunities. The youngest have not yet had time to establish themselves in the labor market.

The difficulty of upward social movement, however, is not linear within each stratum. Theoretically, we should have expected reductions of upward social movement with accentuated advancement as we rose in the social structure.[13] This may be better understood by examining the possibilities for an individual to go from a certain lower stratum to any higher stratum. From Table 6.6 we see that among the mobile individuals of the lower-lower stratum, obviously, 100% move upward socially. Among those of the upper-lower, this proportion is about 87%, showing a 13% reduction compared to the previous one. From there on, the individuals start from a higher plateau; they have less space for moving upward, and, logically, the difficulties increase. All this should have been reflected in increasing differences of upward social movement in relation to the previous stratum. Indeed, the proportion of upwardly mobile people among those of the lower-middle stratum falls to about 63%, and the difference in relation to the previous stratum increases to 24%, almost doubling. A similar pattern exists in the middle-middle stratum. However, when one examines the upper-middle stratum the difference in upward social movement in relation to the previous stratum is seen to be smaller; that is, it goes from close to 36% to 21%, with a reduction of only 15%. But this area of the social pyramid, as we know, is quite hermetic. The only possible upward social movement is to go to the upper class, and close to 21% did just this. There are indications, though, that the upward movement was relatively easier in this particular area of the social structure. That is, the number of jobs created at the upper level (and the access to property), although small in absolute terms,

13. At this point we are not yet considering the distance covered in terms of mean values for different strata. This will be presented in Chapter 8.

TABLE 6.7. Differences in Upward Social Movement by Age Group (%)

Strata Considered	Total	(51–64)	(41–50)	(31–40)	(20–30)
			Age Groups		
Upper-middle/ Middle-middle	14.5	13.1	17.2	15.3	11.5
Middle-middle/ Lower-middle	27.6	20.6	26.6	30.3	29.9*
Lower-middle/ Upper-lower	24.0	16.5	22.6	22.8	29.7
Upper-lower/ Lower-lower	12.5	26.1	12.1	9.6	10.2**

*The difference between this type of movement and the one below it (29.7%) was not significant at the level of 5%.
**The difference between the values 9.6 and 10.2 was not significant.

was substantial enough to advance a relatively large portion of the heads of family. Included in this category are numerous occupations of the university level (lawyers, engineers, doctors, dentists, economists, architects) which supplied mobility via education, as well as occupations which supplied mobility through capital, as in the case of industrialists, ranchers, and other property owners.

To what extent is this tendency changing with the passage of time? In other words, how do the young differ from the oldest people in terms of social "conquests" between generations? To answer this question it will be necessary to look at all of these phenomena by age group. Table 6.7 shows the differences in upward social movement (in relation to the previous stratum) by age group. We will examine some instances.

We have already seen that moving from the lower-lower stratum to the upper-lower stratum indicates, in a rough way, a departure from rural poverty and an entrance into urban poverty. The conventional hypothesis argues that tertiarization and the creation of jobs of low qualification typical of the informal urban sector have been speeded up in Brazil in recent years, and, consequently, that it would be reasonable to expect an increase in movement from the lower-lower stratum to the upper-lower for the youngest populations who have entered into the market most recently. The data, however, demonstrate the contrary. The proportion of people 51–64 years old who left rural poverty and entered urban poverty was close to 26%; among those 20–30 years old, it was close to 10%, and among those 31–40 years old, less than 10%.[14] This suggests that

14. This should not induce the reader to conclude that structural mobility disappears in developed societies. Various studies show that it merely loses its relative importance. See Hauser, 1975; Duncan, 1966; Rothman, 1978.

the youngest had passed over urban poverty and were succeeding in placing themselves in numerous middle class positions. Indeed, movement to the upper rungs on the ladder follows this pattern. Entrance into the different middle class strata has been more frequent among the youngest than among the oldest. The phenomenon begins to stabilize itself when the upper-middle stratum is reached. Entrance into that stratum is equally small for all the age groups, being a little higher for those 41–50 years old.

At any rate, the data allow us to conclude that upward mobility is easier today than it was yesterday. Consequently, the growth of the middle class is a relatively recent phenomenon, the product of changes in the labor market, of the creation of urban employment, and of greater occupational differentiation, all mentioned in Chapter 4. All this permits us to affirm that industrialization, urbanization, and rural-urban migration join together to increase occupational differentiation and mobility. We are dealing with a mobility induced by economic transformations, especially by those which spring from a decrease in rural employment. However, the youngest heads of family were taking advantage of a labor market much more diversified than that which their fathers faced several decades before. The data appear to leave no doubts that the mobility that took place between fathers and sons is the main phenomenon responsible for the formation of a middle class. Clearly, this class still is far from being the middle class of the advanced nations, where it is composed of occupations of a high level of qualification, but it unquestionably brings together occupations practically nonexistent 40 to 50 years ago.

Types of Mobility

The data shown so far allow us to say that intergenerational mobility for heads of family in Brazil has been intense, concentrated mostly in the structural base, associated basically with transformations in the labor market, and, therefore, related to migration and to the increase in job opportunities in urban zones. We saw also that, among mobile individuals, the proportion of those who ascended is four times greater than that of those who descended. And the fact stands out that upward social movement was more frequent in the intermediate age groups than it was in the age groups of either extreme.

We have seen that mobility may have various origins. This section is devoted specifically to an examination of the various types of intergenerational mobility and their origins. More precisely, we will identify and contrast total mobility, upward mobility, downward mobility, immobility, upward and downward proportions, structural mobility, circular mobility, and the Yassuda mobility index. Measurements of these different types of mobility were presented in Chapter 3.

TABLE 6.8. Types of Social Mobility by Age Group (%)

Types of Mobility	Age Groups				
	Total	(51–64)	(41–50)	(31–40)	(20–30)
1. Total mobility	58.5	52.4	58.8	61.0	59.3
2. Structural mobility	32.9	29.3	34.0	35.1	31.0
3. Circulation mobility	25.6	23.1	24.8	25.9	28.3
4. Upward mobility	47.1	41.7	48.0	50.1	46.4
5. Immobility	41.6	47.5	41.2	39.0	40.7
6. Downward mobility	11.3	10.8	10.8	10.9	12.9
7. % of Upwardly mobile	80.6	79.4	81.7	82.1	78.2
8. % of Downwardly mobile	19.4	20.6	18.3	17.9	21.8
9. Mobility without exchange	76.0	74.1	77.6	78.2	72.0
10. Mobility with exchange	24.0	25.9	22.4	21.8	28.0
Mobility index (Y)	63.6	63.5	63.6	64.1	64.6

Table 6.8 summarizes the results for intergenerational mobility. Total mobility refers to the proportion of individuals who, in 1973, were already in positions different from those of their fathers, without taking into account whether this movement was upward or downward. As we have seen, total mobility is an indicator of the degree of fluidity in the social structure. A stagnant society based exclusively upon attributed criteria tends to keep sons in the same positions as fathers. In a dynamic society, however, inheritance has less weight and the sons tend to move away from the fathers' positions.

The data in Table 6.8 show that, in the Brazilian social structure reflected by the status of the heads of family, nearly 59% of the individuals move away from their fathers. This was most emphatic in the 31–40 age group—that is, among individuals who began to work in the decade of the fifties, a period which saw the beginning of a strong expansion in industrial jobs, as well as in opportunities in the areas of commerce and service indirectly linked to industrialization. The smallest measurement of total mobility was observed among individuals 51–64 years old who began their careers in the decades of the twenties and thirties. For them, as the data of Chapter 4 show, opportunities for employment and for new occupations were severely limited. The great majority of Brazilians who started to work in that epoch depended upon rural employment and upon a limited, homogenous occupational structure. In brief, mobility increases as age decreases, excepting the youngest group (20–30 years old). Thus we can say that social dynamism in Brazil has been greater in the recent past than in the remote past.

Analyzing the first set of mobilities in the table, we see that most total mobility derives systematically from structural mobility—that is, from labor market transformations that have taken place between the times of fathers and of sons, and, in particular, from the shrinkage of the agricultural market and the creation of new jobs in the urban zone. As we have seen, this is the expected pattern for the beginning stages of development. Mobility changes from structural to circulation only when society has already attained a reasonable level of development and job-creation, so that the opening up of the social structure comes to depend upon rearrangements of people within the same structure. For this reason, sociologists are always alert to identify differences in participation in each of the types of mobility, in relation to the total mobility.

The data in Table 6.8 suggest that the role of structural mobility in the composition of total mobility varies from age to age. To examine these fluctuations more directly, we have put together Table 6.9, which reflects the types of mobility on a percentage basis. For example, a value of 29.3 found for structural mobility among people 51–64 years old represents about 56% of total mobility. For the 41–50 and the 31–40 year age groups, the proportion of structural mobility was even higher, and indicative that changes of status depended fundamentally upon new jobs. Again, the greatest descent observed occurred in the youngest group (20–30 years old). For this group, structural and circulation mobility were almost equal. This means that in the remote past the impact of new jobs was more important for generating mobility; however, in the recent past, mobility stemming from the composition and rearrangement of individuals within the social structure has gained importance.

The second group of mobility types in Table 6.8 (four, five, and six) incorporates data that refer to direction. The proportion of upward mobility in every age group is always higher than that of downward mobility and of immobility (with only one exception). Again, the people who progressed furthest in relation to their fathers were those 31–40 years old who entered the labor market during the decade of the fifties and who established their positions during the early sixties. This group also shows the smallest proportion of immobility. In a society which is rapidly becoming urbanized and which dislocates large masses of workers from the country to the city, one expects a much higher

TABLE 6.9. Percentages of Structural and Circulation Mobility (%)

Type of Mobility	Total	(51–64)	(41–50)	(31–40)	(20–30)
Total	100.0	100.0	100.0	100.0	100.0
Structural	56.2	56.0	57.8	57.5	52.3
Circulation	43.8	44.0	42.2	42.5	47.7

proportion of upward mobility than of downward, as the data show. As we have said, the status scale used contains an urban tendency, so that in the lowest levels the only possibility for descent would be a return to the country.

The same pattern can be observed in mobility types seven and eight. They indicate the proportions of mobile people who rose and who descended. For the entire sample we discover that for every 100 individuals who, in social terms, separated themselves from their fathers, 80 bettered their positions and 18 fell on the social scale. Even though we know that the greater part of this mobility was structural and of short distances, it is undeniable that the proportions observed indicate a very favorable performance by Brazilian society during the period. Finally, if the urban sector had not expanded, the overwhelming majority of the Brazilian population would be in low status positions in the rural zone (laborers, fishermen, rubber workers, etc.).

Mobilities nine and ten, measured by Hutchinson's formula, indicate in a primitive way that for every 100 people who achieved social mobility, close to 76 headed for spots that opened up either through new jobs or through retirement and other departures from the work force; 24 people owed their mobility to rearrangements within the existing opportunity structure.

Now a brief commentary on the mobility index (Y). As seen in Chapter 3, this measurement constitutes a coefficient of the opening up of the social structure. It assumes a value of 1.0 in the case of perfect mobility and 0 in the absence of circulation mobility. Y is a measurement of net mobility, that is, a measurement which relates structural mobility with circulation mobility. In the case of Table 6.8, we multiply the values of Y by 100 in order to standardize them in terms of the other measures of mobility. We found a value of 63.6% for the total sample. This is very far from 0—that is, from a situation in which circulation mobility is absent. In fact, the intergenerational mobility situation in Brazil tends more toward a case of perfect mobility than it does toward immobility.[15]

When we analyze the behavior of Y by age group, we discover that the values encountered are very close to each other, rising slightly for the younger groups as a consequence of the increase in circulation mobility.

The measurements and commentary presented so far leave no doubts as to the occurrence of a high volume of intergenerational mobility in Brazil. We have seen also that a large part of this mobility was structural and that it stemmed from transformations in the labor market. That is, many new occupations were created between the times of fathers and sons, so that for the sons to go up, there was no need for others to go down. However, this phenomenon

15. For a look at the problems and concerns involved in comparative studies, see Kerckhoff, 1978.

TABLE 6.10. Mobility by Exchange and Without Exchange

Social Stratum	Descending Individuals	Immobile Individuals	Ascending Individuals	Total
Upper	635	270	—	905
Upper-middle	775	399	211	1,385
Middle-middle	2,508	2,221	1,404	6,133
Lower-middle	808	1,904	1,406	4,118
Upper-lower	293	732	2,053	3,078
Lower-lower	—	12,873	15,815	28,688
Total	5,019	18,399	20,889	44,307

varied throughout the social structure. It was localized more in the base and was practically absent at the top of the social pyramid.

High proportions of structural mobility are more frequent in developing societies than in stabilized societies. In the latter, much upward mobility depends upon the descent of employed persons, or upon retirement, death, or other departures from the work force. In this type of society, the structures are more stable and more closed. In Brazil one observes a great flexibility in the base and a relative rigidity at the top of the pyramid. In this area, the greater part of mobility is circulation mobility.

But in exactly what level of the pyramid is structural mobility replaced by circulation mobility? Table 6.10 presents the absolute numbers of the sample studied, and shows that the "turning point" of the phenomenon is located in the middle-middle stratum. Up to that level, most mobility stems from occupation of new jobs. From there on, the number of those who descended exceeds that of those who rose, indicating that the upward movement occurred only through exchange or the separation of a certain number of individuals from the work force. It is important to remember, however, that for the sons there was an opening up of opportunities in all the levels, although this was more apparent in the lower levels.

International Comparisons

It is always tempting to contrast the total Brazilian mobility with that which occurs in other societies. Comparisons of this type are still precarious. The significance of occupations differs from society to society; the methods for measuring the status hierarchy often varies; the measuring does not always refer to the same periods or to similar stages of development, etc.[16] In short, the difficulties of precise comparisons between societies are enormous. Even

16. Admittedly, the social structures and the points of departure in these societies are very different. For a complementary look at the problem, see Lagos, 1963.

so, sociologists are striving to surmount or bypass these problems to make possible comparisons which have a minimum of reliability.

Miller, in 1960, achieved a comparison of this type among 18 societies after having bypassed the greater part of the problems mentioned. After almost 20 years, another comparative study came out which involved ten societies (Klein-ing, 1978). The latter also used a status scale of six points (similar to that of the present study) and analyzed age groups comparable to those of the present study. The ten countries were studied between 1973 and 1975. All of the data, however, was not based upon national samples.

Table 6.11 presents the data for total mobility in the ten countries considered. In the case of Brazil, because we possess a national sample, the corresponding information is inserted, and the original results, which refer to São Paulo, are included below the data for Brazil. With the proper caution, we have examined the data.

The fact which stands out in this table is that Brazil shows rates of mobility above the mean in most cases. For example, when we analyze the 31–40 and the 41–50 year age groups, Brazil stands above all the other countries.[17] In fact, the only country with intergenerational mobility higher than that of Brazil is the United States. For the youngest group (20–30 years), three countries are more dynamic than Brazil: the United States, England, and Yugoslavia. The others show a dynamism equal to (Switzerland) or lower than that of Brazil. For the oldest group (51–64 years), three countries are more dynamic than Brazil: the United States, England, and Indonesia (Jakarta).

How great has been the gain in mobility in the various age groups? With the exception of Yugoslavia, whose difference in mobility rates between the oldest group (51–60 years) and the youngest (20–30 years) was very high (28%), all the other countries show differences of less than 10%. Indonesia, Argentina, West Germany, and Switzerland remained well below this value. The United States is at the mean, with a 5% difference. Brazil and Italy are a little above the mean with 7%. Austria and England are found well above the mean, with a 9% difference between the two groups. Thus, Brazil tends more toward the countries which progressed a great deal in terms of mobility (Austria, England, Italy, and the United States) than toward those who progressed slightly (In-donesia, Argentina, West Germany, and Switzerland).[18]

It is interesting to note that in almost all the countries, the total mobility rate decreases in the younger age groups and increases in the older age groups, with the exception of Indonesia (Jakarta). This shows that, in a general way, mobility is greater today than it was yesterday, although it is true that several

17. We must remember that the same level of total mobility in various countries may be reached through quite diverse mechanisms, some tending more toward structural mobility, others toward circulation. See Kerckhoff, 1974.

18. The analysis in Chapter 10 is done with the help of statistical regressions.

TABLE 6.11. Total Intergenerational Mobility in Ten Countries (%)

Countries	Age Group					
	(71–80)	(61–70)	(51–60)	(41–50)	(31–40)	(20–30)
United States (1975)	54	58	60	64	62	65
Great Britain (1975)	46	52	54	59	59	63
Switzerland (1973)	40	48	—	55	—	59
Austria (1975)	45	43	47	52	54	56
West Germany (1974)	41	44	49	53	54	52
Italy (1974)	39	45	49	53	54	56
Yugoslavia (1972)	25	35	41	58	54	69
Argentina (1972)	36	40	46	48	50	48
Indonesia (Jakarta 1974)	—	—	56	46	53	51
Brazil (1973)	—	—	52	59	61	59
São Paulo (1974)	43	51	55	69	67	70

Note: The age groups are approximate. Numbers between parentheses following the names of countries indicate the years studied. Brazil is represented in this table by the national sample of heads of families, men 20–64 years old, described in Chapter 3.

countries are reaching a stabilized plateau. In the case of São Paulo, the tendency is the same. Mobility has increased substantially for the youngest groups. Brazil as a whole is also moving in this direction, recording the reverse only for the 20–30 year age group which represents individuals who are still establishing themselves in the market, and many of whom are still in school. In Brazil the phenomenon follows the pattern only beginning with the 31–40 year age group.

Indices of Association

How does origin influence the social destiny of Brazilian families in general? The influence of origin can be identified in various ways.[19] One of the simplest and most direct is to look at the proportion of people in a certain level of the status scale in relation to the proportion of the work force located at that level. The last row in Table 6.1, at the beginning of this chapter, shows the distribution of the total work force in the various strata. This distribution has been used as a standard against which all the percentages in the main part of the table are compared. Dividing the percentage of each instance by the corresponding total percentage gives an index of the influence of origin upon social destiny (Blau and Duncan, 1967:35). The relation obtained (index of association) measures the extent to which mobility from one level to another was due to chance or to other factors. A value of 1.0 indicates that the observed mobility is equal to expected mobility, presupposing statistical neutrality. Values higher than 1.0

TABLE 6.12. Influence of Origin upon Social Destination

	Individual's Status in 1973					
Father's Status	1	2	3	4	5	6
Upper	*8.5*	*2.6*	*1.5*	0.5	0.3	0.1
Upper-middle	*4.3*	*4.6*	*1.6*	0.6	0.4	0.2
Middle-middle	*2.4*	*2.3*	*2.0*	0.8	0.6	0.3
Lower-middle	*1.1*	*1.4*	*1.2*	*1.9*	0.9	0.1
Upper-lower	0.9	*1.2*	*1.1*	*1.5*	*1.5*	0.3
Lower-lower	0.3	0.4	0.7	0.9	*1.1*	*1.4*

indicate the great importance of origin, while values less than 1.0 indicate the opposite.

Table 6.12 presents the results of this procedure applied to Table 6.1. To facilitate the analysis, we have italicized those values greater than 1.0, which indicate a heavy involvement of social inheritance in present status. As we see, the weight of social origin begins to predominate markedly at the middle-middle stratum, repeating here the phenomenon already observed for circulation mobility.

From this perspective, we discover that of the 36 cells in the matrix, 19 are italicized. The highest values are found in the principal diagonal, especially at the top of the pyramid. Even so, values far from 1.0 are relatively rare. If we use 2.0 as a cut-off point, we see that only six cells are greater than 2.0, all of them, of course, at the top of the pyramid.

It is also important to note certain peculiarities of mobility. For example, the value of origin for individuals who reach the upper stratum falls drastically from stratum to stratum. In the upper level, the value reaches 8.5; in the upper-middle, it has fallen to 4.3; in the middle-middle, to 2.4. The value in the lower-middle stratum is nearly neutral, and below that, it is totally dissociated. This phenomenon is due to the relatively large influx of individuals of other origins into the upper stratum, a fact which will be analyzed in detail in Chapter 8.

The weight of heritage is greater at the top of the pyramid. If heritage were a dominant factor in social determination at all levels, then those above the level of manual labor would all be concentrated in the six cells of the principal diagonal and the values of the other cells would be well below the expected frequency. This does not occur. Values exceed 1.0 in 19 cells. Besides this, high values are observed only in the two highest cells on the principal diagonal (8.5 and 4.6). From there, besides the mentioned influence of heritage, the values fall steadily. In sum, there is a great deal of intergenerational mobility in the matrix as a whole, and it seems to depend little upon social inheritance.

Conclusion

In conclusion, the picture of intergenerational mobility in Brazil shows a prevalence of upward social movement throughout the entire structure, and, principally at the base of the pyramid, the predominance of structural mobility with a relatively small influence of paternal social inheritance. Many of these changes are due to the accelerated industrialization and urbanization through which Brazil has passed in the last 40 years. These changes have not dislocated the high status groups for the benefit of a society of fully open classes. Neither have they permitted the other extreme, that is, they have not maintained the old forms of stratification and social control: the new groups have not needed to dislocate the old in order to occupy higher positions. On the contrary, the new middle class formed quickly through the increase in the number of jobs and through occupational differentiation in the urban zone.[19] We are seeing an opening up through expansion and not through a better utilization of existing positions.

Has the structural type of social mobility exhausted itself in Brazil? No. Brazil has a long way to go in decreasing the proportion of low status individuals in the rural zone, who today constitute almost one third of the heads of family. Modern agriculture produces much more with fewer people in the fields. The increase in productivity per man and per land area is marked by extreme urgency in Brazil. The fact that we have a very large lower-lower stratum constitutes a reasonably secure forecast that much upward social movement can still be achieved in Brazil through structural paths. This does not mean that structural mobility in the future will be equally as easy as that of the past. The cities are beginning to show signs of saturation and of competition for employment and upward movement. From here on, the role of circulation mobility should grow in importance, especially in the middle levels. Experience, on-the-job training, urban life, increase in contacts, schooling, and aspirations should act as powerful factors in circulation mobility in the coming decades.

19. Cardoso argues that this pattern is valid for all Latin American societies which have industrialized. See Cardoso, 1969:134–35.

7
Intragenerational Mobility in Brazil

We saw in Chapter 5 that Brazilians enter the labor market at an early age and in low social positions. We saw also that social origin has a limiting effect upon entry and upon the distance that people travel in the social structure. The lower the origin, the earlier is the entry and the shorter is the distance covered. We discovered also that this pattern stood out more in the past than it does in the present. There are signs that people are making up for their initial disadvantages. It seems relevant to find out under what conditions and over what period of time this "recuperation" occurs. We are also interested in knowing the characteristics of those who achieve upward mobility vis-à-vis those who do not. Finally, it is necessary to know to what extent these factors are changing through time. All these questions fall into the field of intragenerational mobility, or career mobility.

The theoretical model for explaining intragenerational mobility assumes that people enter into certain occupations and job ranks and remain in them for some time. Once these positions are attained, people try to move to others every time opportunities arise for economic or social advancement. The mobility here may be structural or circulation. The approach of this study of intragenerational mobility will be the same as that of Chapter 6—that is, the individual's occupational status in his first job will be compared to his occupational status in 1973. As in Chapter 6, the analysis will be based upon matrices of status changes and, therefore, it will be descriptive in character.[1]

1. Recently, various proposals for the use of status change matrices have been based upon modifications of the Markov chains. This study is beginning with simpler and more descriptive

103

General Tendencies of Intragenerational Mobility

Table 7.1 presents data for occupational statuses in the first jobs and in the current ones (that is, the status of individuals in 1973).[2] The percentages of the diagonal remain relatively high, but here again one observes a large amount of social mobility.

TABLE 7.1. Occupational Matrix of Intragenerational Mobility

Beginning Status	Individual's Status in 1973							Total Beginning Status
	1	2	3	4	5	6	Total	
1. Upper	72.8	14.2	9.6	1.2	1.9	0.3	100.0	0.6
2. Upper-middle	24.9	47.3	19.4	6.3	1.3	0.8	100.0	0.7
3. Middle-middle	16.7	24.8	45.0	8.8	3.9	0.8	100.0	6.9
4. Lower-middle	2.8	7.3	17.1	59.5	10.3	3.0	100.0	7.3
5. Upper-lower	4.0	9.0	24.6	34.0	22.1	6.3	100.0	25.2
6. Lower-lower	0.7	2.6	13.4	18.7	17.0	47.6	100.0	59.2
Total Status in 1973 N = 53,764	3.4	6.5	18.7	24.7	16.7	30.0	100.0	100.0

Generally, the status change matrix indicates that about 42% of the individuals remained immobile and 58% were in positions different from those at the start of their careers. In other words, the total mobility was practically identical to the total mobility observed in the comparison of generations (58%). The comparisons between intra- and intergenerational mobility will be detailed in the following section. Here, we will show the general characteristics of career mobility among heads of families in Brazil.

Intragenerational mobility also depends upon time. Normally, the time involved in intragenerational mobility is less than the time involved in intergenerational mobility. However, that study is based upon a survey which asked

procedures since it is the first to be carried out in Brazil based upon a national sample. The reader interested in this methodological alternative may consult Sorensen, 1975.

2. The respondents told the IBGE Foundation interviewers what they did in their very first jobs. The occupations mentioned were annotated and codified in detail. In the case of more than one occupation, only the one which the respondent judged more important was noted. For details of the collecting of these data see Fundação IBGE, *Instruções da folha de registro de domicílios* and *PNAD-1 Mão-de-Obra*, Rio de Janeiro, 1973.

for the father's occupation *at the time at which* the respondent began to work. Therefore, the father's status and the son's initial status refer to the same time.[3] For example, a person who was 25 years old in 1973 and who began to work at 15 entered the labor market in 1963. His initial status is referring to 1963; the status of his father also is referring to 1963. This being the case, the intra- as well as the intergenerational mobility covers a period of ten years, from 1963 to 1973. Nevertheless, two basic differences must be brought out here. One is that, for the majority of fathers, their status and their own careers were already more or less established in 1963, while the sons' professional trajectory was only beginning; and the sons were not really professionals, but rather children helping their fathers in whatever ways they could. The other difference is that the majority of the sons were very young. In 1973, the sons still had a long road to travel, a path to be traveled in an occupational structure quite distinct from the one experienced by their fathers. It was a path, therefore, with different probabilities for upward mobility.

Putting the question in another way, the ten years which separated the individual's initial status from his status in 1973 have different meanings according to whether one considers the father's or the individual's status as the point of departure. In the first case, we compare the current status with the status established by someone who has already passed through the phases of an informal market, sporadic work, etc. All those phases were excluded from the father's career simply because we have no pertinent data. In the second case, we compare the current status with a contingent status just being formed and generally linked to the temporary work of children, as we saw in Chapter 5. This initial employment is far from characteristic of an individual's autonomous position in society. In most cases, we are dealing with activities that were supplementary and sporadically carried out as part of the family's work, generally in the rural zone. Technically, and for the purposes of analyzing intragenerational mobility, we should consider only the individuals who began to work at age 20 or older—that is, in circumstances offering a high probability of autonomy.[4] This type of inquiry will be carried out in Section 3 of this chapter.

Intragenerational mobility depends also upon the point of departure. The lower the beginning, the greater the potential space to be covered in the social

3. Fixing the precise time of the career beginning has been an important procedure for comparisons of mobility among different social groups. Modern studies have asked for the first occupation in a certain age group or even in those of a specific age. PNAD/73, unfortunately, did not adopt this procedure, and this has created additional difficulties for positioning the cited occupations.

4. Most studies of intragenerational social mobility in advanced countries exclude part-time, occasional jobs (which are often held by students) from what is considered the first job. This is the position of Ornstein, 1976; Blau and Duncan, 1967; and various others.

TABLE 7.2. Evolution of Social Structures (%)

Social Strata	Situation of Fathers	Situation of Sons	
		First Job	in 1973
Upper	2.0	0.6	3.4
Upper-middle	3.1	0.7	6.5
Middle-middle	13.8	6.9	18.7
Lower-middle	9.3	7.3	24.7
Upper-lower	6.9	25.2	16.7
Lower-lower	64.9	59.8	30.0
Total	100.0	100.0	100.0
N =	44,307	53,764	53,764

structure. If individuals enter into low status occupations at lower levels than those of their own fathers, then clearly the sons will have a greater probability of upward social movement than do those who have entered at the top of the pyramid.[5] Again, the picture differs according to whether we consider the fathers or the sons as the point of departure.

Therefore, before continuing the analysis, we must look at the beginning social conditions of the sons vis-à-vis those of their respective fathers. Table 7.2 reproduces previously discussed data which refer to differences in the social structure between fathers and sons in their first jobs. Due to early entry into the labor market, the sons tend to begin in occupations with a lower status than those of their fathers. After all, the father is an adult and, in most cases, at the peak of his career. The son is a child just beginning in the labor market.[6]

In Brazil, the fact that in many cases the sons' points of departure are lower than that of their fathers is explained by the high number of children who enter the informal sector of the labor market in occupations of low qualification and remuneration. While the individuals have little time to achieve career mobility, they do, however, have ample social space in which to move. This is an important point for an adequate understanding of the significance of the accentuated intragenerational mobility discussed below. Comparisons between the two types of mobility should take into account that we are dealing with two quite different initial social structures; we see this clearly in Table 7.2.

The impact of the equalization in the social structure of the heads of family in 1973 is largely a reflection of the lowering of status seen at the entry into the labor market. Taking the two lower strata together, we discover that among

5. In the same way, when one enters into a high-status job at a level higher than the parent's position, the probability of downward mobility is high.

6. This phenomenon of the relative lowering of the father's status is found in numerous societies, including advanced ones. See Featherman and Hauser, 1978; Pasqualini, 1973; Miller, 1960.

the fathers the lower class amounted to about 72% of the total; among the sons, at the beginnings of their careers, the lower class amounts to 85% of the total. Thus, the initial stage was lower for about 13% of the sons. If the upward intragenerational mobility were only 13% above the intergenerational, then we would conclude roughly that no significant change took place although the two periods being considered had quite different characteristics. As we will see below, the percentage of mobile individuals who ascended, in the case of intragenerational mobility, was about 93% (Table 7.8); for intergenerational mobility, it was 81% (Table 6.8). The 12% difference is due largely to the lowering of that first social step.[7]

Such commentary should not lead the reader to conclude that intragenerational mobility in Brazil is insignificant. As we will see, career mobility among heads of family has been considerable, coming very close to intergenerational mobility. Furthermore, there are numerous internal variations in the career mobility matrix which deserve special attention.

Mobility in the Different Social Strata

The data in Table 7.1 tell us that most upward mobility occurred in the base of the pyramid. In 1973, most people in the two lower strata were in positions higher than those of the beginnings of their careers. About 52% of those who began in rural occupations of the lower-lower stratum were in better positions; a good part of them had advanced into the middle class (almost 40%). Of those who began in low-status, urban zone occupations (upper-lower stratum), about 72% had achieved upward mobility. And these people moved to middle class occupations in even greater numbers than did their rural counterparts.

The upward intragenerational mobility in the two lowest strata was about 53% and 72%, respectively; the percentages of those who were in the middle class were about 35% and 68%, respectively. The argument that this mobility is due to the low beginning career level does not explain the high percentages of people who passed from the lower class to the middle. A comparison of Tables 7.1 and 6.1 suggests that people are more eager to leave their own beginning positions than to leave their fathers' positions. In other words, a good career beginning is better than a good inheritance for individuals in the lowest strata.[8]

---

7. The lowering of the first step is a well-known phenomenon, the product of a combination of family background, age, and schooling. See Muller, 1973.

8. Theories of labor market segmentation argue that the good beginning depends upon taking advantage of jobs in the primary market, and not in the secondary. This is a fruitful alternative explanation which is already giving satisfactory results. See, for example, Gordon, 1972; Leigh, 1976; Hodson, 1977; Piore, 1975.

Intragenerational mobility was also the product of structural transformations in the labor market. Table 7.1 shows that the percentage of rural workers among the total number who entered the work force was 59%; among their fathers, as the reader will remember, that percentage was almost 65% (Table 6.1). On the other hand, this percentage for low-status urban workers (upper-lower stratum) rose to 25% of those entering the work force, while among their fathers it was less than 7%. These differences indicate rapid structural changes having occurred in the labor market, all of them accompanied by a growing occupational differentiation between fathers and sons. As we have seen, the father's status and the initial status of the son were measured for practically the same time periods. Many of the sons' initial statuses derive from childhood rural jobs. Even so, there were more fathers than sons in the rural zone.

What happened to people who began to work in middle class occupations? Clearly, the beginning stage was higher for them, and the space for upward movement was reduced. On the other hand, the jobs in their area were not created in the same proportion as were lower status jobs (Chapter 4). Thus, one expects less upward social movement here than in the strata discussed above. In fact, the values of the diagonals in the three middle strata rise significantly in relation to the previous ones, which indicates a higher degree of immobility (Table 7.1). For example, about 60% of the individuals who began in lower-middle status jobs remained, in 1973, in the same initial position. These include electricians, masons, plumbers, carpenters, rugmakers, drivers, barbers, elevator operators, etc. Note further that about 13% of these people descended on the social scale; this problem could be associated with age and will be examined below. Even so, about 27% rose on the social scale, going on to jobs of higher qualification, prestige, and income.

Of those who started out in the middle-middle stratum (draftsmen, musicians, broadcasters, purchasers, office workers, foremen, small landowners), a relatively small percentage remained in the same position (45%). In spite of the smaller space open to these individuals, the percentage of those who rose on the social scale was greater than for the lower-middle stratum—almost 42%. The volume of downward mobility, although there was more room to descend, was small—almost equal to that of the lower-middle stratum (13.5%). Thus, it seems that to begin a career in middle-middle stratum professions is a good start and a reliable guarantee of upward mobility.[9]

What is the overall behavior of the entire intragenerational mobility matrix, and how does it compare with that of intergenerational mobility? Table 7.3 shows that upward mobility was greater in the first case. As we saw, close to 54% of the individuals were in positions better than those of their fathers; in

---

9. We have not commented upon the other two social strata because they include very low percentages of individuals who started out in them.

TABLE 7.3. General Patterns of Inter- and Intragenerational Mobility (%)

Type of Mobility	Intragenerational	Intergenerational
Upward	54.2	47.1
Immobility	41.9	41.6
Downward	3.9	11.3
Total	100.0	100.0

terms of career, close to 47% in 1973 enjoyed higher statuses than those with which they had started. The percentage of immobile people was practically the same in both cases; the percentage of the descendants was smaller for intragenerational mobility, due at least in part to the low starting point.

There are two ways to interpret these data. When one considers that the traveling space was greater for intragenerational mobility (a function of the low starting level), the data suggest that 7% or more of the upward movement loses most of its social significance. When one takes into account, however, the period of time the individual worked in the labor market as a child, "marking time," the upward movement increases in importance. If we consider the period after this wait as a point of departure, we will conclude that these people achieved more in less time, all this suggesting the occurrence of a rapid and recent transformation in the Brazilian occupational structure. In other words, new jobs and new occupations emerged more quickly during the sons' careers than they did during the fathers'. Besides this, the sons seem to have been able to take better advantage of the new opportunities, achieving their upward movement in less time. This aspect will be developed in more detail later in this chapter.

Looking at the percentages of upwardly- and downwardly-mobile people in the two types of mobility (Table 7.4), and considering that the precise job situation occurred well after the beginning of the job declared by the respondent, one verifies that the sons seem to have progressed more in less time than their fathers. That is, the progress in one's own career was greater than the initial leap away from the fathers. The increase of 13% in upward intragenerational mobility (already discussed) was due in large part to the very low initial stage of people who entered the labor market as children.[10]

10. Nevertheless, this increase occurred in a period of time when there was one phase of delay and another of an actual career. Remembering the large number of individuals who began to work in more definite careers at the age of about 20 years, it is apparent that many of them at that time had already spent eight to ten years working as children—that is, as aggregate members of the family structure.

TABLE 7.4. Types of Mobility for Mobile Individuals (%)

Types of Mobility	Intragenerational	Intergenerational
Upward	93.4	80.6
Downward	6.6	19.4
Total	100.0	100.0

TABLE 7.5. Intragenerational Mobility by Social Strata (%)

| Types of Mobility | Social Strata | | | | | | |
	Upper	Upper-middle	Middle-middle	Lower-middle	Upper-lower	Lower-lower	Total
Upward	—	24.9	41.5	27.2	71.6	52.6	54.2
Immobility	72.7	47.2	45.0	59.5	22.0	47.4	41.9
Downward	27.3	27.9	13.5	13.3	6.4	—	3.9
Total	100.0	100.0	100.0	100.0	100.0	100.0	100.0

What happened in each of the social strata in terms of upward and downward mobility? As we saw, people of different social strata have different probabilities of rising or falling on the social scale. Low strata individuals have ample space for upward movement. For them, rising depends basically upon the opening of new spots in higher levels and also upon their personal qualifications, experience, and contacts. Upper strata individuals have little space for upward movement and much for downward movement. Rising depends a great deal upon exchanges of positions, departure of other individuals from the work force, or (again) upon the creation of new positions of high status. Downward movement can stem from a disappearance of positions, from exchanges, from professional obsolescence, or from a loss of power.

But upward movement does not depend solely upon available space; it depends also upon the rigidity of the structure in the upper levels; or, to use an earlier image, it depends upon the steepness of the mountain. Thus, space for progress does not necessarily mean effective conditions for progress.[11]

What has been the behavior of each stratum in terms of rising or falling on the social scale? Table 7.5 shows the relevant data.

This table has numerous peculiarities that make it different from Table 6.5, which related to intergenerational mobility. One of these, already discussed,

11. The situation for downward movement is more or less the same. If the structure suddenly loses many spots, the fall is rapid and far. If the reduction is slow, the fall depends a great deal upon individual resources (education, contacts, dependence, etc.).

has to do with the relatively low level of downward mobility in all the strata, and, in particular, in the upper, upper-middle, and middle-middle strata. Everything indicates that people who begin in the middle-middle strata or higher tend to remain in it or to rise even more. Thus the high proportions of immobile people in these strata. A good career beginning seems to be a reliable guarantee of not descending. The same did not occur for intergenerational mobility. Many people who originated in high-status families suffered substantial descents (Table 6.5).

There is 7% more upward mobility in the case of intragenerational mobility than in intergenerational (Table 7.3). In certain strata, however, the difference is even greater. For example, in the upper middle, intragenerational upward mobility is about 25% (Table 7.5), against about 15% for intergenerational upward mobility (Table 6.5). The approximate figures for the middle-middle are 42% and 23%. This suggests that a person's entrance into an occupation of these statuses is a better guarantee of upward mobility than a social origin in these same strata. In Brazil, starting a career in middle class occupations is an excellent beginning, better even than being a middle class son. In other words, initial individual status seems to have a slightly greater impact upon a person's career than does the father's status.[12] This is in keeping with prevailing sociological theory, according to which the variables from the recent past have more influence in determining status than those of the remote past (Kelley, 1973).

What is the effect of time upon upward mobility? Do older individuals rise further than the young? In the case of intergenerational mobility, individuals of the intermediate age groups rise further than do those of the extremes (Table 6.6). For intragenerational mobility, the pattern is more or less the same for the middle-middle and lower-middle strata, but it changes for the others. Mobility in the upper-middle, for example, is higher at the extremes and lower in the intermediate age groups, meaning that the oldest individuals reach high status through their experiences, contacts, and relations; all this suggests a relative scarcity of open positions for their group. On the other hand, we observe that more than 50% of young people (20–30) years) who began their career in the upper-middle stratum had already entered the upper class in 1973 in spite of their youth; this suggests a greater availability of high status spots.

One observes in the lower-middle stratum also more upward mobility among the youngest and less among the oldest. Among mobile people of 20–30 years, about 93% of those who began to work in low status, urban zone occupations eventually rose in the social scale. This fact in itself indicates that people took full advantage of the new occupational opportunities that arose in the great

---

12. The net effect of this variable, though, continues to be relatively small. See specific details in Chapter 10.

TABLE 7.6. Upward Mobility of Mobile Individuals by Age Groups (%)

Social Strata	Age Groups				
	Total	(51–64)	(41–50)	(31–40)	(20–30)
Upper	—	—	—	—	—
Upper-middle	47.2	60.0	47.2	33.9	54.2
Middle-middle	75.5	74.5	81.0	76.0	69.0
Lower-middle	67.2	67.7	70.2	70.0	60.2
Upper-lower	91.8	85.9	91.1	93.6	93.4
Lower-lower	100.0	100.0	100.0	100.0	100.0

cities, as we made clear in Chapter 4. Among the oldest (51*64 years), although it was quite high, upward mobility fell to about 86%.[13]

The discussion of the preceding two paragraphs leads us to conclude that occupational opportunities have expanded more for the young in the recent past than they did for the old in the remote past. This is particularly true for those who began their careers in occupations of low (upper-lower) and of high qualification (upper-middle) in the urban zone.[14]

The difficulty of upward social movement from stratum to stratum is not linear. For career mobility also the difficulties increase as one rises on the social scale. Looking at the Total column of Table 7.6, we see that among mobile individuals of the lower-lower stratum 100% (obviously) rose on the scale. Among those of the upper-lower, this percentage falls a little, but only to about 92% (smaller than in the case of intergenerational mobility). From there on the difficulties increase substantially. Among mobile individuals who began in the lower-middle, the percentage of those who moved upward falls to about 67%. Curiously, it increases again for those of the middle-middle, and one observes that the two age groups that contributed the most to this were the 41–50 year olds (with 10.8%) and the very young—the 20–30 year olds (with 8.8%). Neither the decrease nor the recovery observed is present in the case of intergenerational mobility. In the latter, the level of difficulty for upward movement increases systematically. In career mobility, it lessens for people who began in the lower-middle and increases again in the subsequent level. These phenomena may be explained in large part by the massive entry of children into urban, low-status occupations. This would bring about a certain inflation of people in that level, which seems to be caused by a high degree of participation by children in the informal market. But among mobile children, almost all eventually rose on the social scale (91.8%).

13. The difference between 93% and 86% in these two groups was not significant at the level of 5%.

14. In developed societies this difference in favor of the young tends to be very small, indicating that employment had evened out long ago. See Simpson and Simpson, 1977.

Mobility of Children and Adults

We have mentioned several times that children in Brazil frequently enter the labor market. We emphasize again that technically this entrance should not be considered as a career beginning, because in many cases, especially in the rural zone, occasional help in agricultural tasks is culturally part of childhood and of the dynamics of the family as a productive unit. We included in the sample of heads of families only those individuals who had already gone through the initial stages of transition, but who could have varied considerably in matters touching on their childhood participation in the labor market. In the analysis of intergenerational mobility, we saw that the earlier individuals began jobs, the lower their initial status and their destiny. How does this phenomenon behave for intragenerational mobility? In what direction does the exclusion of individuals who began to work on an occasional basis influence the general pattern of intragenerational mobility?

To test the hypothesis that people achieve more upward movement to the extent that they delay the beginning of their careers, we must look at the matrices of status change for each age. Although possible, this becomes a quite complicated analysis. To test the hypothesis that the exclusion of occasional childhood work would cause the elevation of the beginning career stages, we need to separate the occasional from the continuous. This is simple, but impossible with the available data.

Research is also the art of the possible. Under these restrictions, what we have been able to do is to contrast the social structures given by the initial and current statuses in two phases of the lives of individuals—before and after 18 years of age. Table 7.7 shows clearly that most of the people who entered the labor market at 18 years or older did so in middle class occupations. The three

TABLE 7.7. Beginning and Current Status by Age upon Entry into the Labor Market (%)

| | Age upon Entry into the Labor Market | | | |
| | Beginning Status | | Current Status | |
Social Strata	Younger than 18 years	18 or Older	Younger than 18 years	18 or Older
Upper	0.0	4.4	2.2	13.6
Upper-middle	0.1	4.9	5.3	16.0
Middle-middle	3.3	34.5	17.6	27.8
Lower-middle	5.9	18.3	24.8	24.1
Upper-lower	25.8	26.9	17.2	13.0
Lower-lower	64.9	11.0	32.9	5.5
Total	100.0	100.0	100.0	100.0
N =	49,124	6,677	47,092	6,517

middle strata account for almost 60% of the entrants. On the other hand, those who entered before the age of 18 are strongly concentrated in lower class occupations: more than 90% of the entrants are thus accounted for. The same occurs with final status. Those who began to work at 18 or older are concentrated heavily in occupations of middle status in 1973. Those who began before age 18 remain concentrated in the base of the pyramid. Thus, intragenerational mobility differs according to whether one takes the child or the adult as point of departure. Apparently, those who begin to work as children begin at the bottom of the social structure and remain there. Those who begin as adults begin with a higher status and then rise even further.

But the structure is far from being closed to those who began to work during their childhood. Table 7.7 shows a reasonable amount of upward mobility for people who started working as children. In fact, under "initial status" we find more than 90% of those who began working as children located in the lower class and only 10% in the other classes. Under "current status," the percentage for the lower class falls toward 50%, the middle class reaches almost 48%, and the upper class a bit more than 2%. No doubt these people in pursuing their careers found ways to recover and to achieve upward mobility. Those who did begin after age 18, however, did progress even further, as shown in Table 7.7.

The most impressive findings are the differences between the two groups in the columns under "current status," beginning with the middle-middle stratum. About 18% of those who started working as children, and 28% of those who started after age 18, are in this stratum. In the upper-middle, the difference is approximately from 5% to 16%; in the upper, it is from 2% to 14%. Everything indicates that the older people enter into the labor market better prepared and in better positions, all of which allows them to move on a more massive scale toward the top of the pyramid.

Types of Mobility

The data examined here lead us to conclude that career mobility in Brazil has been as profound as mobility between generations, and that if it was not more profound it was only because so many people still enter the labor market at a very early age. Indeed, analysis of people who began working at age 18 or older showed that their upward mobility was substantial, and that a high percentage of them reached the top of the social pyramid. On the other hand, comparison of the social structures showed that Brazilian society is becoming considerably more flexible thanks to changes in the labor market and to the growing occupational differentiation which took place especially in the urban zone.

In the case of intergenerational mobility, we saw that most movement occurred at the base of the social structure; that is, the movement was of short distance for most people, and it stemmed from the indicated changes, from migration, and from urbanization. What can we say with respect to intragenerational mobility. Table 7.8 presents the same forms of measurement used in the analysis of intergenerational mobility.

Analyzing the first group of mobilities, we discover that, as in the case of intergenerational mobility, most movement is of a structural nature. This movement is induced by changes in the labor market. We see also that the smallest amount of total mobility is found among the oldest (51–64 years), and the greatest amount among the intermediate age groups. At this point, however, there is an interesting difference. Table 6.8 indicated a total mobility of 58.5%, with 32.9% (56.2% or 58.5) due to the structural changes taken place between fathers and sons. In Table 7.8 we discover almost the same amount of total mobility (58.1%), but structural mobility accounts for 37.8% (or 65.1% or 58.1). In this case, then, structural mobility plays a clearer role in bringing about social mobility.

Were there more structural changes between the beginning and the current points of individual careers than there were between fathers and sons? It has been shown that there was a lowering of status at the entrance into the labor

TABLE 7.8. Types of Social Mobility by Age Group (%)

Types of Mobility		Age Groups			
	Total	(51–64)	(41–50)	(31–40)	(20–30)
1. Total mobility	58.1	53.4	59.5	60.9	56.4
2. Structural mobility	37.8	43.3	38.6	41.0	36.2
3. Circulation mobility	21.9	10.0	20.6	19.9	20.2
4. Upward mobility	54.2	49.5	55.9	57.7	52.2
5. Immobility	41.9	46.6	40.4	39.1	43.6
6. Downward mobility	3.9	3.9	3.7	3.7	4.7
7. Percentage of ascendants	93.4	92.7	93.8	93.8	92.5
8. Percentage of descendants	6.6	7.3	6.2	6.2	7.5
9. Mobility without exchange	93.0	92.1	93.4	93.4	91.2
10. Mobility with exchange	7.0	7.9	6.6	6.6	8.8
Mobility index (Y)	54.7	59.1	56.9	54.8	50.3

market. This lowering was due principally to the high incidence of children in low status occupations in the rural zone. This caused large differences between initial and current statuses, which in turn indicated greater structural mobility. But most of the upward movement was due to the structural mobility located in the 51–64 year age group, where it reached 81.0%. The other groups remained close to the mean of the total. This reflects the already-discussed fact that the entrance of children at low levels was more frequent in the past than it is in the present. Looking at it from another angle, circular mobility doubles when one goes from the oldest group (51–64) years) to middle-aged people and then to the youngest. For the latter, mobility based upon exchange and competition is increasing.

Furthermore, we must emphasize that the oldest group (51–64) showed the lowest level of total mobility. What can be said for all this is that those who entered the market in the decades of the twenties and thirties had less chance for career mobility; and career mobility depended more upon market transformations than upon individual betterment. For those who started working in the forties and fifties, circulation mobility was increasingly important, although even today structural mobility still predominates.

Analysis of the second group of mobilities shows a small decrease in upward mobility in relation to the observation for intergenerational mobility. Even so, the percentage of the upwardly mobile is greater than the percentage of the immobile and the downwardly mobile. The rates of upward mobility are higher in the intermediate age groups and lower in the extremes for the reasons already discussed: the oldest had time, but few opportunities to rise; the youngest had opportunities but did not have sufficient time to further their careers. This also explains the relatively higher percentage of descending individuals (4.7%) in the 20–30 year age group.

The percentage of upwardly- and downwardly-mobile individuals (lines 7 and 8 in Table 7.8) show from another angle the same phenomenon: the intermediate groups achieved more upward movement, but the differences are insignificant. On the other hand, the mobilities with and without exchange (lines 9 and 10 in Table 7.8) portray the labor market's structural changes, although with less details than do the structural and circular mobilities above.[15]

Generally, we can say that the Brazilian social structure shows signs of increasing flexibility in terms of career mobility; the large amount of upward movement stands out. Other than this, the data referring to structural mobility indicate an intense movement around new spots. Mobility through exchange

15. The mobility index (Y) is much more sensitive to age in the case of intra- than it is for intergenerational mobility (Table 6.9). Basically, the index grows smaller with age, reflecting the importance of time for establishing careers. As we have seen, the oldest groups show the highest intragenerational mobility indices.

TABLE 7.9. Mobility with Exchange and without Exchange

Social Strata	Descending Individuals	Immobile Individuals	Ascending Individuals	Total
Upper	88	235	—	323
Upper-middle	106	180	95	381
Middle-middle	502	1,676	1,546	3,724
Lower-middle	521	2,339	1,070	3,930
Upper-lower	859	2,991	9,712	13,562
Lower-lower	—	15,112	16,732	31,844
Total	2,076	22,533	29,155	53,764

has been relatively low in the case of career mobility. The occupational structure has expanded and differentiated so as to induce upward movement without corresponding descents or withdrawals of individuals in the labor market. In the case of career mobility, contrary to that of intergenerational mobility, this pattern has been maintained consistently in the various levels of the social structure. Table 7.9 shows the absolute numbers for the movements. In all strata, more people moved up than moved down.

Association Index

What is the influence of career beginning upon an individual's social destiny? Working with change matrices gives us only an approximate vision of the phenomenon. To achieve this end, we have again calculated the association index for the entire occupational matrix contained in Table 7.1. The results are shown in Table 7.10. The weight of the point of departure is a bit heavier here than it was in the case of intergenerational mobility (Table 6.11), and it becomes more pronounced after the upper-middle stratum. In intergenerational mobility it already stands out in the middle-middle stratum.

TABLE 7.10. Influence of Origin upon Social Destination

Beginning Status	Individual's Status in 1973					
	1	2	3	4	5	6
1. Upper	21.4	2.2	0.5	0.0	0.0	0.0
2. Upper-middle	7.3	7.3	1.0	0.2	0.0	0.0
3. Middle-middle	4.9	3.8	2.4	0.3	0.2	0.0
4. Lower-middle	0.8	1.1	0.9	2.4	0.6	0.1
5. Upper-lower	1.2	1.4	1.3	1.4	1.3	0.2
6. Lower-lower	0.2	0.4	0.7	0.7	1.0	1.6

The weight of the initial position continues to be relatively high. Of the 36 values on the matrix, 17 are higher than 1.0. Few, however, are higher than 2.0, which is considered high. At the top of the pyramid, the values are higher than in the case of mobility between generations. For example, the association index in the upper stratum is 21.4, which means that a beginning in this level is a very reliable guarantee of remaining in the upper class. Although this pattern occurred for intergenerational mobility also, the value, was not so high; that is, to be born in the upper class was a good guarantee, but not quite as good as a first job in the upper class.

Thus, if the point of departure were the only determinant of an individual's social status, all excess values would be concentrated in the six values along the principal diagonal. This does not happen. Nineteen values are higher than 1.0. High values are observed mainly in the values next to those on the diagonal. The matrix as a whole shows much mobility. Indeed, a more detailed analysis which determines the net effects of each of these variables (Chapter 10) will show that in inter- as well as in intragenerational mobility the weight of initial status is not as great as it is in societies that are stagnant or structured in castes. Other variables, especially education and differentiated job opportunities, have a much more significant impact upon the social achievements of Brazilian heads of family.

8

Mobility and
Social Distance

The analyses in the two previous chapters identified different patterns of social mobility in the base and in the top of the social pyramid. Locating mobility in particular areas of the social structure is one of the advantages of using status change matrices. Generally, the inter- and intragenerational mobility matrices show that there is more upward mobility in the base than in the top of the social pyramid in Brazil. They also show that most people travel relatively short distances, and that a minority travels greater distances. Everything suggests that the many rise little while the few rise a great deal in Brazil. This pattern, which is common even in developed societies (Miller, 1960), is an unequalizing force in itself and deserves more detailed analysis.

The transition matrices prove useful again, for one way to analyze the question is to study individually the social distances run by individuals located in different levels of the social structure, particuarly by those of the lower and the middle classes. This is the objective of this chapter.[1] To do so, not only will status be categorized into six levels, as was done in the two previous chapters, but the values of the 259 occupations found in Valle Silva's scale will be used.

Lower Class Mobility

It is worth repeating that the term "class" is used in a liberal way in this study, as referring to the group formed by the strata with similar mean values

---

1. This chapter is restricted to intergenerational mobility. In this sense, it is a further detailing of Chapter 6.

of occupational statuses. Two strata are to be considered in the lower class: the *lower-lower* and the *upper-lower* strata. As we have seen, these two strata include occupations of low qualification, education and income. The values of the occupational statuses in these strata are very close. In fact, these two strata are distinguished more by their rural or urban loci than by any difference in mean values for their occupational statuses. The lower-lower stratum includes 16 rural occupations and the upper-lower 61 urban occupations. The social positions of the occupations of the first stratum have a mean value of 4.70 on Valle Silva's scale. The mean value for the second stratum is 5.80. The social distance between these two strata, then, is relatively small—1.10 points. This is the smallest distance in the entire structure (see Table 8.1).

As we saw, the proportion of upward intergenerational mobility in these two cases is greater than the proportions of downward mobility and of immobility. In the lower-lower stratum, 55% of the individuals rose in relation to their fathers. In the upper-lower stratum, this was even more intense—about 66% moved upward on the social scale. Thus, mobility was accentuated in both cases, but more markedly for people who began their occupation trajectory in the urban environment.

What can we say about the course run by ascending individuals in these two strata? This question can be approached in terms of *degrees* and of *distance* (in points) traveled.

Speaking in degrees, we discover that in both strata many people traveled the smallest possible distance; that is, they moved to the stratum immediately above their point of departure. For example, we have seen that 55% of the lower-lower stratum individuals achieved upward intergenerational mobility. Table 8.2 shows that of those who rose, about 32% traveled one degree. In other words, about one third of the lower class, mobile individuals remained in the lower class, their upward movement being attributed to the structural mobility brought about by rural-urban migration. Fully two thirds traveled greater distances. About 38% entered into the first level of the middle class.

TABLE 8.1. Value of Social Positions by Strata

Social Strata	Mean Value of Social Position	Difference in Relation to the Stratum Below It
Upper	63.71	32.87
Upper-middle	30.84	13.83
Middle-middle	17.01	7.54
Lower-middle	9.47	3.63
Upper-lower	5.84	1.14
Lower-lower	4.70	—

These are people who originated in the lowest level of the rural zone and who entered into manual occupations which required a certain level of preparation, such as electricians, masons, carpenters, barbers, radio technicians, and even lathe operators. Grouping together the two strata of destination, we see that about 70% of the mobile individuals originating in the lower-lower stratum entered into urban occupations, most of them manual, but of a higher level of qualification. It is one thing to leave the rural zone to be a trash collector or a shoeshiner in the urban zone, but it is quite another to become a lathe operator or a radio technician. The trash collector has a value 5.56 on Valle Silva's scale, the shoeshiner 3.76, the lathe operator 10.82, and the radio technician 12.99. Even though these occupations are all considered within the one category "manual," there are substantial differences in status between the upper-lower and the lower-middle strata. We must note also that about one quarter of the mobile individuals originating in the rural zone entered into occupations of much higher qualification and income in the middle-middle stratum. These include, among others, medium-sized rural landowners, farm technicians, surveyors, and other urban occupations which require better preparation, such as accountants and bursars, draftsmen, notaries, linotypists, copy editors, and construction foremen. Thus, about one quarter of these individuals traveled 3 degrees from their paternal status; this is more than a moderate mobility. From there on, as Table 8.2 shows, the difficulties increase a great deal for the sons of the lower-lower stratum.

The percentage of the upper-lower stratum individuals who were upwardly mobile in relation to their fathers was about 66% (Table 6.1). Table 8.2 shows that about 53% of these traveled only one degree, entering into predominantly manual occupations (with some qualification) of the lower-middle stratum, while about 45% went on to mostly non-manual occupations in the middle-middle and higher strata. Thus, 55% traveled one degree and 45% two or more

TABLE 8.2. Distances Traveled by Sons of the Lower Strata

Social Strata		Distances Traveled in Relation to Point of Departure, by Strata					Mean Distance Traveled
		Upper-lower	Lower-middle	Middle-middle	Upper-middle	Upper	
Lower-lower	D	1.14	4.77	12.31	26.14	59.01	7.36
	(%)	(31.6)	(38.3)	(23.9)	(4.5)	(1.7)	(100.0)
Upper-lower	D	—	3.63	11.17	25.00	57.87	10.84
	(%)	—	(53.3)	(31.0)	(11.0)	(4.7)	(100.0)

D = Distance in points on Valle Silva's scale.
% = Percentage of upwards.

degrees.[2] The greatest concentration of those who traveled the longer distances is in the middle-middle stratum, with 31%. We must not disregard, however, the 11% who traveled three degrees and the 4.7% who moved four degrees, reaching the top of the structure. Brazil has been a very mobile society with large groups rising quite a bit and small groups traveling very large distances. This is one source of present inequality.

The distance from one degree to the next (in points) is not constant. Actually it increases exponentially as one rises on Valle Silva's scale. This scale is sufficiently sensitive to reflect the fact that the number of available positions in the social structure is inversely proportional to their level. Table 8.1 shows the mean values of each stratum and the distance in points from the previous stratum. More specifically, when we say that about 46% of the sons of the upper-lower stratum traveled two or more degrees (Table 8.2), we are referring to people who left the position with a value of 5.84 and who reached positions with values of 17.01, 30.84, and 63.71 respectively, having traveled distances of 11.17, 25.00, and 57.87 points on the social scale. When we say the same for the sons of the lower-lower stratum, we are referring to distances covered of 4.77, 12.31, 26.14, and 59.01 points, respectively. Thus we must examine more closely the question of proportions and distances run for each social stratum, as well as mean distances.

Table 8.2 indicates that the mean distance traveled by the sons of the lower-lower stratum was 7.36 points, while for those of the upper-lower it was 10.84, or 47.0% more than the former.[3] Thus, the upper-lower stratum showed more mobility (Table 6.1) and more mean distance covered than did the lower-lower stratum, even though the latter potentially had more space available in which to rise—only to rise, as a matter of fact. To be born into the urban lower class guarantees greater probability for upward mobility than to be born into the rural lower class. This seems to be in accord with the urban occupational differentiation pointed out in Chapter 4. In addition, among those who rose, the mean distances traveled also are greater. This is reflected in Table 8.2. The mean distance covered by those who rose in the social structure is greater for individuals with an urban origin than it is for those with a rural origin. But the same table shows that most people (about 53%) are far from this mean; they traveled a distance of 3.63 points, indicating that the mean is pushed upward by a minority who rose a great deal. In this sense, the means conceal the persistence of great social inequalities in both the urban and the rural zones.

When the positions reached by the two strata are compared, the relative

2. The idea that many rise little and few rise much should be looked at with certain reservations in light of these data. Nevertheless, it takes on more significance when the distances traveled (in points) are examined. This is done in the next paragraphs.

3. The author is grateful to Dr. Archibald O. Haller for suggesting this procedure.

differences are great. For example, of the urban-originated ascendants, 11% traveled an average of 25 points and entered the upper-middle stratum. Of those with a rural origin, 4.5% traveled 26 points and reached the upper-middle stratum. Similarly, 4.7% of the urban-originated individuals traveled the enormous distance of about 58 points, entering the upper stratum, while 1.7% of the rural-originated individuals traveled 59 points to do the same. Thus, birth in the urban lower class expands one's social horizons further than does birth in the rural lower class. The weight of the urban social differentiation pointed out in Chapter 4 is revealed here.

We can summarize by affirming that the two lower strata achieved ample vertical mobility. In both cases, the sons enjoy higher statuses than their fathers do. The social mobility in these two strata seems to be strongly associated with the massive rural-urban migration that has occurred in Brazil in the last few decades.

Almost all the fathers examined in the lower-lower stratum held rural occupations. A good percentage of their sons moved to occupations in the urban lower class (and the others went even further). Simple migration must have provoked this upward movement. Even though they were of a low level (and some of them in the informal sector), the upper-lower stratum (urban) occupations offered mobility for whoever came from an origin still lower. It is important to note, however, that most of the people who rose on the social scale entered into the middle class strata (about 66%). The indication is that those who migrate to the city tend not only to occupy new positions but also to replace the native city dwellers, who themselves ascend in the work force. In this sense the rural-urban migration tends to promote social mobility both in the migrants and the non-migrants. This will be better demonstrated in Chapter 9.

The mobility found in the upper-lower stratum seems to be due to two factors: first, many of the fathers of this stratum had already migrated to the urban zones some time before. This would have offered to their sons more and better contacts, as well as more experience and possibilities to learn new jobs; second, these urban conditions themselves seem to have facilitated training, apprenticeship, and even formal schooling for the sons. In fact, 33% of the sons of this stratum completed grade school; this percentage did not pass 16% in the lower-lower stratum. Similarly, only 11% of the former were illiterate, while this percentage for the lower-lower reached 32%.

It seems beyond doubt that much of the movement of individuals originating in the lower class was associated with the intense rural-urban migration, and that it should be characterized as structural mobility. But there was circulation mobility as well. The majority of those who went to or who were born in the city entered into occupations which required some qualification. Most of this qualification seems to have been acquired in the market itself, especially in the subsector of civil construction. In the case of the upper-lower stratum, there are indications of a higher level of formal education. This qualification, attained in school, created a large part of the already-mentioned circulation mobility.

In sum, the idea that many rise little and few rise much can be accepted only with certain qualifications in the case of the lower class. Even though most individuals with this origin are still concentrated in the base of the pyramid, a reasonable proportion go further, particularly those who were born into low-status families in the urban zone. An intense dynamism at the base of the social structure is undeniable, even though this may be induced by structural transformations and a low beginning social position. In other words, the new occupational opportunities in the urban zone, although meager from an absolute point of view, were sufficient to promote much social mobility in the lower class.

Middle Class Mobility

Upward mobility for people originating in the middle class is generally more difficult than it is for lower class individuals. It bears repeating that the number of available positions in the social structure is inversely proportional to the level of the positions. The higher the level, the smaller the number of positions. The data in Chapter 6, for example, show that about half the sons of the lower-middle stratum remained in their fathers' positions; 34% rose and about 20% fell (Table 6.1). In part, this is due to the fact that the social space available to these people was much more limited than it was for lower class individuals. We saw also that from the lower-middle stratum on, the proportion increases of industrial sector occupations and of jobs which require more qualification. Also, there are indications that the market becomes formal and comes to require more formal education.[4]

Most of the upward mobility of the lower-middle stratum was of short distance. Table 8.3 shows that about 63% of the ascending individuals rose only one degree, with the probability of going beyond that plateau falling consid-

---

4. Interpretation of the more moderate mobility in the middle class can take two lines of argument. On the one hand, the fact may be seen as stemming from the supply of professionals, as a problem of a scarcity of well-educated people. On the other, it also seems legitimate to argue that the problem is one of demand, that society has not been able to create large numbers of middle-level jobs and that, therefore, the number of spaces is smaller than that of the job seekers. In fact, the problem seems to be more of demand than of supply, in this case. The data indicate that more than one third of the lower-middle stratum individuals completed at least junior high school. This is an excellent "mark" in a society in which about 82% of the labor force only completed grade school or less.

TABLE 8.3. Distances Traveled by Sons of the Middle Strata

Social Strata		Distances Traveled from Point of Departure, by Social Stratum			Mean Distance Traveled
		Middle-middle	Upper-middle	Upper	
Lower-middle	D	7.54	21.37	54.24	16.26
	(%)	(63.3)	(25.6)	(11.1)	100.0
Middle-middle	D	—	13.83	46.70	26.11
	(%)	—	(62.4)	(37.6)	100.0
Upper-middle	D	—	—	32.87	32.87
	(%)	—	—	(100.0)	100.0

D = Distance in points on Valle Silva's scale.
% = Percentage of upwards.

erably. About 26% traveled two degrees and entered into the upper-middle stratum; 11% reached the upper class. Here, more clearly than in the case of the lower class, most ascending individuals of the lower-middle traveled short distances while the minority traveled far. However, this situation is different from that of the lower strata. Table 8.3 shows that the rising middle class individuals traveled very long distances compared to lower class people. More specifically, those of the lower-middle stratum traveled an average of 16.26 points; those of the middle-middle traveled 26.11 and those of the upper-middle 32.87 points. The individuals of the two lower strata traveled distances of only 7.36 and 10.84 points, respectively. Thus, the average course run by ascending individuals of the lower-middle stratum is twice that of the lower-lower stratum, and about half again as great as that of the upper-lower.

The social space is smaller for the Brazilian middle class, but the mean distances traveled are long. In other words, the middle class has benefited more in terms of distance traveled, although few have been able to take advantage of this.

There is a further qualification to make on this point. Comparing the middle strata with the lower, on the average, upward mobility diminishes and downward mobility increases (Table 6.1). This pattern is common in nearly all known systems of stratification, at least some of the phenomenon being attributed to the reduced space available in the top of the pyramid and to the factor of age. This leads us to consider the percentages of upward mobility in the middle strata as having a different significance than they do in the lower strata. For example, the quarter of the sons of the middle-middle stratum who rose on the social scale should not be considered a small proportion. Even in more advanced societies with flexible structures, the sons of the middle-middle stratum have little space for movement. Few are the modern social systems which show 25% upward mobility for individuals of middle-middle origin (Miller, 1960; Kleining, 1978).

How do the three middle strata compare in terms of distance run? The mean distance traveled by individuals originating in the lower-middle stratum was 16.26 points. This is quite a large distance to open up between fathers and sons. But most of those who rose traveled about 7.54 points, moving to the stratum immediately above—that is, to the middle-middle. Besides being much smaller than the mean distance, this movement has a particular significance, since it reflects changes from predominantly manual occupations to non-manual ones. This change was very rare in the past and indicates not only changes in the occupational structure but also educational improvements. The percentage of people who moved to the upper-middle stratum is not small (26%)—they traveled a mean distance three times greater than did the lower class. These people, whose fathers held manual occupations, are now technicians, administrators, landlords, etc.

The average distance traveled by people of middle-middle stratum origin was 26.11 points, or about 60% more than that achieved by the lower-middle. Here again the large concentration of those who rose was in the stratum immediately above (about 62%), but the mean distance traveled by this group was almost 14 points on the social scale. Those who jumped two degrees and entered into the relatively hermetic upper stratum traveled an enormous distance of almost 47 points! In sum, few people rose from the middle-middle stratum, but those who did rise traveled far.

What happened, in terms of social mobility, to the sons of the upper-middle stratum? Here the space was even smaller, as their fathers had already reached an elevated plateau. The greatest probability was to descend on the social scale. For those who rose, the only leap possible was to enter the upper class, which is normally quite hermetic and very much determined by self-recruiting. In spite of all this, the data of Chapter 6 showed that about 15% of the sons of the upper-middle stratum entered the elite and that 28% remained stable, which in itself is an accomplishment.[5] The data indicate also that about 28% also fell only one degree on the social scale, this being associated largely with the youngest groups. Together, about 75% of the sons of the upper-middle stratum were clustered around their fathers' positions. If the top of the pyramid was insufficient to generate new positions in a way that promoted upward movement of large masses of the work force, we cannot disregard the fact that it did offer space to most of its own members and even to persons of other origins.

5. Clearly, this type of judgment applies in a situation of intense structural mobility such as that of Brazil. In stable societies, where upward mobility depends a great deal upon circulation mobility, this type of phenomenon would be an impediment to mobility for those who are below. See Parkin, 1971:53–55.

Self-Recruitment

What is the proportion in the upper class of individuals of another origin? This question is often raised by social stratification scholars. The size and social origin of the elite are commonly taken as indicators of the rigidity or flexibility of the social structure (Kahl, 1957:268–70; Hutchinson, 1960: Chap. 9).

But to speculate upon the origin of the elite we need another type of data. So far we have studied tables designed to show the social destination of individuals born into the various social strata. To answer the question above, however, we need data which indicate the social origins of individuals who, in 1973, composed the various strata, especially the upper stratum. Such data make up Table 8.4

These data may be surprising, but professionals who are accustomed to this type of data are familiar with the phenomena they reveal.[6] In fact, when we look at the heads of family who comprised the highest stratum in the Brazilian social structure in 1973 (according to the PNAD/73 sample) we discover that only 175% came from that stratum itself (Table 8.4). In other words, for every ten people of the upper class, less than two come from the upper class itself. The degree of social heterogeneity in this stratum in Brazil is surprising: about 14% come from the upper-middle stratum; more than one third from the middle-middle; 10% from the lower-middle, and almost one quarter from the two lower strata. One might wish to attribute this heterogeneity to the status scale, but the fathers in the sample unquestionably knew an upper class quite different from that of 80 or 100 years before, when the elite recruited its members only and exclusively from within the elite itself.

The upper-middle stratum shows the same pattern of heterogeneity. Only 14.3% are self-recruited and about 7% come from the upper class. Almost 80% of the upper-middle stratum individuals came from families whose fathers were members of lower strata. About 32% came from the middle-middle; that is, their fathers worked in non-manual professions of little qualification and prestige, such as office workers, accountants, and warehousing superintendants. Today the sons of these professionals work in high status occupations through either education (liberal professions) or capital (industrialists, merchants, etc.). About 13% came from the lower-middle stratum (manual occupations also of little qualification), and approximately 34% came from the rural or urban lower class.

Table 8.4 shows also that each of the current social strata recruited more than 18% of its members from low-status, rural zone families. This is in large part a reflection of the enormous numbers of peasants in past times, to the

---

6. Various studies have shown that the elite is becoming permeable in Brazil and in the rest of Latin America. See Cardoso, 1969:51–82; Lipset and Solari, 1967.

TABLE 8.4. Social Origin of the Current Strata (%)

Father's Status	Individuals' Status in 1973					
	1	2	3	4	5	6
1. Upper	17.5	7.3	3.0	1.0	0.6	0.2
2. Upper-middle	13.8	14.3	4.9	2.0	1.2	0.6
3. Middle-middle	34.0	31.6	27.2	11.0	9.1	5.0
4. Lower-middle	10.0	12.9	10.9	18.1	8.6	1.4
5. Upper-lower	6.3	8.1	7.8	10.4	10.3	2.1
6. Lower-lower	18.4	25.8	46.2	57.5	70.2	90.7
Total	100.0	100.0	100.0	100.0	100.0	100.0

rural-urban migration, and to the high fertility rate of this group, which helped spread its sons to the various strata.

Table 8.5 shows the proportions of self-recruitment for all the social strata. The lower-lower stratum shows the expected highest self-recruitment index, since it is difficult to imagine that a peasant today would have come from a family of non-peasants. But the other social strata show relatively low self-recruitment indices, suggesting again great changes having taken place in the Brazilian social structure. As an illustration and basis of a (rather uncertain) comparison, we might remember that self-recruitment of the elite in the United States is about 14%; in Brazil it is almost 18%. For occupations corresponding to the middle-middle stratum, the picture is practically the same (Blau and Duncan, 1967:39). A recent study (1973) which grouped North American occupations into five status levels shows more self-recruitment than Brazil does in nearly all strata. (Featherman and Hauser, 1978:66). In sum, the number of spaces open in the top of the Brazilian social pyramid may not have been sufficient to bring about the social equality desired by Brazilians, much less to attend to all those who are trying to enter. However, the two highest strata did recruit sons of all the other social strata to fill the positions that opened up. In other words, the new spaces were excessive for the fertility patterns of the elite and insufficient for the masses of candidates for upward mobility.

Nevertheless, upward mobility toward the upper-middle and the upper strata seems to have taken several paths. First, there is the case of medium-sized landowners and landlords who simply expanded their businesses and facilitated their sons' entering into these two strata. This is basically an upward mobility via accumulation of capital. Second, there are those who, through education and strategic contacts, become parts of the public and private bureaucracies, thus characterizing an upward mobility via education and relationships. Third, there is the case of the liberal professionals who serve the "new middle class" and whose numbers, therefore, must rise with those of the middle class; this mobility combines education and capital. Finally, there is a large number of

TABLE 8.5. Percentage of Self-Recruitment*

Social Strata	Index of Self-Recruitment
1. Upper	17.5
2. Upper-middle	14.3
3. Middle-middle	27.2
4. Lower-middle	18.1
5. Upper-lower	10.3
6. Lower-lower	90.8

*In the specialized literature this measurement is given as a "self-recruitment index" which varies from 0 to 1 (Blau and Duncan, 1967:40).

people who enter the upper-middle stratum and the upper class by having taken advantage of new opportunities arising, especially in the commercial sector. Capital, opportunities taken, and an entrepreneurial spirit give the impulse to this group's upward mobility. In sum, upward mobility for these two strata was achieved by various paths and by individuals who began at very different points. Brazilian society opened up various alternatives for social mobility for this group.

And the role of education?[7] The fact is that about a quarter of those who are today in the upper-middle stratum possess university degrees. This level of education is extremely high in a country where most heads of family have not even finished grade school. It is more surprising, however, to discover the reverse; that is, that almost half of the people who compose the upper-middle stratum have finished only grade school or even less. In this sense their social attainment was very far from their educational attainment. They climbed in spite of their meager formal education.

Intergenerational Mobility: Summary

How might we summarize the situation of intergenerational mobility in Brazil? So far we have seen that 80% of all mobile persons achieved upward mobility, while only 20% went down on the social scale. But what is the degree of the system's general fluidity? How has the fluidity of the Brazilian social structure behaved when fathers and sons are compared?

A series of techniques has been used in the analysis of structural fluidity.[8] One of these is based upon correlations between the statuses of ancestors and descendents—in our case, fathers and sons. Fluidity is given by an equation:

$F = 100 \times (1 - r^2_{pf})$ where
r^2_{pf} = correlation between the respective statuses of fathers and sons.

7. An analysis of the net effects of education will be presented in Chapter 10.

8. For a look at the various techniques available in modern sociology, see Broom, 1977; Rogoff, 1953; Haller and Spenner, 1977.

By itself, r^2_{pf} measures the variance of paternal status transmitted to the son independently of the direction of the mobility. Thus, $(1-r^2_{pf})$ measures the variance of the status not transmitted; that is, it measures the degree of the system's fluidity. (The multiplication by 100 is to facilitate reading.) When F = 0, the status of the sons will be determined totally by the status of the respective fathers. When F = 100, mobility will be due exclusively to the achievements of the sons and to the flexibility of occupational opportunities.

The value found for the occupational status matrix of Table 6.1 (Chapter 6) was F = 78.1. This value, although it does not indicate direction, shows a high degree of circulation in the Brazilian social structure. It also indicates that most status was due to individual and structural factors and not to paternal inheritance. In the United States, one of the societies with the greatest circulation, the level of fluidity found in 1962 was F = 84.0, or about 8% more than in Brazil (Blau and Duncan, 1967:64).

What happened to the Brazilian structure after all these upward and downward movements? Table 8.6 repeats the data presented in Table 7.8 and adds one other column for the purpose of comparing what happened between generations. In the last 80 years, Brazil has undergone a marked decrease in the lower class and an expansion of the middle class. Among the fathers of the heads of family studied, the middle class comprised little more than one quarter of the population. Among the sons this class has almost doubled, becoming about 49% of the population.

Close examination of the internal situation of the middle class in the last column reveals a greater growth in the extreme strata and a certain social vacuum in the middle-middle stratum. The greater expansion clearly took place in the lower-middle stratum: the size of this stratum for the sons is 156%

TABLE 8.6. Change in the Brazilian Social Structure

Class and Social Stratum	(1) Fathers' Situation	(2) Sons' Situation	(2–1) Expansion/ Reduction	(2–1) : (1) × 100 Expansion/ Reduction in Relation to Fathers
Upper class	2.0	3.5	1.5	85.0
Upper stratum	2.0	3.5	1.5	85.0
Middle class	26.2	48.5	22.3	85.1
Upper-middle st.	3.1	6.3	3.2	103.2
Middle-middle st.	13.8	18.4	4.6	33.3
Lower-middle st.	9.3	23.8	14.5	156.0
Lower class	71.8	48.0	−23.8	−31.4
Upper-lower st.	6.9	16.0	9.1	131.8
Lower-lower st.	64.9	32.0	−32.9	−50.7

greater than for the fathers. This expansion, as well as the growth by almost 132% of the upper-lower stratum, is due in large part to the increase in opportunities for urban, manual occupations. The difference in the upper-middle stratum is also large (103%), while that of the middle-middle is only 33%. The first concerns individuals going from one status to another within occupations predominantly non-manual and high-level. The second percentage reflects the difficulties of individuals leaving manual jobs and entering non-manual, more highly qualified jobs. In other words, a great amount of mobility seems to have occurred within each of the occupational niches (manual and non-manual), it being more difficult to pass from one to the other.

The lower class shrank by about 24%. However, this included two antagonistic movements. The lower-lower stratum shrank by approximately 33%, and the upper-lower increased by 9%. Currently, the size of the upper-lower stratum among the sons is about 132% greater than it was among the fathers. The lower-lower is about 51% smaller among the sons. These movements reflect the structural mobility pointed out in Chapter 6 and the changes in the agricultural labor market, the shifts of the rural-urban migration, and the accelerated urbanization which all took place in Brazil especially after 1950.

The upper class continues very small, reflecting an unequal and funnel-shaped pyramid. In absolute terms, the upper class, which constitutes a proxy of the Brazilian elite, is still quite limited. In relative terms, however, the upper class among the sons is 85% larger than it was among the fathers. More important than this expansion is the internal transformation occurring in this class. As we have seen, the elite can no longer self-recruit its members, and is slowly becoming a quite heterogeneous stratum.

In sum, despite the great social disparities which persist in Brazil, it seems unquestionable that the Brazilian social pyramid is changing in form. To say that Brazil today is a middle class society is unrealistic. But the changes that have occurred undoubtedly are taking Brazil in that direction.

During the 80 years studied, the performance of Brazilian society (measured by the intergenerational mobility of the heads of family) seems to have been quite reasonable. The data reflect great dynamism in the occupational structure for the heads of family, especially at the base of the social pyramid. Assuming that the status of the family head principally determines the status of his family group, we can conclude that Brazilian families enjoy better social opportunities today than yesterday. Occupational differentiation and employment opportunities are pathways to upward mobility for a large part of the heads of family and for the families themselves. In this sense, it seems unquestionable that Brazil advanced socially a great deal.

We believe, however, that the greatest problems of social equalization have yet to arise in Brazil. Although there is still much space for structural mobility based on rural-urban migration, most of the population today is already in the large cities. Although there is much to be achieved with this type of mobility, from now on the importance of vertical mobility should increase. The mobility will increase which depends upon competition among individuals for jobs in the urban zones. Strong, new pressures will exist in the cities which will be strengthened by mobility itself. We will enter, then, into a new phase of development. Up to now, much upward mobility stemmed from a career beginning or from an origin low in the social structure, and from the creation of new jobs of a relatively low level. From here on, it will depend upon the social system finding other ways to promote upward mobility; in particular, it will depend upon the system moving more in the direction of circulation mobility.

9

Mobility and Regional Development

Mobility depends upon opportunities and opportunities depend upon development. In the end, mobility hangs upon the development of the social system under consideration. The marked regional differences which persist in Brazil's development are reflected in the available jobs and in the occupational differentiation. These differences in occupational opportunity tend to create social niches which are more or less favorable to the process of social mobility. Although individual characteristics also influence mobility, they cannot act, of course, in a vaccuum, but only within the context of concrete opportunities. From this interaction of forces, we expect to see different levels of mobility and of inequality in the regional social structures.

This chapter examines the role of this structural variable (regional development) in the social mobility of the Brazilian heads of family. At this time, there is no precise classification for hierarchizing the regions of Brazil in terms of development. This is a primary methodological difficulty in the analysis of mobility and regional development. To get around it, we shall treat the regions as discrete variables, ordered according to their levels of urbanization and non-agricultural labor, taking these indicators as proxies for occupational differentiation.

A second methodological limitation, already mentioned in Chapter 3, involves the lack of coverage by the PNAD/73 in the rural areas of the Northern region and part of the Central-West. As we saw, these regions were underrepresented in the rural occupations because of their enormous expanse and other geographical difficulties. At this point, it is nearly impossible to correct

TABLE 9.1. Regional Distributions by Levels of Urbanization
and Non-Agricultural Labor[1] (%)

Regions	Urbanization	Non-Agricultural Labor
Brasília	96.7	95.5
Rio de Janeiro	91.1	91.7
São Paulo	85.0	81.4
East	59.4	54.2
South	52.0	45.9
Northeast	45.4	41.8

Source: PNAD/73. Fundação IBGE. Author's adaptation.

this bias. In view of this, our only alternative is to exclude from the analysis the Northern and the Central regions, and to include the remaining six regions defined by the PNAD/73 itself.[2] These regions have been ordered on the basis of Table 9.1.

This chapter has three parts. In the first, we shall examine the relationship between regional development and social structure. We shall study the occupational status distribution among the heads of family in each region, as well as the principal social and individual characteristics of the people. In the second part, we shall analyze the differences in mobility among the Brazilian regions, focusing, again, upon inter- and intragenerational mobility. In the third part, we shall present a preliminary analysis of the connection between social mobility and geographical mobility—that is, mobility and migration.

Region and Social Structure

The data in Table 9.2 show a clear connection between regional and social inequalities.[3] The bases in the regional social pyramids differ from one to the other. The largest is found in the Northeast, where nearly 53% of the people interviewed in 1973 were still located in the lower-lower stratum, reflecting the conditions of severe poverty which persist in the rural environment. After the Northeast come the South and the East, although with much smaller per-

1. To calculate the level of urbanization, we used the number of urban households divided by the total. To calculate non-agricultural labor, we used the proportion of people in the labor force engaged in non-agricultural occupations.

2. Brasília (Federal District), Rio de Janeiro (the States of Rio de Janeiro and Guanabara), São Paulo (the State of São Paulo), East (Minas Gerais and Espirito Santo), South (Paraná, Santa Catarina and Rio Grande do Sul), Northeast (from Bahia to Maranhão).

3. Numerous studies have identified enormous disparities in income among Brazilian regions and States. See Langoni, 1973; Costa, *Forum Eduçacional* 1; Costa, 1978.

TABLE 9.2. Social Structure by Regions (%)

Social Strata	Brasília	Rio	São Paulo	East	South	Northeast
Upper	6.0	5.9	4.5	2.5	3.2	1.3
Upper-middle	10.2	8.6	7.8	6.3	5.0	3.0
Middle-middle	24.1	20.7	18.6	17.0	16.2	16.2
Lower-middle	34.6	33.2	33.2	17.7	17.8	13.5
Upper-lower	21.3	22.9	18.3	12.5	11.8	14.2
Lower-lower	3.8	8.7	17.6	44.0	46.0	52.8
Total N	4,188	4,813	7,296	6,998	7,166	10,179

centages of rural occupations. The South, as we know, is permeated with landed estates where the participation of labor is high and mechanization is low. The East, besides being partially within what we might call the Brazilian dust bowl (neighboring the Northeast), is a region of quite recent industrialization and urbanization, which explains the strong retention of manpower in the rural sector up to 1973. São Paulo, with a vigorous but highly mechanized agriculture, reduced the size of the lower-lower stratum to less than 18%. The much reduced size of this stratum in the new and the old capitals is due to their administrative functions.

Looking in more detail at the participation of rural occupations in the Brazilian social structure, we discover that the lower-lower stratum in the Northeast is three times as large as it is in São Paulo. The East and the South are about the same, but they are still about 2.5 times the size of São Paulo in terms of low-status, rural occupations. Considering that much of the Brazilian social mobility was due to the reduction of agricultural occupations, we conclude that São Paulo must have played a large role in determining general mobility in Brazil.[4] This will be discussed in the next section.

Rio, Brasília and São Paulo present the greatest proportions of individuals in occupations typical of the urban lower class. In the case of Rio and Brasília, these occupations include activities peripheral to the bureaucratic structure which dominated and dominates these regions. Many occupations are linked to the small services which support the administrative machinery (office boys, messengers, low-qualification services such as carwashers, porters, and snack vendors). In São Paulo, the proportion is slightly smaller (18.3%); here, we see occupations stemming from an accelerated urbanization which took place in the midst of a strong industrialization (weavers, cobblers, bakers, hod car-

4. This hypothesis assumes that the individuals' beginning statuses have been at approximately the same level.

riers, doormen, watchmen, salesclerks). In the other three regions, the percentages of these occupations are lower and more stable, although slightly greater in the Northeast (13.2%). These occupational categories include a large part of the urban poor and are important in the composition of manpower in the peripheries of Brazilian cities. It is also here that informal work takes on relevance. The contingent of people who work these occupations in the cities would be even greater if we had included women and children in the sample. This is another way of saying that urban poverty seems to attain less to the heads of family and more to the other members of the family unit.

What is the behavior of the various middle-class strata in the regions considered? For the lower-middle stratum (which includes occupations whose apprenticeship takes place more on the job than in school), we see, again, that Brasilia, Rio, and São Paulo stand out with about one third of their people in this class. The East and South are basically similar but have half this proportion in the lower-middle. Finally, the Northeast has little more than 10% of its heads of family in this stratum. The labor market linked to public administration, commerce and industry in Brasília, Rio, and São Paulo, respectively, has been much more vigorous in generating lower-middle stratum occupations. This becomes clear when we compare these regions with those which still depend more upon agriculture, mining, and other primary sector activities. And the general picture in the Northeast is worse, where the three sectors of the economy still suffer chronic difficulties which bring about a low level of diversification in the occupational structure and limited possibilities of forming a solid middle class.

The middle-middle stratum, which includes numerous occupations linked to public and private administration, shows its highest percentage in Brasília, where about a quarter of the heads of family can claim that level of occupational status. Brasília is followed by Rio de Janeiro, which, in a way, reflects the labor market characteristics of the old capital besides the present commercial vigor. The other regions, with São Paulo standing out a bit, are clustered together with percentages varying from about 16% to 19%.

The picture for the upper-middle stratum again shows great variations among the Brazilian regions. The greatest percentage, about 10%, is in Brasília, and reflects the federal administration. Rio and São Paulo follow Brasília, showing similar sizes in their upper-middle strata. The percentages fall substantially in the East and South, and in the Northeast the upper-middle stratum reaches only 3%. The size of the upper-middle in Brasília is about three times that of the upper-middle in the Northeast, and twice as great as it is in the South.

A similar situation is found for the upper stratum. Here again we see great inequalities among the various regions, particularly in the Northeast. About 6% of the occupations in Brasília and Rio are upper class, followed by São

Paulo with 4.5%. From there the figures are lower. The South shows about 3% with upper class status; the East shows 2.5% and the Northeast little more than 1%. It bears repeating that upper class status in the occupational classification of Valle Silva does not constitute an immediate indicator of wealth. But it does reflect various characteristics of a high standard of living. Being a member of the upper stratum signifies a broader more cosmopolitan lifestyle, broader cultural, educational and social horizons, and a pattern of material life substantially above the mean of the Brazilian population. It is in the upper stratum where we find the industrialists, the large merchants, the bankers, the liberal professionals and other people with high income.

What is the composition of the "classes" of these six regions? Table 9.3 uses a liberal terminology and groups the strata together into the three conventional social classes. The largest pyramid base is seen again in the Northeast (66%), followed by the South and the East (around 57%). Urban and rural poverty weighs most heavily upon heads of family and upon the families themselves in these three regions. The labor market has a rudimentary level of differentiation which keeps more than 50% of the families in lower class conditions. In contrast, middle class occupations have come to predominate in Brasília, Rio, and São Paulo. In these three regions, more than half of the families are in the middle class. In these three cases, the form of the social structure is no longer that of a pyramid but that of a barrel, although with a pointed top.

On the individual side, the most highly contrasting characteristic among the regions has to do with the education levels of the heads of families. The Brazilian labor force in general shows quite a low level of formal schooling: more than three quarters never finished grade school. This general picture, however, encompasses numerous interregional variations which are even more dramatic. Table 9.4 presents the figures for education in the six regions. Almost half the heads of family in the Northeast have no schooling at all. This, of course, is a manpower at the lowest level of formal preparation. This individual deficiency, however, exists along with the limited occupational differentiation

TABLE 9.3. Class Structure by Regions (%)

Social Classes	Brasília	Rio	São Paulo	South	East	Northeast
Upper	6.0	5.9	4.5	3.2	2.5	1.3
Middle	68.9	62.5	59.6	39.0	40.9	32.7
Lower	25.1	31.6	35.9	57.8	56.6	66.0
Total	100.0	100.0	100.0	100.0	100.0	100.0

TABLE 9.4. Educational Situation by Regions (%)

Level of Schooling	Brasília	Rio	São Paulo	South	East	Northeast
University	13.4	7.2	5.3	3.6	2.6	1.6
High school or equivalent	9.0	8.3	5.7	3.5	3.0	2.3
Jr. high school or equivalent	16.6	16.9	10.3	7.7	7.1	3.6
Grade school completed	17.1	27.2	29.7	24.1	19.2	7.6
Grade school incomplete	34.5	30.1	35.6	44.0	44.6	36.5
No schooling	9.4	10.3	13.4	17.1	23.5	48.4
Total	100.0	100.0	100.0	100.0	100.0	100.0
N =	5,395	6,661	8,861	8,339	6,998	12,200
Mean*	5.3	4.4	3.9	3.2	2.9	1.8

*The schooling mean was calculated by giving the following values to the levels under consideration: no schooling = 0; grade school incomplete = 2; grade school completed = 4; jr. high = 8; high school = 11; university = 15.

which predominates in that region. In this case, it is impossible to say which is the cause and which the effect. Thus, we prefer to assume that this coexistence stems from historical deformations. Coincidentally, the percentage of people engaged in rural occuptions with qualification (52.3%) is almost equal to the percentage of heads of family with no schooling.

The proportions of people with no education become smaller in all the other regions. One notices, however, that close to a quarter of the heads of family in the East still remain in this category.

Table 9.4 suggests that the "great expectation" for individuals of the poorest regions is to complete grade school; in the richest it is to complete junior high school. In fact, only 15% of the individuals in the Northeast and East completed grade school or went further; in Brasília, Rio, and São Paulo, more than half of the heads of family finished grade school or more. In these regions, however, the number of individuals who finished junior high school fluctuates greatly. In São Paulo, this percentage is little more than 20%; in Rio it rises to 30%; and in Brasília it reaches almost 40%. The occupational structure in São Paulo, although more diversified, still shelters and promotes a large number of people with less than a junior high school education. In Brasília and in Rio, the power of the diploma and of credentials apparently is much greater, as it is becoming a necessity for employment and upward mobility.

In sum, the differences in education among the Brazilian regions are still quite strong. The heads of family in Brasília show an education level more than three times as great as that of the Northeast. The education level in Rio almost triples that of the Northeast, and that of São Paulo doubles it. It bears repeating, though, that the average education in these regions, in absolute terms, is nothing extraordinary. The mean level of 3.98 tells us that the heads of family working in São Paulo in 1973 had not completed even grade school; this is a more than modest level for the most highly developed state in the country.

Mobility and Regional Development

One of the basic strategies of contemporary models in the study of mobility is to analyze the impact of work opportunities upon the attainment of individual social status. As we know, the regional disparities present differences of opportunity, and, therefore, we expect different levels and types of social mobility. In this section we shall locate these differences and their repercussions in terms of inter- and intragenerational mobility.

Before we present our results, however, we must emphasize a limitation stemming from the way in which the data for this entire research were collected. Upon examining intergenerational mobility in the different regions, we are quite likely to discover that fathers and sons have originated in different regions. Thus, an individual's destination may be reached in a region different from that of his father, and, unfortunately, the data do not permit us to distinguish the two. Consequently, it is very difficult, if not impossible, to contrast the work opportunities of the fathers with those of the sons at the regional level. The same problem occurs with intragenerational mobility: the point of departure may be in another region; the first stages and even the establishment of a career might have taken place in a region different from that in which the individual was interviewed. The data portray conditions only in the region of destination and not in the region of origin. In view of these difficulties, we shall try to avoid inter-regional comparisons which refer to the "region of fathers," "region of sons," or "region of social destination."

In addition, the analysis of inter- and intragenerational mobility becomes overly confused when one compares status change matrices in the six regions. For this reason, the test refers only to the types of mobility observed in the six regions, and points out the principal differences between fathers and sons or between career beginning and the position attained by 1973.

Table 9.5 presents the results of the matrices of status change in the six regions for the case of intergenerational mobility. The data show quite distinct social structures in each of the six regions, and this is valid as much for the fathers' status distribution as it is for the sons'. Individuals who were in the Northeast, South and East in 1973 had a low and markedly rural social origin.

TABLE 9.5. Intergenerational Structural Changes by Regions (%)

Social Strata	Brasília			Rio			São Paulo			South			East			Northeast		
	F	S	(S − F)	F	S	(S − F)	F	S	(S − F)	F	S	(S − F)	F	S	(S − F)	F	S	(S − F)
Upper	3.9	6.0	2.1	3.7	5.9	2.2	2.7	4.5	1.8	2.1	3.2	1.1	1.2	2.5	1.3	0.7	1.3	0.6
Upper-middle	4.8	10.2	5.4	4.8	8.6	3.8	3.0	7.8	4.8	2.2	5.0	2.8	3.3	6.3	3.0	1.7	3.0	1.3
Middle-middle	20.4	24.1	3.7	20.1	20.7	0.6	14.1	18.6	4.5	9.6	16.2	6.6	13.3	17.0	3.7	11.3	16.2	4.9
Lower-middle	9.7	34.6	24.9	18.0	33.2	15.2	13.7	33.2	19.5	6.3	17.8	11.5	7.9	17.6	9.7	4.6	13.5	8.9
Upper-lower	5.8	21.3	15.5	12.8	22.9	10.1	10.2	18.3	8.1	5.3	11.8	6.5	5.0	12.5	7.5	5.0	13.2	8.2
Lower-lower	55.4	3.8	−51.6	40.6	8.7	−31.9	56.3	17.6	−38.7	74.5	46.0	−28.5	69.3	44.1	−25.2	77.7	52.8	−24.9
Total	[	100.0	]	[	100.0	]	[	100.0	]	[	100.0	]	[	100.0	]	[	100.0	]

F = Father
S = Son

140

Almost 80% of the fathers of individuals who were in the Northeast came from the lower-lower stratum; among those of the South, this percentage is about 75%, and in the East, it is almost 70%. This low and rural origin also predominates (at lower levels) among individuals who were in the other regions.

It is interesting to note the flooding of the upper-lower stratum which occurred from father to son in all the regions, but particularly among people who were in the three least urbanized regions—that is, the Northeast, East and South. Although they were the least urbanized and least industrialized, much of the expansion in employment was concentrated in lower-tertiary services in the urban centers. If it weren't for the high rate of emigration from the Northeast and East, the proportions of people in the upper-lower would be even greater. In the other regions, there was more dispersion toward the other social strata.

The middle class, made up of the three middle strata, underwent the fastest growth in the three most advanced regions. Among individuals in Rio, the difference between the size of the fathers' middle class (42.9%) and that of the sons' (62.5%) was almost 20%; in São Paulo, that difference was almost 30%, and in Brasília, 35%. The sons in these three regions are better off than their fathers not only in relative terms but also in absolute terms. We observe that the middle class occupations predominate in all three. But the original plateaus of the people who were in these regions were quite different. In Rio, about 43% of the individuals' fathers occupied middle class positions. In Brasília this percentage reached about 35%, and in São Paulo, about 30%. Of these three regions, São Paulo has the smallest middle class (about 60%), but it was the region which showed the lowest initial plateau; that is, it showed the smallest proportion of middle class fathers (many of them originally from other regions).

To clarify the analysis, we can look at the various types of mobility occurring in the six regions. Table 9.6 reproduces the same measurements presented earlier for the entire sample and for the different age groups. The striking differences between regions characterize Brazil as one of the most heterogeneous societies in Latin America, and as one which is differentiating itself in a most unequal manner. For example, the level of mobility of the population of Brasília was almost double that of the Northeast. Most of the population in the three most advanced regions (Brasília, Rio, and São Paulo) achieved upward intergenerational mobility, while immobility predominated in the other three. In the Northeast, only one third of the population is better off than their fathers; in São Paulo this figure almost doubles, and in Brasília it is more than 68%.

It is most interesting to note the differences in the levels of structural mobility. In Brazil in general, structural mobility predominates and circulation mobility is relatively minor. In other words, many individuals rose in the structure, "pushed up" by newly opened positions, while few rose through

TABLE 9.6. Types of Intergenerational Mobility by Regions (%)

Types of Mobility	Regions					
	Brasília	Rio	São Paulo	South	East	Northeast
1. Total mobility	81.0	72.2	69.2	49.7	49.1	42.3
2. Structural mobility	51.6	38.3	38.7	28.5	25.3	23.9
3. Circulation mobility	29.4	40.9	30.5	21.2	23.8	18.4
4. Upward mobility	68.1	54.6	57.6	40.6	38.3	33.5
5. Immobility	19.0	27.8	30.8	50.3	50.9	57.7
6. Downward mobility	12.9	17.6	11.6	9.1	10.8	8.8
7. Percentage of upwardly mobile	84.0	75.7	83.2	81.7	77.9	79.2
8. Percentage of downwardly mobile	16.0	24.3	16.8	18.3	22.1	20.8
9. Mobility without exchange	81.0	67.8	45.9	77.6	71.7	73.7
10. Mobility through exchange	19.0	32.2	54.1	22.4	28.3	26.3

exchange or through someone else's withdrawal from the labor market. Structural mobility, however, is relatively low in São Paulo (about 46%) and much higher in the other regions. The case of Brasília can be explained by the fact that the new capital provided a large quantity of new jobs. In the case of the three poorest regions, however, much of the mobility was due to the new, low-status jobs in the urban zones. In fact, returning to Table 9.5, the greatest expansion of the upper-lower stratum, which groups together occupations of low qualification and low income, occurred precisely in these three regions.

For intragenerational mobility, the data show equally accentuated differences in dynamism in the six regions studied. Entry into the labor market in Brazil occurs at an early age, and the majority of people enter into the lowest levels of the social structure. The general picture examined in the previous chapters, however, encompasses the regional differences, which are very great. Thus, Table 9.7 reveals that entry into low-status occupations in the rural zone is much more frequent in the poor regions than in the richer ones. The shrinking of this category is less pronounced in the poor regions than in the rich. For example, more than three quarters of the individuals who were in the Northeast in 1973 began to work as farmhands, fishermen, etc., and more than half

TABLE 9.7. Intragenerational Structural Changes by Regions (%)

Social Strata	Brasília			Rio			São Paulo			South			East			Northeast		
	S	P	(P − S)	S	P	(P − S)	S	P	(P − S)	S	P	(P − S)	S	P	(P − S)	S	P	(P − S)
Upper	1.4	5.6	4.2	0.8	4.9	4.1	0.8	4.5	3.7	0.5	3.4	2.9	0.5	2.5	2.0	0.2	1.4	1.2
Upper-middle	1.4	10.4	9.0	1.0	8.8	7.8	0.9	8.2	7.3	0.5	5.4	4.9	0.5	5.9	5.4	0.4	3.1	2.7
Middle-middle	16.7	24.7	8.0	12.0	21.7	9.7	7.1	18.8	11.7	4.6	16.5	11.9	4.0	17.3	13.3	3.5	16.0	12.5
Lower-middle	10.2	34.5	24.3	10.9	33.8	22.9	9.3	33.6	24.3	5.7	18.5	12.8	5.5	18.9	13.4	4.1	14.4	10.3
Upper-lower	26.6	20.9	−5.7	45.4	23.4	−22.0	31.6	18.3	−13.3	16.8	12.4	−4.4	23.0	13.2	−9.8	15.2	13.8	−1.4
Lower-lower	43.7	3.9	−39.8	29.9	7.4	−22.5	50.3	16.6	−33.7	71.9	43.8	−28.1	66.5	42.2	−24.3	76.6	51.3	−25.3
Total	[	100.0	]	[	100.0	]	[	100.0	]	[	100.0	]	[	100.0	]	[	100.0	]

S = Start
P = Present

143

remained in these occupations. In São Paulo, on the other hand, half began as farmhands but only about 15% remained in that position. The heads of family who are in Brasília today also showed a heavy rural origin and a high level of mobility in the lower-lower stratum. This has been the predominant situation in the labor market for two or three decades.

The career beginning in urban occupations of low social status is also frequent. This is the case for shoeshiners, janitors, deliverymen. The upper-lower stratum, though, showed noticeable reductions in Rio and in São Paulo, and relatively small ones in the Northeast, in the South, in Brasília, and in the East. Indications are that in these regions most occupations are of low status and that they serve the great urban centers.

Significant proportions of middle class career beginnings are found only in the two capitals, in the old (about 24%) and in the new (about 28%), due to the high number of occupations available in the upper tertiary in Rio and in Brasília. This phenomenon is rare in the other regions. Even so, São Paulo stands out for presenting great differences between the initial middle class and that observed in 1973. Less than 20% of the heads of family began working in middle class occupations; more than 60% were in these occupations in 1973. Upward intragenerational mobility in São Paulo was enormous, although Brasília maintained the largest middle class (in relative terms, of course).

Table 9.8 presents the different types of intragenerational mobility by regions. We observe again a big difference in total mobility between the first three and the last three regions. The majority of heads of family in the Northeast, the South, and the East remain at their career starting points, while much more intragenerational upward mobility takes place in Brasília, Rio, and São Paulo.

It is interesting to note, however, that structural mobility is more or less the same in all the regions, even though it decreases a bit in the Northeast and the East. It indicates that the vast majority of people move in the direction of new positions and not through exchanges or replacement.

On the basis of Tables 9.6 and 9.8 we can conclude that inter- and intragenerational mobility are closely associated with the level of urbanization and industrialization in the individuals' regions of destination. The population in Brasília, Rio, and São Paulo has taken good advantage of the opportunities for mobility presented to them, thus creating a very dynamic side of Brazilian society. The Northeast, on the other hand, continues to show a static side. There, the social structure changes little from generation to generation and from point to point in the individual career. There is little dynamism and few signs of social development. The East and the South resemble the static Brazil more than they do the dynamic Brazil. The job opportunities in these regions seem to have responded to an employment problem, but have not resulted in

TABLE 9.8. Types of Intragenerational Mobility by Regions (%)

Types of Mobility	Regions					
	Brasília	Rio	São Paulo	South	East	Northeast
1. Total mobility	75.7	69.7	69.1	49.1	50.8	42.0
2. Structural mobility	45.5	44.5	47.0	32.5	34.0	26.9
3. Circulation mobility	30.2	22.7	22.1	16.6	16.8	15.1
4. Upward mobility	72.0	64.6	65.8	45.8	46.0	38.7
5. Immobility	24.3	30.3	30.9	50.9	49.0	58.0
6. Downward mobility	3.7	5.1	3.3	3.3	5.0	3.3
7. Percentage of upwardly mobile	95.1	92.7	95.2	93.4	90.4	92.2
8. Percentage of downwardly mobile	4.9	7.3	4.8	6.6	9.6	7.8
9. Mobility without exchange	95.0	92.7	95.0	93.0	90.4	91.6
10. Mobility through exchange	5.0	7.8	5.0	7.0	10.6	8.4

large waves of social mobility. Many of the individuals working there have a high probability of staying immobile during their entire lives.

Migration and Social Mobility

Migration is a common feature of modern societies, and generally acts as a mechanism to control regional, economic, and social disparities. Employment restrictions and the low occupational differentiation in certain regions act to expel or repel individual people, while the better conditions in other regions tend to attract people. Theories of attraction and repulsion have become influential in sociological theory (Stouffer, 1940; Bake, 1954), and the most advanced models have begun to indicate a series of intervening variables in the decision to migrate (Blau and Duncan, 1967: Chap. 7; Lopreato and Hazebrigg, 1972: Chap. 14; Featherman and Hauser, 1978: Chap. 7).

In this study we shall say little about conditions prior to the decision to migrate. The data for characteristics of regions of origin are quite poor at the moment. On the other hand, the PNAD/73 provides abundant data for the regions of destination, which allow us to compare the social roles of natives and migrants in the locale in which they were found in 1973. Thus, the sample permits us to test some of the basic hypotheses of the works about migration and mobility. Although the findings are still divided, the most recent studies have produced enough empirical evidence to demonstrate that individuals who migrate generally achieve more mobility than do those who remain in their place of birth. Some studies have suggested that, depending on their education level, people in a new region end up with a better social position than that of the natives.

The PNAD/73 sample does not provide elements for comparing individuals who departed with those who stayed, but it does enable us to compare those who arrived (migrants) with the natives, in the labor force under consideration. The data presented here bring out first the differences in social origin and career beginning between migrants and natives, and, second, they show the achievements of the two groups in terms of inter- and intragenerational mobility.

Before we begin the analysis itself, we must mention some limitations to this exercise. First, the definition of migrant used here is a conventional one; that is, a migrant is an individual who, in 1973, resided in a state different from that in which he was born. The data do not tell us in which of the two places the individual matured, where he began his career, how many times he entered and left this state, and other important events in his professional life. In the second place, this study brings out only two types of individuals: (a) those who were born in and who remained in the state in which they were found in 1973; (b) those who were born in one state and, in 1973, were working in an other. Thus, those who were born outside the country were excluded, even those who arrived in Brazil as children and who constructed their entire professional career there. This is an analysis, then, only of internal migrations. In the third place, we have excluded from study all individuals who did not declare their state of birth, as well as those who made imperfect responses to the questions on social mobility.[5]

Table 9.9 shows the distribution of migrants and natives. For the entire sample, 65% of the heads of family were natives, and 35% migrants. The region with the greatest contingent of migrants (not counting Brasília) is the South, where more than half of the heads of family were born outside of Paraná, Santa Catarina, and Rio Grande do Sul. Rio de Janeiro also was quite attractive to people of other regions; 48% of its heads of family were born in

---

5. Consequently, the initial sample of 58,256 was reduced to 54,906 individuals.

TABLE 9.9. Distribution of Natives and Migrants by Regions

Type of Individual	Total		Brasília		Rio		São Paulo	
	N	%	N	%	N	%	N	%
Natives	35,602	65.0	10	0.2	3,833	52.0	6,706	70.0
Migrants	19,304	35.0	5,612	99.8	3,533	48.0	2,882	30.0
Total	54,905	100.0	5,622	100.0	7,366	100.0	9,588	100.0
	South		East		Northeast			
	N	%	N	%	N	%		
Natives	3,556	48.0	8,190	91.0	11,025	87.4		
Migrants	3,817	52.0	773	9.0	1,595	12.6		
Total	7,373	100.0	8,963	100.0	12,620	100.0		

other states. São Paulo is in third place, with 30% of its heads of family being migrants. The Northeast and the East have characterized themselves more by expulsion than by attraction of people from other regions of Brazil.[6]

What are the main differences between natives and migrants in terms of the points of departure and destination—that is, of the father's status, and people's beginning status and their status in 1973? Table 9.10 presents these three distributions. The two groups differ very little in matters of social origin. The great majority of natives and migrants come from fathers who were farmhands, fishermen, rubber workers, etc., as does the majority of the Brazilian population. The small differences in the other categories slightly favor the natives (with the exception of the upper stratum).

Equally small differences are seen in the first job situations. Two notes should be made here. The first is in reference to the smaller proportion of migrants who began their careers in the rural zone. Indications are that migration in itself removed them from rural work and placed them directly into urban work. The high percentage of natives who entered into agricultural work is due in large part to the rural contingent which still remains in the Brazilian labor force.

The second note has to do with the higher proportion of individuals who began to work in middle-middle stratum occupations. Various occupations are included in this stratum which are typically agricultural, but of a higher status.

6. According to 1970 census data for migration in all of Brazil, the order of regions and their attraction is São Paulo, Rio, and the South. This discrepancy is the result of numerous differences between the PNAD/73 sample studied here and the total population. The more important differences have to do with age groups, civil status and differences in fertility.

TABLE 9.10. Social Structures of Natives and Migrants (%)

Social Strata	Father's Situation		Situation at First Job		Situation in 1973	
	Native	Migrant	Native	Migrant	Native	Migrant
Upper	1.8	2.5	0.5	0.8	3.1	3.9
Upper-middle	3.0	3.3	0.7	0.8	6.0	7.2
Middle-middle	13.7	14.7	5.8	9.3	18.1	19.1
Lower-middle	9.7	8.6	6.9	8.0	22.1	29.3
Upper-lower	7.5	6.2	25.1	25.8	15.2	19.7
Lower-lower	64.3	64.8	61.0	55.3	35.5	20.2
Total	100.0	100.0	100.0	100.0	100.0	100.0
N =	27,412	14,381	33,039	17,701	33,039	17,701

Such is the case for middle-sized landowners, farm managers, agricultural technicians, surveyors, and similar occupations. This seems to have given the migrants a certain advantage in this stratum. We must remember, however, that many of them must have come very early to the cities, where they began their careers in urban occupations—as office help, typists, storeroom clerks, construction foremen, draftsmen.

More pronounced differences, however, are found in current status—that is, status in 1973. In general, the migrants show a higher status than do the natives. This occurs in all levels of status except, of course, the lower-lower. One must note here, though, that nearly all the migrants are concentrated in urban oc-cupations (about 80%). The natives, then, still constitute a higher proportion of people in agricultural occupations, having less people in urban occupations (about 65%). Above all, the advantage the migrants show is in great part due to Brasília being included in the total sample, for in Brasília everyone is a migrant and most of the occupations there offer high status.[7] At any rate, we have a picture in which the migrants attain better positions than do the natives, including as natives, of course, those born and reared in the large, medium-sized, and small cities and in the rural zones. The migrants' world is predom-inantly urban and offers great occupational differentiation. The natives' world is more heterogeneous: it is rural and urban; it includes sectors that are vigorous in terms of employment, and others that are extremely backward. To migrate, in this sense, was to travel toward the better opportunities.

7. In the beginning, this fact led the author to consider eliminating Brasília from the analysis of migration. However, to do so would be to eliminate the principal attracting pole for migration in Brazil today, and thus to introduce another kind of bias. For this reason, Brasília was retained for purposes of analyzing inter- and intragenerational mobility.

To what extent do natives and migrants differentiate themselves in terms of intergenerational mobility? Table 9.11 forms a matrix of status change between generations where data for natives and migrants are presented together. The percentages outside the parentheses refer to the natives, and those within parentheses refer to the migrants.

For individuals born into families of farm laborers of the lower-lower stratum, upward mobility was more pronounced among migrants (about 70%) than among natives (about 47%). This is explained by the urban predominance of the migrants. The tendency is the same, although less pronounced, for the sons of the upper-lower stratum.

In the middle class, the general tendencies are these: the migrants are more mobile than the natives in all strata; in all three strata, the migrants achieve more upward mobility than the natives, with the most marked differences being in the middle-middle and the upper-middle.

To summarize the general patterns of intergenerational mobility, Table 9.12 shows the types of mobility already discussed in other parts of this study, except that here they are separated by natives and migrants. The migrants' total social mobility is almost 30% greater than that of the natives; their upward mobility is almost 36% higher. One sees also that most of the mobility for both groups is structural, although much more pronounced among the migrants.

What can be said about career mobility for the two groups? The two start out more or less at the same point, with slight exceptions in favor of the

TABLE 9.11. Intergenerational Mobility of Natives and Migrants (%)*

Father's Status	Individual's Status in 1973						Total	Total for Fathers
	1	2	3	4	5	6		
1. Upper	30.0	23.4	25.8	11.8	5.4	3.6	100.0	1.8
	(30.1)	(21.5)	(28.0)	(13.6)	(5.1)	(1.7)	(100.0)	(2.5)
2. Upper-middle	13.6	29.3	28.8	15.5	5.5	7.3	100.0	3.0
	(17.5)	(28.7)	(28.7)	(15.5)	(6.7)	(2.9)	(100.0)	(3.3)
3. Middle-middle	7.8	13.6	38.0	17.5	9.4	13.7	100.0	13.6
	(9.5)	(16.0)	(33.4)	(20.6)	(13.1)	(7.4)	(100.0)	(14.7)
4. Lower-middle	3.7	8.5	21.3	46.5	15.2	4.8	100.0	9.7
	(3.6)	(8.7)	(22.7)	(46.4)	(14.5)	(4.1)	(100.0)	(8.6)
5. Upper-lower	2.3	6.5	19.9	36.5	24.1	10.7	100.0	7.5
	(4.6)	(9.4)	(21.8)	(33.7)	(23.5)	(7.0)	(100.0)	(6.2)
6. Lower-lower	0.9	2.3	12.2	16.6	14.8	53.2	100.0	64.3
	(1.1)	(2.6)	(14.4)	(28.6)	(22.5)	(30.8)	(100.0)	(64.8)
Total for individuals in 1973	3.1	6.0	18.1	22.1	15.2	35.5	100.0	100.0
	(3.9)	(7.2)	(19.7)	(29.3)	(19.7)	(20.2)	(100.0)	(100.0)

*Numbers in parentheses refer to migrants.

TABLE 9.12. Types of Intergenerational Mobility (%)

Types of Mobility	Natives	Migrants
1. Total mobility	52.8	68.0
2. Structural mobility	26.7	42.9
3. Circulation mobility	26.1	25.1
4. Upward mobility	41.6	56.5
5. Immobility	11.2	11.6
6. Downward mobility	47.2	31.9
7. Percentage of the upwardly mobile	78.7	83.0
8. Percentage of the downwardly mobile	21.3	17.0
9. Mobility without exchange	73.0	79.5
10. Mobility through exchange	27.0	20.5

migrants. Nevertheless, Table 9.13 shows that the migrants' mobility, again, is higher than that of the natives. For example, among those who started in the lower-lower stratum, about 66% of the migrants rose on the social scale; among the natives, only 45% rose. All other strata show a similar pattern for natives

TABLE 9.13. Intragenerational Mobility of Natives and Migrants (%)*

Beginning Status	Individual's Status in 1973							Total per Beginning
	1	2	3	4	5	6	Total	
1. Upper	76.1	10.8	10.8	1.1	0.6	0.6	100.0	0.5
	(67.6)	(18.8)	(8.3)	(1.5)	(3.8)	(0.0)	(100.0)	(0.8)
2. Upper-middle	21.1	45.4	24.7	6.2	1.3	1.3	100.0	0.7
	(30.3)	(50.0)	(12.0)	(6.3)	(1.4)	(0.0)	(100.0)	(0.8)
3. Middle-middle	16.3	24.8	44.8	9.7	3.5	0.9	100.0	5.8
	(16.6)	(25.3)	(45.5)	(7.7)	(4.5)	(0.4)	(100.0)	(9.3)
4. Lower-middle	2.9	7.1	17.4	59.4	10.1	3.1	100.0	6.9
	(2.5)	(7.3)	(16.7)	(59.7)	(10.9)	(2.9)	(100.0)	(8.0)
5. Upper-lower	3.9	8.6	24.2	33.7	22.1	7.5	100.0	25.1
	(4.0)	(9.6)	(25.2)	(34.7)	(22.4)	(4.1)	(100.0)	(25.8)
6. Lower-lower	0.7	2.6	13.1	14.5	14.3	54.8	100.0	61.0
	(0.8)	(2.3)	(13.5)	(26.5)	(22.8)	(34.1)	(100.0)	(55.3)
Total for individuals in 1973	3.1	6.0	18.1	22.1	15.2	35.5	100.0	100.0
	(3.9)	(7.2)	(19.7)	(29.3)	(19.7)	(20.2)	(100.0)	(100.0)
N = 33,039 (N) = 17,701								

*Numbers in parentheses refer to migrants.

and migrants throughout the entire professional career; this reinforces our finding that most mobility is associated with rural-urban migration.

Looking at the general measurements of mobility shown in Table 9.14, we can say that our previously observed picture is repeated. Structural mobility predominates in both groups, but it is a little higher among migrants. Migrants also show a higher level of total mobility and of upward mobility. On this last point, the difference is quite pronounced. Upward mobility among migrants is about 62%, and among natives it is 50%. The difference is approximately the same as that observed for intergenerational mobility.

The general picture for social mobility among natives and migrants is the same one found in various other contemporary societies. Geographic (horizontal) mobility brings about social (vertical) mobility. Various studies indicate that economic opportunities induce geographic mobility. People who live somewhere other than their place of birth tend to achieve a higher occupational status than do those who remain in their birthplace. Although both points of departure are quite low in intergenerational terms, such is not the case for intragenerational mobility. Here, the migrants' point of departure is slightly higher than that of the natives. In spite of this, they achieve more mobility than the natives.

The general pattern of migration and mobility in Brazil runs counter to the popular conception that migration is a force of deterioration in the cities, among citizens, and among the migrants themselves. The results found here join the data of various other studies which show migration to be a force of advancement for migrants as well as for natives, and that it acts to equalize the social

TABLE 9.14. Types of Intragenerational Mobility

Types of Mobility	Natives	Migrants
1. Total mobility	53.6	65.4
2. Structural mobility	35.4	41.2
3. Circulation mobility	18.2	24.2
4. Upward mobility	49.7	61.6
5. Immobility	46.3	34.6
6. Downward mobility	4.0	3.8
7. Percentage of upwardly mobile	92.5	94.2
8. Percentage of downwardly mobile	7.5	5.8
9. Mobility without exchange	92.0	94.0
10. Mobility through exchange	8.0	6.0

structure.[8] This suggests that a drastic diminution in migration would mean a deceleration for social mobility and, consequently, an increase in social inequality—unless the rural segment also quickly begins to create jobs and to differentiate itself at the same speed as the urban segment. And that is an unrealistic proposition. In sum, indications are that migration has acted as a compensatory mechanism for the enormous regional disparities than exist in Brazil. To inhibit migration would imply increasing the effects of disparity.

8. We must note, however, that when we consider only the metropolitan areas, the natives are in higher social positions than are the people who have migrated there. A recent study, using the same occupational scale, brought out this fact. See Martine and Peliano, 1978: Chap. 3.

10
Mobility and
Social Development

The portrait of mobility in Brazil reveals a society which has been quite dynamic throughout the twentieth century. During this period, the country passed through numerous changes which had marked repercussions upon the social structure. The society's transformation from rural to predominantly urban was one of the most powerful factors in changing Brazilian social structure and in creating a relatively large middle class.

One often hears references to the fact that the Brazilian middle class is disappearing or is becoming more proletarian. The data say just the opposite. In spite of the strong expansion of jobs in the lower tertiary in the urban zones, middle class occupations for the heads of family increased substantially throughout the twentieth century. These jobs simply did not exist in the times of our fathers and grandfathers. During this period, Brazil began and established its industrialization, creating a large number of industrial occupations. Even more important were the enormous expansion of service sector occupations, peripheral to industry itself, and the sharp increase in commercial activities connected not only to industrialization but also to urbanization.

We have seen also that the "feminizing" of the Brazilian work force intensified a dualism in the labor market, which brought about a certain social promotion for men, particularly for heads of family. Women (and children) occupying the jobs of lower status permitted the male heads of family to hold higher-status jobs.

The data have shown that social mobility has been intensifying in the recent period, especially in the more developed regions. In fact, the clearest signs of upward mobility show up among individuls 30–50 years of age and in the more advanced regions. The social equalization observed in São Paulo, Rio de Janeiro, and Brasília have had to coexist with a strong social inequality in the other regions.

The general tendency in Brazil is an intense structural mobility stemming from changes in the economy and in the labor markets. Nevertheless, circulation mobility, which depends more upon the improvement of individual capabilities and upon competition among labor market participants, is showing clear signs of growth. Again, this is most important in the advanced regions and among the younger individuals.

But, how can we evaluate conjunctively the impacts of structural and circulation factors upon social mobility? How can we isolate the net effects of each of these variables in determining the status of heads of family in Brazil through time, and thus discover the most refined mechanisms of social mobility? This is the objective of the analysis presented in the following section. The analysis was carried out with the help of multiple regression models, and is based upon a random subsample of 5,826 cases.[1] The value of each occupation according to the Valle Silva scale was considered in the regressions being studied. These refer to the occupations of individuals in 1973, to their first jobs and to the occupations of their fathers (Valle Silva, 1974). An education variable was used in terms of mean years of schooling.[2] Thus, all the variables included in the model were continuous.

Avenues of Social Mobility

In the previous chapters we have seen that age, formal education, beginning occupational status, paternal status, region and migration are all related to the current social status of Brazilian heads of family. Those analyses were based upon status change matrices, and therefore it was difficult to identify the net effects of each of the variables. Our aim in this section is to capture precisely the net contributions of each variable and of all of them together, as well as to identify the mechanisms and trajectories by which they act.

Our adopted procedure includes the above-mentioned variables in a conventional regression model, in which the individual's occupational status in 1973 is taken as a dependent variable, while the father's occupational status, status

1. This sample was representative for age groups and for regions. The number of instances was reduced further due to defective information for variables included in the regression model. See the specific N's for each model in the next section.

2. The education variable was transcribed in the following way: no schooling = 0; grade school incomplete = 2; grade school complete = 4; junior high school incomplete = 6; junior high complete = 8; high school incomplete = 10; high school complete = 11; university incomplete = 14; university complete = 16.

TABLE 10.1. Means of Variables in the Model, by Region

Variables	Total	Brasília	Rio	São Paulo	East	South	Northeast
				Regions			
Age (years)	39.6	38.2	40.1	39.8	40.0	39.5	39.9
Present status	10.6	14.4	12.5	11.5	9.9	9.4	8.3
Education	3.3	5.3	4.4	3.9	2.9	3.2	1.8
Father's status	8.1	10.9	10.4	8.2	7.6	7.2	6.5
Status at first job	5.9	7.9	7.5	6.3	5.3	4.9	4.8
N =	4,418	447	508	751	718	628	1,101

at first job, education, age, and migration ("dummy") are taken as independent variables.[3] Before presenting the results of this study, let us look at how the six regions and the four age groups differentiate themselves in terms of these variables.

Table 10.1 shows the means for the variables in the six regions studied. The age distribution of heads of family is similar in all regions; Brasília stands out with an average that is more than one year from the national mean. This is practically the only variable with a homogenous distribution, and it reflects a demographic dynamic that is quite standard among the regions. The other variables reflect the intense social inequalities already discussed in Chapter 9. For example, the average status of heads of family in the Northeast is about 42% lower than it is in Brasília. In terms of education, the work force as a whole is extremely poor (with less than four years of schooling), but the heads of family in the Northeast have only a third of the schooling of those who live in Brasília and half that of the heads of family in general. The Northeast shows equal disadvantages in the father's status and in the individual's status at first job.

How are these phenomena distributed through the various age groups? Is Brazil improving or becoming worse in terms of individual status? Data here confirm an already-observed fact about occupational status: the highest average statuses are found predominantly in the middle age groups. Education is showing a slow improvement through time, although from an absolute point of view the situation is still poor. The same occurs with the status at the first job and the father's status. On the basis of these individual variables, Brazil is improving gradually. This, of course, refers to a relative improvement through time and in relation to a point of departure.

What is the role of each of these variables (and of all of them together) in

3. A linear function relating these variables was tested for the total sample, by age group and also by regions. The model assumed the following specific form:

$$Y = a + b_1 x_1 + b_2 x_2 \cdots + b_6 x_6$$

TABLE 10.2. Means of Variables in the Model, by Age Group

	Age Groups				
Variables	Total	51–64	41–50	31–40	20–30
Age (years)	39.6	—	—	—	—
Present status	10.6	9.1	11.3	11.2	10.0
Education	3.3	2.4	3.3	3.6	3.7
Father's status	8.1	7.6	8.1	8.5	8.0
Status at first job	5.9	5.2	5.9	6.1	6.2
N =	4,418	824	1,116	1,415	1,063

determining the current status of heads of family? The aggregated results of the model are shown in Table 10.3. The variables used explain about 43% of the current status in the total sample. The highest percentage of variance explained by the model occurred in Brasília (about 50%), and the smallest was seen in São Paulo (about 36%). Thus, the model explains more in Brasília than it does in São Paulo.[4]

To understand this fact better, let us examine the net contributions of each variable in each region. Education stands out in all regions. In Rio de Janeiro, for example, each year of school adds about two points to social status.[5] In the South and in the East, each year of school guarantees 1.82 and 1.67 points, respectively. The smallest net contributions of education are found in the extreme cases: that is,São Paulo (1.36); Brasília (1.40); and the Northeast (1.27). In the two most highly developed regions, this fact seems to be explained by the relatively high mean education (Table 10.2), and in the Northeast by the low level of occupational differentiation (Table 4.6). In the former case, education, although meager in absolute terms, begins to show declining effects; in the latter, labor market restrictions still do not permit education to be utilized for upward mobility at the same rate that other regions make use of it.[6]

There is an interesting general pattern in all the regions: the background variables (father's status, status at first job, migratory status) have little importance, while individual variables (education and age) make an enormous

4. The percentages of explained variance are quite reasonable when compared with explanations reached through similar models in other studies. For example, Blau and Duncan accounted for about 43% using education and father's status, education and individual starting status. See Blau and Duncan, 1967:147. Featherman and Hauser (1975:256) accounted for about 43% with a model of seven variables for the American population in 1973. Iutaka and Bock (1973:312–222), using data from six Brazilian cities, accounted for about 34% of the variance.

5. To appreciate better the entire scale, see Appendix I.

6. It would be hasty, though, to underestimate the role of education, which in all six regions is the most outstanding of all the variables included in the model. For the sample as a whole, each year of school added 1.45 points to an individual's position on the status scale.

TABLE 10.3. Net Effects (β) and Explained Variance (R²)

| Variables | Regression Coefficients β | | | | | | |
	Total	Brasília	Rio	São Paulo	East	South	Northeast
Age	0.443	0.320*	0.178*	0.490	0.437	0.708	0.414
Age²	−0.004	−0.003*	−0.001*	−0.005	−0.004	−0.007	−0.004
Father's status	0.064	0.051*	0.013*	0.030*	0.164	0.156	0.059
Education	1.451	1.100	2.022	1.360	1.673	1.820	1.274
Status at first job	0.344	0.571	0.058*	0.349	0.240	−0.119*	0.472
Migration	−0.079*	3.722*	0.017*	−0.077*	−0.559*	0.782*	−0.532*
Constant	−6.252	−11.681	−2.303	−6.064	−6.533	−13.184	−4.384
Explained variance (R²)	0.427	0.498	0.439	0.359	0.474	0.408	0.375
N**	4,418	447	508	751	718	628	1,101

*Not significant at 5%.
**The difference between the N's and the total sample is due to defective responses for one or more of the variables included in the model.

contribution to explained variance. This suggests a movement from attributed criteria to achieved criteria. Table 10.4 allows us to compare each variable within each region and also against the total. For example, for the total sample, education (β = 0.495) shows strong and similar impacts. Its relative importance increases even further in Brasília and in Rio de Janeiro, reflecting the advantages of education in cities with a high concentration of jobs in the upper tertiary, as in the cases of the old and new capitals. In the Northeast and South, where the opportunities for work are more limited and where the level of social differentiation is fairly low, age produced a greater impact than education did. But, how to explain São Paulo? What accounts for the greater relative partic-

TABLE 10.4. Net Effects (β) and Explained Variance (R²)

Variables	Total	Brasília	Rio	São Paulo	East	South	Northeast
Age	0.450	0.242	0.148*	0.523	0.479	0.768	0.533
Age²	−0.406	−0.188	−0.075*	−0.514	−0.425	−0.698	−0.515
Father's status	0.057	0.049	0.011*	0.027*	0.149	0.177	0.048
Education	0.495	0.411	0.634	0.454	0.534	0.584	0.420
Status at first job	0.185	0.357	0.374	0.192	0.098	−0.040*	0.221
Migration	−0.003*	0.013	0.000*	−0.003*	−0.016*	−0.038*	−0.020*
Constant	−6.253	−11.618	−2.303	−6.064	−6.533	−13.184	−4.384
Explained variance (R²)	0.427	0.498	0.439	0.359	0.474	0.406	0.375
N =	4,418	447	508	751	718	628	1,101

*Not significant at 5%.

ipation of age and the lesser impact of education? A definitive answer can be reached only if we dissociate the direct and indirect effects of each variable, as we shall do in the following paragraphs. We see, meanwhile, that education is strongly determined by the father's status (Table 5.12), suggesting that the impact of the father's status in determining the son's status is not a direct process but an indirect one, via education and other variables. For this type of study we can examine the β coefficients and do a path analysis. The values of the coefficients are presented in Table 10.4.

In fact, the effects of each variable are brought about in direct and indirect ways. The studies of association indices presented in Chapters 6 and 7 sought to delineate, for example, the role of social inheritance in determining current status. The regression models permit us to move toward a path analysis,[7] so as to separate the direct and indirect effects of paternal inheritance measured by the impact of the father's status upon the son's status. Table 10.5 confirms that most of the effect of inheritance is brought about indirectly, via education and status at first job. To understand these results better, we must look carefully at the model. The diagram shows that the father's status is transmitted to the son in two ways. One is direct, and associates father with son. The other is indirect, subdivided into two trajectories: through education and through the individual's status at first job.[8]

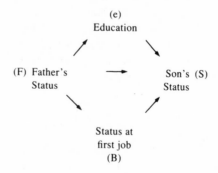

The estimate of these trajectories is fixed:

$$r_{SF} = W_{SF} + (W_{SE} \cdot r_{FE}) + (W_{SB} \cdot r_{FB})$$

7. Path analysis has been used extensively in the past few years in studies of the determination of social status. See Blau and Duncan, 1967: Chap. 5; Pastore, 1973: 62–75.

8. There is also another indirect trajectory in which the effects of the father's status begin through education, then pass to beginning status at first job and from there to current status. However, the correlation between education and status at first job is very low (on the order of about 0.30) and stems from the early entry into the labor market (Chapter 5). Hence, the exclusion of this model.

where

W_{SF} = Total effect of father's status (f) upon that of the son (S)

W_{SE} = Direct effect of father's status upon that on the son

W_{SB} = Indirect effect via education (E)

W_{SF}, W_{SE}, and W_{SB} = Weights ("Beta") in the Regression Equation[9]

The results in Table 10.5 show also that the direct influence of paternal inheritance varies from region to region. In Rio and in São Paulo, it is less than 10%. Brasília stands beside the Northeast, with about 13%, but for different reasons and with quite different social structures.[10] In the South and in the East, we find the highest weight of direct influence of paternal inheritance.

TABLE 10.5. Effects of Father's Status upon Son's Present Status, by Region

Types of Effects	Total	Brasília	Rio	São Paulo	East	South	Northeast
Total	0.397	0.423	0.325	0.330	0.457	0.389	0.393
(%)	*(100.0)*	*(100.0)*	*(100.0)*	*(100.0)*	*(100.0)*	*(100.0)*	*(100.0)*
Direct	0.080	0.005	0.002	0.029	0.149	0.106	0.050
(%)	*(20.0)*	*(13.0)*	*(7.0)*	*(9.0)*	*(32.6)*	*(27.6)*	*(13.5)*
Indirect	0.317	0.368	0.303	0.301	0.308	0.283	0.340
(%)	*(80.0)*	*(87.0)*	*(93.0)*	*(91.0)*	*(67.4)*	*(73.0)*	*(86.5)*
Via education	0.240	0.227	0.291	0.226	0.252	0.281	0.236
(%)	*(60.0)*	*(53.8)*	*(89.5)*	*(68.5)*	*(55.0)*	*(72.0)*	*(60.0)*
Via status at first job	0.077	0.141	0.012	0.075	0.056	0.002	0.104
(%)	*(20.)*	*(33.4)*	*(3.5)*	*(22.5)*	*(12.4)*	*(0.0)*	*(26.5)*

How does the influence of paternal inheritance behave through time? Analysis of the different age groups shown in Table 10.6 suggests that the influence of the father's status via education has been the most prominent influence in all the age groups, but that it was much stronger in the past than in the present. On the other hand, the influence of the father's status via status at first job is growing. This shows that the educational discrimination dictated by social inheritance was much stronger in the older groups than in the younger ones.

9. $\beta \, SF \cdot E = {}^{b}SF \cdot E \dfrac{S_F}{S_S} \, ; \, \beta \, SE \cdot F = b_{PE} \cdot P \dfrac{S_E}{S_S} \, ; \, \beta_{SB} = b_{SB} \cdot P \dfrac{S_B}{S_S}$

10. In Brasília the proportion of people in the middle class is high; in the Northeast the majority is concentrated in the lower class. In both cases the father's status has about a 13% influence in determining the son's status.

TABLE 10.6. Effects of Father's Status upon Son's Status,
by Age Group

Types of Effects	Age Group				
	Total	(51–64)	(41–50)	(31–40)	(20–30)
Total	0.397	0.312	0.452	0.382	0.385
(%)	(100.0)	(100.0)	(100.0)	(100.0)	(100.0)
Direct	0.080	−0.016	0.066	0.074	0.030
(%)	(20.0)	(−5.1)	(14.6)	(19.4)	(7.8)
Indirect	0.317	0.328	0.386	0.308	0.355
(%)	(80.0)	(105.0)	(85.4)	(80.6)	(92.0)
Via education	0.240	0.285	0.328	0.178	0.216
(%)	(60.0)	(91.0)	(72.8)	(46.8)	(56.0)
Via status at first job	0.007	0.043	0.056	0.130	0.139
(%)	(20.0)	(14.0)	(12.6)	(33.8)	(36.0)

Mobility and Poverty

The general picture of Brazilian social structure through time shows clear signs of increasng flexibility caused by changes in the economy and in the labor markets. As a result of these structural changes, Brazil is forming a middle class based upon changes of occupation. But circulation mobility definitely is beginning to emerge, the signs indicating that in one or two decades it will predominate—unless, of course, a serious economic crisis occurs.

In this respect, one can conclude that Brazil is advancing socially: job opportunities and the occupational differentiation of the last few decades offer clear improvements in occupational status for most Brazilian heads of family. Although it is still bad today, the Brazilian social structure was much worse in the past—that is, in our fathers' and grandfathers' generations. For them there were fewer and less desirable jobs. Although there are still problems and limitations, the present generation has occupational opportunities that are unquestionably better than those available at the beginning of the century or even right after the war. This is due mostly to industrial expansion, urbanization, and the tertiarization of urban labor markets. And with the better occupational opportunities for the heads of family have come better educational and occupational opportunities for the sons.

However, when we compare the above description with the recent social clamor from the end of the seventies, it seems that we are dealing with different countries. Socio-economic analyses of present-day Brazil reveal intense rural and urban poverty, malnutrition, low income, marginality, and a poor quality of life, all of this touching a large part of the Brazilian population. How do we explain this? Which might be wrong, the above description or these analyses?

In fact, both are correct. The description of the behavior of the social structure and of mobility reveals our evolution through time. It is a temporal comparison of relatives. The socio-economic diagnosis of the present shows our current poverty in absolute terms.[11] We conclude, then, that Brazilian society is limiting for most Brazilians; but we must conclude also that it was even more limiting in the remote past. In other words, if the situation is bad today, it was worse yesterday. Our picture of mobility compares what we are with what we were. Our picture of the present compares what we are with what we should be.

The problem of poverty is chronic and persistent in Brazil, in spite of all the mobility achieved. It is true that the situation would be worse if not for the mobility achieved. But the situation, without doubt, could be better in view of our economic growth in the last three decades. It is this which creates dissatisfaction and which aggravates the current rural and urban poverty in Brazil. We grow, yet remain poor. Workers rise in the social structure, but continue to be needy. In short, the gains made by social mobility are far from satisfying current Brazilian aspirations. Also, part of present inequality is due to the long distance mobility of small groups.

Thus, it is wrong to think that a high rate of upward mobility can necessarily equalize society or diminish present dissatisfaction. In Brazil's case the opposite occurred: with rates of growth, high mobility rates, a high degree of inequality, a high degree of dissatisfaction. Perhaps the dissatisfaction plays an important role in Brazil's development today. Development depends largely upon society's efficiency in organizing itself to strive for better conditions. Individuals who rise in the social structure gain a few points on the status scale, but many points on the scale of social aspirations.[12] This leads them to want more status, better living conditions, good jobs, education. Any attempt to smother these desires artificially only prolongs the problem, increases tension, and retards social development. Modern societies progress with the help of tension and transaction. As tension is inevitable, social development comes to depend upon a good and rapid apprenticeship in the various forms of transaction. And, apparently, transaction is learned only by acting: advancing and regressing, making errors and correcting them.

Social mobility, then, is far from being an anesthetic for a dissatisfied so-

11. Evaluations of the present often try to examine the present relatives, also—that is, the degree of inequality current in the society. Other times they focus on the advances attained by the rich vis-a-vis the advances attained by the poor. Such analyses, though, neglect any comparison of the same family unit through time, as is done in studies of inter- and intragenerational mobility.

12. In addition, much dissatisfaction is generated when people see the enormous differences between mobility attained by small groups and that attained by the large masses of the population.

ciety, especially when it is a new phenomenon, as it is in Brazil, and when it begins at an extremely low social level. Mobility is a progressive process which creates satisfactions and dissatisfactions. But it is precisely these forces together which permit and induce a better organization of social institutions and groups, of managers and workers, of the governing and the governed. Policies which ignore or impede social mobility and which try to operate society as a machine with predetermined means and ends are extremely dangerous.

The dynamics observed in the Brazilian social structure and described in this monograph were the result of innumerable decisions and changes involving many social groups which reacted at times according to governmental policies, at times against them, and many times simply ignored them. Structural mobility was a reflection of advances and regressions in the economic sectors, of decisions made by innumerable economic and social agents, of the great population movements, of migration, of industrialization, of urbanization, etc., making it difficult to associate it with the role of this or that government.

Mobility and Social Development: Proposals

With the growing and exaggerated participation of the state in the post-war Brazilian economy, the role of Government today is considerable. The Government is the largest producer and the largest consumer in Brazil. Direct or indirect government investments strongly influence the private sector in it's decisions to expand or cut back. Government investments generate much employment. A redirectioning of governmental macropolicies could contribute greatly to expanding and diversifying even more the employment opportunities of the next decades, resulting in more massive mobility and social equalization.

This redirectioning would mean creating policies for the rural and urban sectors and, with each of these, an even more detailed specification of mechanisms capable of generating and diversifying employment. Take, for example, the rural world: here, agriculture carries the heavy responsibility of helping to pay for our foreign debt, a responsibility that will not be assumed easily by any other sector in the next two or three decades. But in addition to this, agriculture must feed the growing urban populations and still resolve or attentuate the grave problem of rural poverty and underemployment.

Specific policies seem to be necessary for each of these three problems, but any policy will affect employment and occupational differentiation in the countryside. Thus, policies governing exports and imports, by the very nature of the products (soybeans, wheat, sugar cane, etc.), sustain vast expanses of land, modern fertilizers, and much mechanization. These policies, although limited as to the quantitative expansion of employment, bring about much occupational differentiation in the countryside, which allows certain portions of the population to be mobile without leaving agricultural activity (although they may even live in the city).

Again because of the nature of the products (beans, rice, manioc, vegetables) and of the available technologies, the policies that support foodstuff production for urban (and rural) consumption tend to stimulate less land and less mechanization, but more chemical and natural fertilizers. This also has a clear impact in terms of occupational differentiation. Above all, the two types of policies tend to generate numerous new occupations in the activities which support agriculture, as in the sectors of fertilizers, construction, equipment, maintenance, general commerce, banks, cooperatives and class associations, all this allowing greater opportunities for mobility clustered around agricultural activities in the countryside and in the small and middle-sized cities.

The policies which attack rural poverty, however, seem to demand other measures: the most urgent is to remove the population from its serious state of undernourishment and illiteracy. Actually, the idea is to take these populations from misery to at least, subsistence. For this, a minimum of resources will be needed for them to produce and consume more foodstuffs. Thus, we arrive at the age-old necessity to redistribute natural and financial resources (fertile land, water, credit). It is true that specific policies for land redistribution and for the occupation of fertile backlands have but a small impact upon occupational differentiation. However, they do generate many jobs and, above all, they improve living conditions for subsistence farmers. At the same time, they improve significantly the education of children in both old and new regions. The participation of children in the labor market is inordinantly high and unproductive as well. As they are, the family and school are powerless to keep children in the classroom, thus necessitating quite specific measures to reverse this pernicious pattern. Much has already been done for secondary and higher education in Brazil in terms of financial support, participation of the private sector, scholarships, loans to be repaid after graduation, diversification of curricula, and professional instruction. We need to develop similar policies for the primary level, especially in the rural zone. In the next two decades we shall need to generate and allocate huge amounts of resources to make it easier for Brazilians to finish primary school. This is the best, perhaps the only, guarantee that the country can count on new generations which are productive, ambitious, and assertive.

Certain specific policies are also needed for the urban environment. Above all, they must guarantee greater employment stability and increase income in the lowest strata in the cities. The aim should not only be an improvement in the standard of living but also an increased demand for continuous and stable sources of food and energy, a demand which is an indispensible condition for a capable, foodstuff-producing agriculture.

But to expand employment in the cities, we must redefine the contours of our industrialization. To the extent that we increase the production of consumer goods (food, transportation, housing, etc.), we shall be able to generate more jobs, to diversify the urban occupational structure, and to improve the workers' standard of living. Job generation and diversification are intimately linked to the nature of products, and they are stimulated by development in the various sectors which participate directly and indirectly in producing those goods. For example, increased industrialization in foodstuffs mobilizes growers, ware-housing, transportation, conservation, manufacture of equipment, supermarkets and commerce in general. Improvement of the quality of life obviously stems from more jobs, from diversified opportunities, from more mobility, and from higher income.

The expansion of these sectors could also allow a substantial improvement for urban female labor. Women have filled the spaces of low qualification left by men in the large cities, in addition to their traditional occupation as domestic servants. Job opportunities for women are still few, marked by the disadvantages of an informal market, and not likely to offer advancement. Correcting our production toward popular consumer goods will permit a strong expansion and formalization in the female labor market and, consequently, an improvement in the family's economic and social situation. In short, if we can put the rural child back into school, diversify job opportunities for the man, and formalize the labor market for the woman, we shall be marching firmly toward a more lasting social equality in Brazil.

Clearly, such profound changes as these do not occur overnight, and neither are they the exclusive responsibility of government. On the contrary, they depend upon a more direct participation by Brazilian workers and entrepreneurs in the larger economic and social policies. If such participation today is small, it is because the Government has become gigantic in areas in which it is dispensible, and has remained out of those areas where its compensating role is absolutely indispensible to correct the imperfections of the market and of capitalism in general. With this unnecessary growth and the inexplicable absence, social institutions have lost the little power they had; society has been transformed into a mere object to be used. Inevitably, this pattern will be reversed, and specific policies will be developed to arm the social institutions and the mechanisms by which workers and entrepreneurs can fulfill their dreams and determine how they want the fruits of their labors used. And this brings us back to the initial theme of this section. We must take advantage of mobility to activate the institutions. As mobility increases, aspirations always grow, and with them tension and, at times, conflict itself. Tension is inevitable; conflict is not. It all depends on how the tension is treated by society.

Reference Material

Appendix

**Occupations Illustrating Occupational Index Values
and Number of Individuals in the EAP—1970**

Stratum	Interval of Scores	Mean Score	Occupations
(1) Upper	40.06–88.75	63.71	Industrialists (and large landowners) (96,342), Administrators of banks and insurance companies (46,106), Labor supervisors (3795), Engineers (43,294), Architects (4752), Chemists (4442), Pharmacologists (3906), Geologists (962), Agronomists (6802), Veterinarians (2726), Physicians (44;354), Dentists (32,286), Economists (9320), Auditors (15,807), Sociologists (455), University professors (17,593), Judges (3604), Attorneys (37,173), Writers and journalists (10,082), Civil pilots (2995), Police commissioners and deputies (5287).
(2) Upper-middle	24.72–38.57	30.84	Cattle ranchers (67,863), Aviculturists and breeders (3801), Other landowners (49,588), Public service administrators (79,685), Other administrators (220,620), Fiscal controllers (29,999), Administrating officials and technicians (26,509), Collectors and tax collectors (10,875), Bookkeepers (116,803), Stenographers (1361), Editors (1056), Interpreters and translators (1330), Programmers (5769), Meterologists (405), Naturalists (852), Registered nurses (5393), Statisticians (2097), Secondary school teachers (97,863), School inspectors (6822), Notaries public and registry officials (6757), Commercial representatives (37,345), Public relations (9902), Insurance brokers (7364), Realtors (31,694), Stockbrokers (10,319), Merchant marine officials (2135), Sports technicians (566).
(3) Middle-middle	9.77–23.33	17.01	Livestock farming administrators (38,476), Surveyors (18,299), Farm technicians (4175), Oil field workers (3416), Merchants (810,209), Hotel and pension owners (23,345), Farmers (124,813), Tellers and cashiers (87,646), Librarians and ref-

Stratum	Interval of Scores	Mean Score	Occupations
(3) Middle-middle (cont.)	9.77–23.33	17.01	erence librarians (5435), Operators and handlers (11,780), Draftsmen (35,813), Physical therapists (3062), Prosthodontists (7213), X-ray technicians (4054), Pharmacists (7743), Laboratory technicians (38,357), Registrars and assistants (29,930), Social workers (1829), Sculptors and painters (4534), Musicians (12,858), Film and theater actors (9833), Broadcasters (5868), Decorators and set designers (4679), Filmmakers and cameramen (1628), Photographers (24,896), Other technicians of cinema (3381), Linotypists (3856), Engravers and photoengravers (2200), Proofreaders, graphics industry (1584), Regional and traveling salesmen (109,945), Other agents and brokers (5841), Buyers (7367), Airline stewardesses (1178), Harbor pilots (2810), Railroad agents (9793), Railroad conductors (4509), Freight inspectors and dispatchers (9749), Postal and telegraph agents (5598), Post office employees (9263), Telegraph and radiotelegraph employees (20,865), Stamp salesmen (1095), Police investigators (16,701), Fiscal inspectors (43,499), Primary school teachers (564,600), Teachers without specialization (37,477), Student supervisors (14,059), Warehouse supervisors (48,316), Typists (59,116), Office Workers (982,364), Construction foremen (40,449), Industrial supervisors, foremen and technicians (50,193), Soccer players (4973), Fighters and other professional athletes (4973), Officers and enlisted men in the armed services (339,511), Firefighters and their officers (9749).
(4) Lower-middle	7.29–12.83	9.67	Metalworkers (8186), Foundrymen (19,197), Laminators and wiredrawers (7810), Sharpeners and grinders (2678), Punch-press operators (3045), Milling machinists and drillers (5455), Lathe operators (78,799), Engine mechanics (221,413), Unspecified mechanics (232,767), Galvanizers and nickel-platers (5314), Solderers (62,416), Copperworkers (9709), Ironsmiths and locksmiths (66,196), Auto body repairmen (17,836), Riveters (1814), Tinsmiths and tinkers (22,744), Farriers (592), Carpetmakers (9609), Textile printers (6062), Electricians (157,687), Radio technicians (31,062), Printers (39,200), Pressmen (11,038), Bookbinders (10,484), Other specific occupation in the graphics industry (3355), Glassworkers and ampule makers (7702), Goldsmiths and watchmak-

Stratum	Interval of Scores	Mean Score	Occupations
(4) Lower-middle (cont.)	7.29–12.83	9.67	ers (15,370), Stone cutters (3120), Marble workers (6467), Stone polishers (19,472), House painters (31,488), Naval repairmen (1192), Unspecified craftsmen (6311), Other occupations in the crafts industries (38,977), Ship supervisors (5866), Firemen on ships (2398), Sailors (9145), Deck hands (3772), Crane operators (4845), Stevadores (26,435), Machinists (15,879), Firemen on trains (2807), Brakemen (3372), Switchmen (9728), Teamsters (759,498), Railway workers (23,611), Telephone operators (33,562), Mailmen (16,963), Linemen (4618), Concrete workers (17,732), Masons (590,616), Painters and whitewashers (131,682), Plasterers (5662), Tilers and parquet workers (11,142), Plumbers (70,748), Glassworkers (4295), Pavers and asphalt workers (9521), Caulkers (5560), Construction heavy equipment operators (17,742), Cabinetmakers (140,085), Carpenters (260,318), Coopers and barrelmakers (559), Upholsterers and auto roofers (16,495), Mattress makers (3336), Wood polishers and varnishers (14,876), Midwives and accoucheurs (4473), Practical nurses (133,716), Barbers and hairdressers (114,574), Civil guards and traffic police (66,716), Jailers and penitentiary guards (4169), Elevator operators (10,284), Overseers (20,419), Sanitation workers (15,090), Cinema operators (2096), Machine operators (96,927).
(5) Upper-lower	1.81–7.65	5.84	Cutters and combers (3332), Rovers (textile) (15,180), Spinners (37,851), Warpers (5216), Rope makers (1715), Weavers (114,873), Bleachers and dyers (5846), Cloth finishers (9503), Belt and harness makers (8167), Tanners (9180), Tailors and dressmakers (393,899), Hatmakers (excluding straw hat makers (1104), Shoemakers (130,437), Handbag and belt makers (3226), Sausage makers (1857), Jerked beef makers (1587), Butchers (18,910), Butter and cheese makers (3373), Candy and confections makers (15,988), Pasta makers (1880), Bakers (74,866), Flour merchants and millers (9594), Milling and sugar mill occupations (13,674), Occupations in grinding and toasting coffee (2506), Occupations in distilleries (5276), Occupations in fish processing (2632), Slaughterhouse workers (32,039), Lacemakers (5360), Netmakers (5608), Embroiderers and menders (25,368), Hatters (31,308), Ceramists and table-

Stratum	Interval of Scores	Mean Score	Occupations
(5) Upper-lower (cont.)	1.81–7.65	5.84	ware makers (21,706), Painters of ceramics (2801), Potters (90,707), Vulcanizers and tire re-cappers (19,865), Fireworks makers (2338), Basket and mat makers (5996), Broom makers (1719), Cigar and cigarette makers (10,020), Firemen, excluding firemen on ships and trains (9259), Packagers and shippers (87,565), Apprentices (20,834), Greasers and oilers (12,504), Sawyers (55,506), Hod carriers (447,045), Boatmen and canoeists, (5009), Cartmen (52,383), Workers in highway maintenance (33,454), Trash collectors (54,191), Unspecified manual laborers (365,812), Domestic servants (1,511,324), Laundresses and starchers (248,551), Fare collectors, buses (53,697), Cooks (89,827), Waiters (82,277), Manicurists and pedicurists (17,318), Shoeshiners (5428), Porters, watchmen, and servants (638,059), Salesclerks and deliverers (737,784), Newspaper and magazine salesmen (10,823).
(6) Lower lower	2.50–4.79	4.70	Plowmen (7215), Tractor drivers (78,720), Small farmers, homesteaders (256,563), Gardeners (41,531), Farmhands (10,009,007), Cattle hands (690,328), Hunters (2585), Fishermen (140,758), Lumberjacks and woodcutters (97,397), Charcoal burners (23,070), Rubber workers (78,365), Herbgrowers (1680), Pickers, huskers, etc. (118,084), Miners (21,938), Quarry workers and rock drillers (39,472).

Source: Valle Silva, 1974.

Note: The hierarchization of the six strata in this study utilized the divisions of the Valle Silva scale as a basic guide. Small changes of positioning occurred for certain occupations, which took into account the nature (manual or non-manual) and the level of qualification of the occupations (office or factory). This, however, did not alter the original hierarchization of Valle Silva, and the number of individuals included in these changes was very small.

Between the lower-lower and upper-lower strata there is a superposing of values upon the upper-lower; one occupation has a value less than the minimum value of the lower-lower stratum: lacemakers = 2.49 (only one individual). Between the upper-lower and the lower-middle strata there are three cases of superposing: sawyers = 7.53 (two cases); wood polishers = 7.29 (34 cases); and carpenters = 7.39 (1074 cases). Between the lower-middle and the upper middle there are four occupations to note: cinema technicians = 12.68 (five cases); stockroom supervisors = 12.79 (174 cases); typists = 12.83 (89 cases); and soccer players = 12.21 (4 cases).

Bibliography

Allardt, E.
1968   "Theories about Social Stratification." In J. A. Jackson, ed., *Social Stratification.* Cambridge: Cambridge University Press.

Almeida, A. L. O.
1974   *Industrialização e emprego no Brasil.* Rio de Janeiro: Instituto de Planejamento Econômico e Social (hereafter IPEA).
1976   *Distribuição de renda e emprego em serviços.* Rio de Janeiro: IPEA/ Instituto de Pesquisas (hereafter INPES).

Almeida, A. L. O., and M. C. Silva
1973   *Dinâmica do setor de serviços no Brasil.* Rio de Janeiro: IPEA.

Alves, D. C. O.
1978   Crescimento industrial e distribuição dos benefícios do progresso técnico. Associate professorship dissertation. Faculdade de Economia e Administração, University of São Paulo.

Andorka, R., and D. Zagorski.
1978   "Structural Factor of Social Mobility in Hungary and Poland." Uppsala, Sweden: IX World Congress of Sociology.

Araújo, B. J.
1976   "Mundanças na estrutura social brasileira." *Ciência e Cultura* 28: 510–525.

Araújo, O. E.
1947   "Pesquisa entre motoristas, operários, continuos e serventes da Prefeitura de São Paulo." *Revista do Arquivo Municipal* 13: 7–135.

Baer, W.
1975   *Industrialização e desenvolvimento econômico no Brasil.* Rio de Janeiro: Fundação Getúlio Vargas.

Bake, E. W., et al.
1954   *Labour Mobility and Economics Opportunity.* Cambridge: MIT Press.

Bancroff, G.
1958   *The American Labor Force.* New York: John Wiley.

Batchieder, A. B.
1965   "Occupational and Geographical Mobility." *Industrial and Labor Relations Review* 18: 570–583.

Baurer, P. T., and B. S. Yamey.
1951   "Economic Progress and Occupational Distribution." *Economic Journal* 51: 741–755.

171

Beals, R.
1959   "Social Stratification in Latin America." *American Journal of Sociology* 58: 327–339.
Bendix, R.
1974   "Inequality and Class Structure: a Comparison of Marx and Weber." *American Sociological Review* 39: 149–161.
Bibby, J.
1975   "Methods of Measuring." *Quality and Quantity* 9: 107–136.
Bielby, W. T., and A. Kalleberg.
1975   "The differentiation of Occupations." Madison, Wisconsin: Institute for Research on Poverty. Discussion Paper no. 309.
Blalock, H.
1960   *Social Statistics*. New York: McGraw-Hill.
Blau, P. M., ed.
1975   *Approaches to the Study of Social Structure*. New York: Free Press.
Blau, P. M., and O. D. Duncan
1967   *The American Occupational Structure*. New York: John Wiley.
Blay, E.
1978   *Trabalbo domesticado: a mulher na indústria paulista*. São Paulo: Atica.
Boalt, G.
1954   "Social Mobility in Stockholm: a Pilot Investigation." *Transactions of the Second World Congress of Sociology* 2: 67–73.
Bogue, D.
1963   *Skid Row in American Cities*. Chicago: University of Chicago Press.
1969   *Principles of Demography*. New York: John Wiley.
Boudon, R.
1973   *Mathematical Structures of Social Mobility*. San Francisco: Jossey-Bass.
Bowles, S., and H. Gintis
1976   *Schooling in Capitalist America*. New York: Basic Books.
Bressan, M.
1971   "Estrutura ocupacional, urbanização e industrialização." Master's thesis, Universidade de Brasília.
Broom, L., and F. J. Lancaster
1977   *Opportunity and Attainment in Australia*. Stanford: Stanford University Press.
Calabi, A. S., and A. E. M. Zaghen
1978   "Segmentação do mercado de trabalho, mobilidade e rotatividade: revisão teórica e evidencias empíricas preliminares." São Paulo: Fundação Instituto de Pesquisas Econômicas (hereafter FIPE). Mimeographed.
Carchedi, G.
1975   "On the Economic Identification of the New Middle Class." *Economy and Society* 4: 1–85.

Cardoso, F. H.
1969   *Mudanças sociais na América Latina*. São Paulo: Difusão Européia do
        Livro.
Cardoso, F. H., and E. Falleto
1970   *Dependência e desenvolvimento na América Latina*. Rio de Janeiro:
        Zahar Editores.
Cardoso, F. H., and O. Ianni
1960   *Cor e mobilidade social em Florianópolis*. São Paulo: Editora Nacional.
Carlsson, G.
1958   *Social Mobility and Class Structure*. Lund, Sweden: Gleerups.
Chase, I. C.
1975   "A Comparison of Men's and Women's Intergenerational Mobility in
        the United States." *American Sociological Review* 40: 483–505.
Clark, C.
1957   *The Conditions of Economic Progress*. London: Macmillan.
Collins, R.
1975   *Conflict Sociology: Toward an Explanatory Science*. New York: Aca-
        demic Press.
Costa, R. A.
1976   "Fontes interestaduais de desigualdade de renda." *Forum Educacional*
        1: 43–64.
1977   "Mobilidade social: alguns resultados empíricos para o Brasil." Rio
        de Janeiro: Fundação Instituto Brasileiro de Geografica e Estatística
        (hereafter Fundação IBGE). Mimeographed.
1978   *Distribuição de renda pessoal no Brasil*. Rio de Janeiro: Fundação
        IBGE.
Crevenna, T., ed.
1950–52 *Materiales para el Estudio de la Clase Media en la America Latina*.
        Washington: Pan American Union.
Cunha, P. V.
1976   "Dualismo no mercado de trabalho." Brasília: IPEA. Mimeographed.
Dahrendorf, R.
1962   *Las clases sociales y su conflicto en la Sociedad Industrial*. Translated
        by M. T. de los Rios. Madrid: Ediciones Rialp.
Davidson, P. E., and H. Dewey
1937   *Occupational Mobility in an American Community*. Stanford: Stanford
        University Press.
Davis, K.
1953   "Reply to Tumin." *American Sociological Review* 18: 394–397.
Davis, K. and W. Moore
1945   "Some Principles of Stratification." *American Sociological Review* 10:
        242–249.
Deasy, L.-C.
1955   "An Index of Social Mobility." *Rural Sociology* 20: 149–155.

Duncan, O. D.
1961   "A Socioeconomic Index of All Occupations." In A. J. Reiss, ed.,
        Occupations and Social Status. New York: Free Press.
1966   "Occupation Trends and Patterns of Net Mobility in the United States."
        Demography 3: 1–18.
Duncan, O. D., et al.
1972   *Socioeconomic Background and Achievement*. New York: Seminar
        Press.
Durkeim, E.
1893   *De la Division du Travail Social*. Paris: Alcan.
Edwards, A. M.
1938   *A Social-Economic Grouping of the Gainful Workers of the United
        States—1930*. Washington, D.C.: U.S. Government Printing Office.
Edwards, R. C., et al.
1975   *Labor Market Segmentation*. Lexington: D. C. Heath.
Ekerman, R.
1976   "Absorção de mão-de-obra nos mercados formal e informal, tecnolo-
        gia e distribuição de renda." São Paulo: FIPE. Mimeographed.
Faria, V. E.
1976   Occupational Marginality, Employment and Poverty in Urban Brazil.
        Ph.D. dissertation, Harvard University.
Featherman, D. L., and R. M. Hauser
1975   "Sexual Inequalities and Socio-Economic Achievement in the U.S.,
        1962–1973." *American Sociological Review* 40: 483–505.
1978   *Opportunity and Change*. New York: Academic Press.
Fernandes, F.
1965   *A integração do negro na sociedade de classes*. São Paulo: Dominus
        Editora.
1968   *Sociedade de classes e subdesenvolvimento*. Rio de Janeiro: Zahar
        Editores.
Fisher, G. G.
1945   *Economic Progress and Social Security*. London: Macmillan.
Fundação IBGE
1970   *Censo Demografico, Brasil*. Brasília: Fundação IBGE.
1973   *Pesquisas Nacionais por Amostra de Domicílios*. Brasília: Fundação
        IBGE.
1974   "Classificação dos grupos de ocupação considerando documento ela-
        borado por Nelson do Valle Silva." Brasília: Fundação IBGE.
        Mimeographed.
1975   *Resumo das pesquisas domiciliares no período 1967–1975*. Rio de Ja-
        neiro: Fundação IBGE. Mimeographed.
1978   *Sinopse preliminar do censo agropecuário*. Brasília: Fundação IBGE.
Frutado, C.
1961   *Formação econômica do Brasil*. Rio de Janeiro: Fundo de Cultura.

Germani, G.
1965   "Estrategia para Estimular la Movilidad Social." in J. A. Kahl, ed.,
        La Industrialización en America Latina. México: Fondo de Cultura
        Economica.
1969   *Sociología de la Modernización.* Buenos Aires: Paidós.

Giddens, A.
1973   *The Class Structure of Advanced Societies.* New York: Harper & Row.

Glass, D. V.
1954a   (ed.) *Social Mobility in Britain.* London: Routledge & Keegan Paul.
1954b   "Social Stratification and Mobility." *International Social Sciences Bul-
        letin* 6: 12–24.

Goldhamer, H.
1968   "Social Mobility." In *International Encyclopedia of Social Sciences*
        14. Glencoe: Macmillan and Free Press.

Goldthorpe, J.
1966   "Social Stratification in Industrial Society." In R. Bendix and S. M.
        Lipset, eds., *Class, Status, and Power.* New York: Free Press.

Gordon, D. M.
1972   *Theories of Poverty and Underdevelopment.* Lexington: D.C. Heath.

Gouveia, A. J.
1965a   "Desenvolvimento econômico e prestígio de certas ocupações." *Amer-
        ica Latina* 9: 66–78.
1965b   *Professores de Amanhã.* Rio de Janeiro: Centro Brasileiro de Pesquisas
        Educacionais.
1971   "A pesquisa educacional no Brasil." *Cadernos de Pesquisa* 1: 1–48.
1977   "A estrutura da população economicamente ativa no Brasil." São
        Paulo: FIPE. Mimeographed.

Grandjean, B. D.
1975   "An Economic Analysis of the Davis-Moore Theory of Stratification."
        Social Forces 53: 543–552.

Granovetter, M. S.
1974   *Getting a Job. A Study of Contacts and Careers.* Cambridge: Harvard
        University Press.

Hall, R. H.
1975   *Occupations and the Social Structure.* Englewood Cliffs, N.J.: Pren-
        tice-Hall.

Haller, A. O., and K. I. Spenner
1977   "Occupational Income Differentiation in Status Attainment." *Rural
        Sociology* 42: 515–533.

Halzerigg, L. E., and M. A. Garnier
1976   "Occupational Mobility in Industrial Societies: a Comparative Anal-
        ysis of Differential Access to Occupational Ranks in 17 Countries."
        American Sociological Review 41: 498–511.

Hauser, R. H., and D. L. Featherman
1977   *The Process of Stratification: Trends and Analysis*. New York: Academic Press.

Hauser, R. M., et al.
1974   "Temporal Change in Occupational Mobility: Evidence for Men in the United States." *American Sociological Review* 40: 274–297.
1975   "Structural Changes in Occupational Mobility Among Men in the United States." *American Sociological Review* 40: 585–598.

Havighurst, R. J.
1957   "Educação, mobilidade social e mudança social em quatro sociedades." *Educação e Ciências Sociais* 2: 114–129.

Herman, L.
1948   "Evolução da estrutura social de Guaratinguetá." São Paulo: *Revista de Administração*.

Hodson, R.
1977   "Labor Force Participation and Earnings in the Core, Peripheral, and State Sectors of Production." Madison: University of Wisconsin, Department of Sociology. Mimeographed.
1978   "Labor in the Monopoly, Competitive and State Sectors of Production." *Politics and Society* 8: 429–480.

Hope, K., ed.
1972   *The Analysis of Social Mobility: Methods and Approaches*. Oxford: Clarendon Press.

Hutchinson, B.
1957   "The Social Grading of Occupation in Brazil." *The British Journal of Sociology* 3: 176–189.
1958   "Structure and Exchange Mobility in the Assimilation of Immigrants to Brazil." *Population Studies* 12: 111–120.
1961   "Fertility, Social Mobility and Urban Migration." *Population Studies* 14: 182–189.
1962   "Urban Mobility Rates in Brazil Related to Migration and Changing Occupational Structure." *America Latina* 6: 47–60.

Hutchinson, B. et. al.
1960   *Mobilidade e trabalho*. Rio de Janeiro: Centro Brasileiro de Pesquisas Educacionais.

Ianni, O.
1963   *Industrialização e desenvolvimento social no Brasil*. Rio de Janeiro: Civilização Brasileira.
1966   *Raças e classes no Brasil*. Rio de Janeiro: Civilização Brasileira.

Iutaka, S., and E. W. Bock
1973   "Determinants of Occupational Status in Brazil." In K. U. Muller, ed., *Social Stratification and Career Mobility*. Paris: Mouton.

Jaffe, A. J.
1959   *People, Jobs and Economic Development*. New York: Free Press.

Jaffe, A. J. and R. D. Carleton
1954   *Occupational Mobility in the United States: 1930–1960*. New York: Kings Crower Press.

Jencks, C., et al.
1972   *Inequality: a Reassessment of the Effect of Family and Schooling in America*. New York: Rinehart.

Kahl, J. A.
1957   *The American Class Structure*. New York: Rinehart.
1965   "Social Stratification and Values in Metropolis and Provinces: Brazil, Mexico." *America Latina* 1: 23–36.
1969   "Urbanização e mudanças ocupacionais no Brasil." *America Latina* 5: 21–30.

Kannappan, S.
1977   *Studies of Urban Labour Market Behavior in Developing Areas*. Geneva: Oficino Internacional del Trabajo.

Kelley, J.
1973   "Causal Chain Models for the Socioeconomic Career." *American Sociological Review* 38: 481–493.

Kerckhoff, A. C.
1974   "Stratification Processes and Outcomes in England and the U.S." *American Sociological Review* 39: 789–801.
1978   "Methodological Problems and Prospects in Comparative Status Attainment Research." Uppsala, Sweden: IX World Congress of Sociology.

Kleining, G.
1978   "Preliminary Results from Comparative Surveys on Social Mobility in Ten Countries." Uppsala, Sweden: IX World Sociology Congress.

Kreps, J. M.
1971   *Lifetime Allocation of Work and Income: Essays in Economics of Aging*. Durham, N.C.: Duke University Press.

Kuznets, S.
1976   "Demographic Aspects of the Size Distribution of Income: an Exploratory Essay." *Economic Development and Cultural Change* 25: 1–94.

Lagos, G.
1963   *International Stratification and Underdeveloped Countries*. Chapel Hill: University of North Carolina Press.

Langoni, C. G.
1973   *Distribuição de renda e desenvolvimento econômico do Brasil*. Rio de Janeiro: Expressão e Cultura.

Leigh, D. E.
1976   "Occupational Advancement in the Late 1960's: an Indirect Test of the Dual Labor Market Hypothesis." *Journal of Human Resources* II (Spring): 155–171.

Lenski, G. E.
1958   "Trends in Inter-Generational Occupational Mobility in the United States." *American Sociological Review* 23: 214–253.
1966   *Power and Privilege: A Theory of Social Stratification.* New York: McGraw-Hill.
1967   "Status Inconsistency and the Vote: a Four Nation Test." *American Sociological Review* 32: 298–301.

Lipset, S. M., and R. Bendix
1959   *Social Mobility in Industrial Society.* Berkeley: University of California Press.

Lipset, S. M., and N. Rogoff
1954   "Class and Opportunity in Europe and the U.S.: Some Myths and What the Statistics Show." *Commentary* 18: 562–568.

Lipset, S. M. and A. Solari
1967   (eds.) *Elites e desarollo en America Latina.* Buenos Aires: Paidós.

Lipset, S. M., and H. L. Zetterberg
1956   "A Theory of Social Mobility." *Transactions of the Third World Congress of Sociology* 3: 155–177.

Lopreato, J., and L. E. Hazebrigg
1972   *Class, Conflict and Mobility.* San Francisco: Chandler Publishing.

Lowrie, S. H.
1938a   "Origem da população da cidade de São Paulo e diferenciação das classes sociais." *Revista do Arquivo Municipal* 4:195–212.
1938b   "Pesquisa do padrão de vida dos operários da limpeza pública da cidade de São Paulo." *Revista do Arquivo Municipal* 4: 336–344.

Lynd, R. S., and H. M. Lynd
1937   *Middletown in Transition.* New York: Harcourt and Brace.

McCann, J. C.
1977   "A Theoretical Model for the Interpretation of Tables of Social Mobility." *American Sociological Review* 42: 74–90.

McClendon, J. J.
1977   "Structural and Exchange Components of Vertical Mobility." *American Sociological Review* 42: 56–74.

MacDonald, K. I.
1972   "MDSCAL and Distances Between Socio-Economic Groups." In K. Hope, ed., *The Analysis of Social Mobility: Methods and Approaches.* Oxford: Clarendon Press.

Marsh, R. M.
1963   "Values, Demand and Social Mobility." *American Sociological Review* 25: 575–583.

Martine, G., and J. C. P. Peliano
1978   *Migrantes no mercado de trabalho metropolitano.* Brasília: IPEA.

Marx, K.
1968   *Oeuvres.* Paris: Biblioteque de la Pléiade.

Matras, J.
1975   *Social Inequality, Stratification and Mobility.* Englewood Cliffs, N.J.: Prentice-Hall.

Miller, S. M.
1960   "Comparative Social Mobility." *Current Sociology* 9: 1–39.
1971   "The future of Social Mobility Studies." *American Journal of Sociology* 71: 257–287.

Moreira, J. R.
1960   *Educação e desenvolvimento no Brasil.* Rio de Janeiro: Centro Latino-Americano de Pesquisas em Ciências Sociais.

Morley, S. A.
1978   "Growth and Inequality in Brazil." *Luso-Brazilian Review* 15 (Winter): 244–271.

Moura da Silva, A.
n.d.   "Distribuição de renda e senso comum." *Ensaios Econômicos.* São Paulo: FIPE. Série IPE-Monografias, no. 10.

Muller, W.
1973   "Family Background Education and Career Mobility." In W. Muller and K. U. Mayer, eds., *Social Stratification and Career Mobility.* Paris: Mouton.

Ornstein, M. D.
1973   "The Impact of Labor Market Entry Factors." In W. Muller and K. U. Mayer, eds., *Social Stratification and Career Mobility.* Paris: Mouton.
1976   *Entry in the American Labor Force.* New York: Academic Press.

Ossowski, S.
1964   *Estrutura de classes na consciência social.* Translated by A. Blachyere. Rio de Janeiro: Zahar Editores.

Pampel, F. C., et al.
1977   "A Social Indicator Model of Changes in the Occupational Structure of the United States: 1947–1974." *American Sociological Review* 42: 951–964.

Parkin, F.
1971   *Class Inequality and Political Order: Social Stratification in Capitalist and Communist Societies.* New York: Praeger.

Parsons, T.
1940   "An Analytical Approach to the Theory of Social Stratification." *American Sociological Review* 45: 841–862.

Pasqualini, R.
1973   "Career Mobility in Italy." In W. Muller and K. U. Mayer, eds., *Social Stratification and Career Mobility.* Paris: Mouton.

Pastore, J.
n.d.   "Recursos humanos e ensino superior." *Ensaios Econômicos.* São Paulo: FIPE. Série IPE-Monografias, no. 10.

1972   "Migração, mobilidade social e desenvolvimento." In M. A. Costa,
        ed., *Migrações internas*. Rio de Janeiro: IPEA.
1973   *Determinantes de diferenciais de salários na indústria paulista*. São
        Paulo: University of São Paulo, Faculdade de Economia e
        Administração.
1976   "Emprego, renda e mobilidade social no Brasil." *Pesquisa e Planeja-
        mento Econômico* 6: 551–586.
1977a   *Política de emprego e mobilidade social*. São Paulo: FIPE.
1977b   "Proporção ocupacional e salários de professionais de nivel médio na
        força de trabalho industrial de São Paulo." *Cadernos de Pesquisa* 20:
        111–123.
1978   "Mobilidade social no Brasil." *O Estado de São Paulo*, September 24.

Pastore, J., and E. E. Ceotto
1974   "Diferenciais de salários de engenheiros, economistas e pessoal de
        ciências básicas." *Cadernos de Pesquisa* 19: 3–12.

Pastore, J., and R. C. Owen
1968   "Mobilidade educacional, mudança social e desenvolvimento no Bra-
        sil: notas preliminares." *Revista da Pontifícia Universidade Católica
        de São Paulo* 35: 477–492.

Pastore, J., and G. G. Perosa
1971   *O estudante universitário em São Paulo*. São Paulo: FIPE.

Pastore, J., et al.
1975   "Theories of Wage Differentials in São Paulo's Industrial Labor
        Force." *Journal of Industrial Relations* 14: 345–357.
1977   "Training, Position and Experience in the Wage Rates of Specialized
        Personnel in São Paulo's Manufacturing Firms." In S. Kannappan,
        ed., *Studies of Urban Labour Market Behaviour in Developing Areas*.
        Geneva: Oficina Internacional del Trabajo.

Payne, G., et al.
1974   "Occupational Mobility in Scotland." *Scottish Journal of Sociology*
        1: 14–27.

Pikes, J.
1968   *Entry into the Labor Force: A Survey of Literature*. Ann Arbor: Institute
        of Labor and Industrial Relations.

Piore, M. J.
1975   "Notes for a Theory of Labor Market Stratification." In R. C. Edwards,
        et al., *Labor Market Segmentation*. Lexington: D.C. Heath.

Poulantzas, N.
1975   *As classes sociais no capitalismo de hoje*. Translated by A. R. Neiva
        Blundi. Rio de Janeiro: Zahar Editores.

Prais, S. J.
1955   "Measuring Social Mobility." *Statistics Journal* 118: 56–66.

Rainwater, L., et al.
1978   "Income Claims Systems in Three Countries." Uppsala, Sweden: IX
        World Congress of Sociology.

Ratinoff, L.
1967   "The New Urban Groups: the Middle Classes." In S. M. Lipset and
        A. Solari, eds., *Elites in Latin America*. New York: Oxford Univer-
        sity Press.

Reiss, A. J.
1962   "Scaling Occupations." In A. J. Reiss, et al. *Occupations and Social
        Status*. New York: Free Press.

Rodrigues, L. M.
1967   Atitudes operárias na empresa automobilística. Ph.D. dissertation,
        University of São Paulo.

Rogoff, N.
1953   *Recent Trends in Occupational Mobility*. New York: Free Press.

Rostow, W. W.
1964   *Etapas do desenvolvimento econômico*. Rio de Janeiro: Zahar Editores.

Rothman, R. A.
1978   *Inequality and Stratification in the United States*. Englewood Cliffs,
        N.J.: Prentice-Hall.

Runciman, W. G.
1966   *Relative Deprivation of Social Justice*. Berkeley: University of Califor-
        nia Press.

Salm, C.
1970   *Aspectos da discriminacão da mulher no mercado de trabalho*. Rio de
        Janeiro: IPEA/Centro Nacional de Recursos Humanos (CNRH).

Sant'Ana, A. M., et al.
1976   *Income Distribution and the Economy of the Urban Household: the Case
        of Belo Horizonte*. Washington: Banco Mundial.

Schervish, P. G., and A. B. Sorensen
1977   "Alternative Theories of the Income Attainment Process." Madison,
        Wisconsin: Institute for Research on Poverty. Mimeographed.

Schnore, L.
1961   "Social Mobility in Demographic Perspective." American Sociologi-
        cal Review 26: 407–423.

Sewel, W. H.
1940   *Construction and Standardization of a Scale for the Measurement of
        Socio-Economic Status*. Tulsa: Oklahoma Experimental Station.

Sewel, W. H., and R. M. Hauser
1975   *Education, Occupation and Earnings: Achievement in the Early Career*.
        New York: Academic Press.

Siegel, B. J.
1955   "Social Structure and Economic Change in Brazil." In S. Kuznets, et
        al., *Economic Growth: Brazil, India and Japan*. Durham, N.C.: Duke
        University Press.

Simonsen, M. H.
1972   *Brasil 2001*. Rio de Janeiro: APEC-Bloch.
1978   "Desigualdade e mobilidade social." *Jornal do Brasil*, May 14.

Simpson, I. H., and R. L. Simpson
1977   "Occupational Permeability and Labor Force Cohort Stability." Chicago: American Sociological Association. Mimeographed.

Singer, P.
1971   "Força de trabalho e emprego no Brasil: 1920–1969." *Cadernos CEBRAP.* São Paulo: Centro Brasileiro de Analise e Planejamento (CEBRAP).
1975   "Emprego e urbanização no Brasil." São Paulo: CEBRAP. Mimeographed.

Smelser, N. J., and S. M. Lipset
1966   *Social Structure and Mobility in Economic Development.* Chicago: Aldine.

Soares, G. A. D.
1969   "Desenvolvimento econômico e estrutura de classes." *Dados* 6: 91–128.
1974   "A nova industrialização e o emprego industrial na América Latina." In C. Mendes, ed., *Crise e mudança social.* Rio de Janeiro: Eldorado.
1977   "A nova industrialização, emprego industrial e segmentação ocupacional na América Latina." Brasília. Mimeographed.

Sorensen, A. B.
1972   "Social Mobility as a Social Indicator." Madison: University of Wisconsin, Department of Sociology. Mimeographed.
1975   "The Structure of Intragenerational Mobility." *American Sociological Review* 40: 456–471.
1976   "Models and Strategies in Research on Attainment and Opportunity." Madison, Wisconsin: Institute for Research on Poverty. Reprint Series no. 191.
1977   "The Structure of Inequality and the Process of Attainment." *American Sociological Review* 42: 965–978.

Sorensen, A. B., and A. L. Kalleberg
1977   "An Outline of a Theory of the Matching of Persons to Jobs." Madison, Wisconsin: Institute for Research on Poverty. Discussion Paper no. 424.

Sorokin, P. A.
1927   *Social and Cultural Mobility.* New York: Harper and Brothers.
1930   "Social Mobility." In *Encyclopedia of the Social Sciences* vol. 11. New York: Macmillan.

Stinchombe, A. L.
1963   "Some Empirical Consequences of the Davis-Moore Theory of Stratification." *American Sociological Review* 28: 805–808.

Stouffer, S. A.
1940   "Intervening Opportunities: a Theory Relating Mobility and Distance." *American Sociological Review* 5: 249–259.

Svalastoga, K.
  1964   "Social Differentiation." In R. E. L. Faris, ed., *Handbook of Modern
            Sociology*. Chicago: Rand McNally.

Szymanski, A.
  1978   "Classes in the Soviet Union." Uppsala, Sweden: IX World Congress
            of Sociology.

Tinker, J. N.
  1977   "Social Mobility and Social Isolation: Tracing the Web of Friendship."
            Fresno: California State University. Mimeographed.

Treiman, D. J.
  1970   "Industrialization and Social Stratification." In E. O. Laumann, ed.,
            Social Stratification. Indianapolis: Bobbs-Merrill.
  1978   *Occupational Prestige in Comparative Perspective*. New York: Aca-
            demic Press.

Treiman, D. J., and K. Terell
  1975   "Sex and the Process of Status Attainment: a Comparison of Working
            Men and Women." *American Sociological Review* 40: 174–200.

Tumin, M. M.
  1953a   "Reply to Kinsley Davis." *American Sociological Review* 18: 572–673.
  1953b   "Some Principles of Stratification: a Critical Analysis." *American So-
            ciological Review* 18: 287–393.

Tumin, M. M. and A. S. Feldman
  1961   *Social Class and Change in Puerto Rico*. Princeton: University Press.

Valle Silva, N.
  1978   Black-White Income Differentials: Brazil, 1960. Ph.D. dissertation,
            University of Michigan.
  1974   "Posição social nas ocupaçõas." Rio de Janeiro: Fundação IBGE.
            Mimeographed.

Velloso, J. R.
  1975   "Training, Employment and the Distribution of Earnings in Brazil."
            Conference on Employment, Underemployment of Graduates. Paris:
            Organization for Economic Cooperation and Development.
            Mimeographed.

Warner, W. L.
  1960   "The Several Types of Rank." In W. L. Warner, et al., *Social Class in
            America*. New York: Harper and Brothers.

Weber, M.
  1947   *The Theory of Social and Economic Organization*. Translated by A. M.
            Handerson and T. Parsons, New York: Free Press.

Wesotowiski, W.
  1962   "Some Notes on the Fundamental Theory of Stratification." *The Polish
            Sociological Bulletin* 3–4: 28–38.

Wright, E. O.
    1976   Class Structure and Income Inequality. Ph.D. dissertation, University
                of California.
    1977   "Operationalizing Social Relations of Production." Madison: Univer-
                sity of Wisconsin, Department of Sociology. Mimeographed.
Wrong, D.
    1970   "The Functional Theory of Stratification: Some Neglected Consider-
                ations." In E. O. Laumann, et al. eds., *The Logic of Social Hierar-
                chies*. Chicago: Macmillan.
Yassuda, S.
    1964   "A Methodological Inquiry into Social Mobility." *American Sociolog-
                ical Review* 29: 16–23.
Zagorski, K.
    1976   "Changes of Socio-Occupational Mobility in Poland." *The Polish
                Sociological Review* 2: 1–34.

Index

185

JACKET DESIGNED BY ED FRANK PRODUCTIONS
COMPOSED BY WEIMER TYPESETTING CO., INC., INDIANAPOLIS, INDIANA
MANUFACTURED BY CUSHING-MALLOY, INC., ANN ARBOR, MICHIGAN
TEST AND DISPLAY LINES ARE SET IN TIMES ROMAN

Library of Congress Cataloging in Publication Data
Pastore, José, 1935–
Inequality and social mobility in Brazil.
Translation of: Desigualdade e mobilidade social
no Brasil.
Bibliography: pp. 171–184.
Includes index.
1. Social mobility—Brazil.   2. Equality.
3. Brazil—Economic conditions.   I. Title.
HN284.P3713   305.5'13'0981   81–69826
ISBN 0–299–08830–8   AACR2